UNDOING TIME

For Catherine and Nathalie, with love,
circling round

UNDOING TIME

The Life and Work of Samuel Beckett

Jennifer Birkett

Irish Academic Press

First published in 2016 by Irish Academic Press
8 Chapel Lane
Sallins
Co. Kildare, Ireland

British Library Cataloguing in Publication Data
An entry can be found on request

ISBN: 978 0 7165 3290 3 (paper)
ISBN: 978 0 7165 3292 7 (PDF)

Library of Congress Cataloging-in-Publication Data
An entry can be found on request

Contents

Acknowledgements

I should like to thank the University of Birmingham for the funding for research leave and travel to libraries which supported the initial stages of this book, and the specialist librarians and their colleagues who maintain the excellent collections of the University Library and its extensive electronic resources. I am grateful to the librarians at the British Library, Trish Hayes and her colleagues at the BBC Written Archive at Caversham Park, and the staff of the Beckett Collection at the University of Reading. The help of Mary Bryden and Kate Lacey at final production stages was much appreciated. Special thanks go to Stan Smith, for first suggesting I write this book, and to the late David Bradby, who generously shared his expertise on Beckett's drama. Lisa Hyde has been a patient and supportive editor. Family and friends, as ever, have been encouraging and forbearing.

Copyright and Permissions

The author and publishers would like to thank copyright holders and publishers for kind permission to reproduce extracts from copyright material as follows.

Excerpts from letters from Samuel Beckett to Alan Schneider of 11 February 1975*; 29 December 1957*; 29 September 1964* and 5 September 1980* © the Estate of Samuel Beckett reproduced by kind permission of the Estate of Samuel Beckett c/o Rosica Colin Limited, London. Reprinted by permission of the publisher from NO AUTHOR BETTER SERVED edited by Maurice Harmon, Cambridge, Mass.: Harvard University Press, Copyright © 1998 by the President and Fellows of Harvard College.

Extracts from Martha Dow Fehsenfeld, Lois More Overbeck, George Craig and Dan Gunn (eds), *The Letters of Samuel Beckett*, © The Estate of Samuel Beckett 2009, published by Cambridge University Press; extracts from George Craig, Martha Dow Fehsenfeld, Dan Gunn, Lois More Overbeck (eds), *The Letters of Samuel Beckett*, © The Estate of Samuel Beckett 2011, published by

Cambridge University Press. Reprinted by kind permission of Cambridge University Press and the Estate of Samuel Beckett. Electronic publication of extracts by kind permission of the Estate of Samuel Beckett c/o Rosica Colin Limited, London.

Extracts from the following works by Samuel Beckett reprinted by kind permission of Faber and Faber Ltd, Grove Atlantic Inc., and the Estate of Samuel Beckett. Samuel Beckett, *Disjecta. Miscellaneous Writings and a Dramatic Fragment,* ed. and intro. Ruby Cohn (London: John Calder, 1983); Samuel Beckett. *The Complete Dramatic Works* (London: Faber and Faber, 1986); Samuel Beckett, *Texts for Nothing and Other Shorter Prose, 1950–1976,* ed. Mark Nixon (London: Faber and Faber, 2010); Samuel Beckett, *The Collected Poems of Samuel Beckett,* eds Seán Lawlor and John Pilling (London: Faber and Faber, 2012); Samuel Beckett, *'Proust' and 'Three Dialogues: Samuel Beckett & Georges Duthuit'* (London: John Calder, 1965); Samuel Beckett, *Happy Days/ Oh Les Beaux Jours by Samuel Beckett. A Bilingual Edition,* ed. James Knowlson (London and Boston: Faber and Faber, 1978); Samuel Beckett, *Company* (London: John Calder, 1980); Samuel Beckett, *Company, Ill Seen Ill Said, Worstward Ho, Stirrings Still,* ed. Dirk Van Hulle, London: Faber and Faber, 2009; Samuel Beckett, *Eleutheria,* trans. Barbara Wright (London: Faber and Faber, 1996); Samuel Beckett, *How It Is,* ed. Edouard Magessa O'Reilly (London: Faber and Faber, 2009); Samuel Beckett, *The Beckett Trilogy. Molloy, Malone Dies, The Unnamable* (London: Pan Books, Picador Edition, 1979); Samuel Beckett, *More Pricks than Kicks* (1934), rpt. London: Calder & Bowers,1973); Samuel Beckett, *First Love* (1973), rpt. in Samuel Beckett, *The Expelled and Other Novellas* (Harmondsworth: Penguin Books, 1980).

Extracts from Samuel Beckett, *Samuel Beckett: The Grove Centenary Edition, Vol. I, Novels,* ed. Paul Auster and intro. Colm Tóibín (New York: Grove Press, 2006), and from Samuel Beckett, *Dream of Fair to Middling Women,* eds Eoin O'Brien and Edith Fournier, (Dublin: The Black Cat Press, 1992). Reprinted by kind permission of Grove Atlantic Inc. and the Estate of Samuel Beckett.

BBC copyright material reproduced courtesy of the British Broadcasting Corporation. All rights reserved.

Extract from © Richard Eyre and Nicholas Wright, 2000, *Changing Stages: A View of the British Theatre in the Twentieth Century,* Bloomsbury Publishing Plc. Reprinted by kind permission of Bloomsbury Publishing Plc.

Extracts from Frost, Everett C. "Fundamental Sounds: Recording Samuel Beckett's Radio Plays." *Theatre Journal* 43:3 (1991), 361–76. © 1991 The

Johns Hopkins University Press. Reprinted with permission of Johns Hopkins University Press.

Extracts from Peter Hall, 'Godotmania', *The Guardian*, Saturday 4 January 2003 (http://www.theguardian.com/stage/2003/jan/04/theatre.beckettat100 16.07); Peter Lennon, 'Evenings with Sam', *Review Guardian*, Thursday 25 January 1990; 'Billie up to her neck in Beckett. Samuel Beckett directing *Happy Days* at the Royal Court, opening June 7th', Arts Guardian, Wednesday May 30 1979, all originally published in *The Guardian*, are reproduced with the kind consent of Guardian News & Media Ltd.

Extracts from Leslie Hill, 'Samuel Beckett (1906–1989)', *Radical Philosophy*, 55 (Summer 1990). Reprinted with the permission of *Radical Philosophy*.

Betsy Jolas gave kind permission for the quotation from 'The Revolution of the Word', by her father Eugene Jolas, as published in his literary magazine *transition* (*transition* No. 16–17 [June 1929]).

Extracts from © James Knowlson, 1996, *Damned to Fame: The Life of Samuel Beckett*, Bloomsbury Publishing Plc. Reprinted by kind permission of Bloomsbury Publishing Plc.

Extracts from James and Elizabeth Knowlson (eds), 2006, 'Beckett Remembering / Remembering Beckett', Bloomsbury Publishing Plc. Reprinted by kind permission of Bloomsbury Publishing Plc. Reprinted in the US by permission of Arcade Publishing, an imprint of Skyhorse Publishing, Inc.

Extract from Derek Mahon, *The Hudson Letter* (1995), by kind permission of The Gallery Press, Loughcrew, Oldcastle, County Meath, Ireland (www.gallerypress.com).

Extract from The Nobel Prize in Literature 1969, Award Ceremony Speech: Presentation Speech by Karl Ragnar Gierow of the Swedish Academy, published on the website of The Nobel Foundation, reprinted with the permission of The Nobel Foundation (http://www.nobelprize.org/nobel_prizes/literature/laureates/1969/press.html#).

Extract from Deborah Philips, 'Interview: Billie Whitelaw', *Women's Review*, Issue 4 (February 1986), reprinted by kind permission of Deborah Philips.

Extract from Juliette Taylor-Batty, 'Imperfect Mastery: The Failure of Grammar in Beckett's *L'Innommable*', *Journal of Modern Literature* 30.2 (2007), © Indiana University Press. Reprinted by kind permission of Indiana University Press.

Extract from David Watson, *Paradox and Desire in Samuel Beckett's Fiction* (Houndmills, Basingstoke: Macmillan, 1991; Copyright © David Watson, 1991). Reprinted by permission of Macmillan Publishers Ltd.

Publishers have also kindly indicated, directly or in website advice, that quotations from the following fall within fair usage: Martin Esslin, 'Samuel Beckett and the Art of Radio', in S.E. Gontarski (ed.) *On Beckett. Essays and Criticism*, rev. edn (London and New York: Anthem Press, 2012); Jonathan Kalb, *Beckett in Performance* (Cambridge: Cambridge University Press, 1989); David Lloyd, *Anomalous States: Irish Writing and the Post-Colonial Moment* (Durham, NC: Duke University Press, 1993).

Despite every effort to trace and contact copyright holders before publication this has not been possible in every case. If contacted, the publisher will be pleased to rectify any errors and omissions at the earliest opportunity.

Author's Note and Abbreviations

Following the publisher's template, the material in this book is considered by genre. Within each section, Beckett's texts are reviewed in chronological order of writing. English versions are used throughout, and where the original was written in French, this is indicated. I have tried where possible to use for reference easily accessible editions, usually from a collection. Details of each edition used are in the Bibliography and the first annotation.

Abbreviations

Trilogy 1979	Samuel Beckett, *The Beckett Trilogy. Molloy, Malone Dies, The Unnamable* (London: Pan Books, Picador Edition, 1979).
Disjecta 1983	Samuel Beckett, *Disjecta. Miscellaneous Writings and a Dramatic Fragment,* ed. and intro. Ruby Cohn (London: John Calder, 1983).
CDW 1986	Samuel Beckett, *The Complete Dramatic Works* (London: Faber and Faber, 1986).
CSP 1995	Samuel Beckett, *Samuel Beckett. The Complete Short Prose, 1929*-1989, ed. and intro. S.E. Gontarski (New York: Grove Press, 1995).
Grove 2006	Samuel Beckett, *Samuel Beckett: The Grove Centenary Edition,* Vol. I, Novels, ed. Paul Auster and intro. Colm Tóibín (New York: Grove Press, 2006).
Van Hulle 2009	Samuel Beckett, *Company, Ill Seen Ill Said, Worstward Ho, Stirrings Still,* ed. Dirk Van Hulle (London: Faber and Faber, 2009).

TN 2010	Samuel Beckett, *Texts for Nothing and Other Shorter Prose, 1950-1976*, ed. Mark Nixon (London: Faber and Faber, 2010).
CP 2012	Samuel Beckett, *The Collected Poems of Samuel Beckett*, eds Seán Lawlor and John Pilling (London: Faber and Faber, 2012).
Letters I	Samuel Beckett, *The Letters of Samuel Beckett, Volume I: 1929-1940*, eds Martha Dow Fehsenfeld, Lois More Overbeck, George Craig and Dan Gunn (Cambridge and New York: Cambridge University Press, 2009).
Letters II	Samuel Beckett, *The Letters of Samuel Beckett, Volume II: 1941-1956*, eds George Craig, Martha Dow Fehsenfeld, Dan Gunn, Lois More Overbeck (Cambridge and New York: Cambridge University Press, 2011).
TLS	*Times Literary Supplement*

Introduction

A Life in Time

For Samuel Beckett, hindsight was the mode of true insight. *That Time,* written in English between June 1974 and August 1975, and first performed at the Royal Court on 20 May 1976, is one of the best dramatisations of his vision of being human. Like all his work, the play is founded, at some distance, in his own life experience, but it is framed, in every sense, in the language of the creative process. This time, unusually, the vision is a happy one, and its representation goes forward with pleasing ease. For Beckett, life was a matter of doing time, while writing was a way of undoing it – a process of transformation by which writer, written, and listeners enter together into a different understanding of not what, but how it is to be human.

Mid-stage, high up, off-centre, is the old white face of the Listener, who is also his own Author, surrounded by a flare of long white hair. His eyes are open, and his breathing is steady and audible. Three voices, all his own, address him in turn, as 'you', coming from both sides and above. He makes no response, except that his eyes close three times, and open three times. His part is to hear and to see, and shape what he sees by the rhythms of his breathing. When the voices finally fall silent, he gives a toothless smile.

The voices speak of and from three different moments in time and space, but their focus on the Listener creates a continuum. The stage directions say that the speech must be continuous, but the switching between voices must be perceptible. In other works, the voices (and the music) of inspiration invoked by the listening author, require his repeated intervention and evaluation to be urged, at last, into a synthesis that he can deem complete.

The emphasis is on the difficulty of the process. In *What Where*, for instance, Beckett's last play for the stage, the raw material has to be tortured and threatened into communicative form.[1] In *That Time*, the artwork shapes itself smoothly to a perfect end, through the medium of an attentive Seer and Listener who has grown old in experience and the skills of his craft. Three evolving narratives cross-cut one another in four sequences, each time in a different order, moving chronologically forward. As stage time advances, different narratives take priority, but all three leach into one another; and they are unified by the artist who, looking inwards and outwards as the words flow by, acknowledges the themes, the insights and the patterns out of which he has repeatedly made himself, in a variety of other productions, and who can now smile at the sense of it all coming together, not in closure, but in the evanescent, moving forms which are those of Everyman's short life. Starting in 'that time', this speaking is 'gone in no time'.[2]

Voice A invokes the child shaped by a desolate Ireland, hiding from the authority of the adults with his picture books and his own imaginary conversations, sitting on a stone in the ruins of the old tower beyond the end of the tram line, caught between tradition and modernity. This moment of first escape is doubled by the moment of final escape, when he went back to see it again, and found only the rusty rails left, and the rail station all boarded up and closed down. The old man returning cannot make his way back to the old refuge, but that was in any case only a trap, one of many to come. Now he can relive the scene in his own story, sitting on a doorstep and talking to himself, and finally fleeing Ireland by the ferry, taking with him only the best of that beginning: the old green greatcoat that was his father's legacy.[3]

Voice B speaks for the lover, channelling the memory of a couple sitting on a long stone in the sun, with a little wood behind and a wheat field before them. It's hard to believe, says the voice, that you ever told anyone that you loved them, it was 'just another of those old tales to keep the void from pouring in on top of you the shroud'.[4] There was no bodily closeness. Standing stock still, the couple played over and over the same old scene. In the end, this lover declares he gave up love, because his body was unresponsive, and there were no words left.

Voice C is the artist, the creative mind that was shaped by the institutions of his cultural heritage. In the Portrait Gallery, coming in out of the cold and the rain, sitting on a marble slab in the old green greatcoat, surrounded by the portraits of the antique dead, staring at one black old picture, a face appeared, which was perhaps, or perhaps not, the viewer's own reflection. This was one of many turning points, generating the questioning about self-knowledge and self-definition ('could you ever say I to yourself'),[5] which went on until the words dried up. There was more free culture in the Public Library, and yet more free culture to be found far away from home, and through the medium of the Post Office. The Library is where this voice finally ends, round a table with all the other old ones, and the room suddenly filled with dust.

The continuity of the piece is founded in the hard, resistant places where the Listener always established himself: a stone in the ruin or rubble, a marble slab, a millstone, a doorstep. Alongside them, there has always been movement, running and fleeing, by tram, train and ferry, looking for better places to be, until all the ways of escape closed down. There is always the debt to his father, and Ireland, and Irish culture, as well as to the culture of the wider European heritage. There is the unrelieved burden of knowledge of women exploited and never really loved, whatever love might be. Whether as child, writer, or lover, the Listener has always been making up stories, and experiencing the shape and feel of places. Finally, the overarching continuity rests in the smiling face, with no teeth and no speech, but still possessed of the capacity to remember, whatever remembering might be, and however diminished. Perhaps, as Derek Mahon has commented, being diminished is itself a source of pleasure; and he reports how Beckett once told him of his enjoyment of being old, losing memory, and losing the words.[6]

This complex stage symbolisation, of the author as the bodily centre of his own experience, focused in the images that wheel round and through the imagination and memory that created them, sets out how Beckett, from his beginnings as a writer in interwar Paris, has always seen himself. Here are all the elements that come together in the process of searching for truthful ways of saying who 'I' am and how it was, in the time 'I' live and have lived. Included are the landscapes, family, community, and long cultural heritage which have made 'me', the limits they set even as they provided a mouth to speak and words to say, and the distance always to be maintained between 'me' and what 'I' say and have said. The words are all theirs, made of their time, not 'mine'. There is no 'I', self-knowing, only a 'you' addressed by 'their' voices. This distanced wording is the only truthful use of pronouns. What is 'mine' is the rehearsal of all this knowledge, in this particular performance of saying: this time, in this theatre, between the rise of the curtain and the departure of the audience, the watchers and listeners who bracket the watching and listening that takes place on stage.

All Beckett's life is in this play, in an elegiac account of flights, failure, disappointment and dust, redeemed by its sharp, energetic vision and the hallucinatory rhythms of its poetry, and lifted out of the merely personal into a shared culture, which is both national and universal. The Listener and Seer is inconceivable outside the whole community of watchers and listeners. This writing is not autobiography, though its elements have their origin in personal experience, nor is it autofiction, that most postmodern of modes. Repeated in many texts, the original experiences have become the raw material of an art that tortures them each time into a different form: human truth, for Beckett, is not merely a matter of history, but of style.

Human Time

This distinctive mixture of the familiar and the fictive may be one reason for Beckett's unique place in contemporary culture, as a citizen of Ireland, Europe, and the world. Hugh Kenner has suggested one way to read those connections: after the Second World War, the sombre vision of Dublin's Beckett, and his quintessentially Irish struggle with suffocation and oppression, reflected the worldwide sense of devastation, and the end of all refuge.[7] The Swedish Academy, awarding in 1969 the Nobel Prize for Literature that Beckett sent his publisher to collect, saw the negatives as positive. The presenter's speech described an intellect and an imagination that spoke to and for Ireland, torn by the Troubles, and to and for humanity, scarred by its post-Second World War initiation into the inhumane:

> Mix a powerful imagination with a logic in absurdum, and the result will be either a paradox or an Irishman. If it is an Irishman, you will get the paradox into the bargain. Even the Nobel Prize in Literature is sometimes divided. Paradoxically, this has happened in 1969, a single award being addressed to one man, two languages and a third nation, itself divided. [...]

> [The] degradation of humanity is a recurrent theme in Beckett's writing and to this extent, his philosophy, simply accentuated by elements of the grotesque and of tragic farce, can be described as a negativism that cannot desist from descending to the depths. To the depths it must go because it is only there that pessimistic thought and poetry can work their miracles. What does one get when a negative is printed? A positive, a clarification, with black proving to be the light of day, the parts in deepest shade those which reflect the light source. Its name is fellow-feeling, charity.[8]

Leslie Hill, writing his obituary for Beckett, made a cognate point:

> Beckett's writing bears witness to the refuse and litter that has never been properly incorporated into the universalising dialectic of European history and culture: to the dispersion of languages, the impossibilities of transmission, the agonies of the flesh, the failure of redemption, the ending of Christianity. [... It] is pertinent to recall that Beckett places Molloy in a world that bears the marks of anti-Semitism and the diaspora. In this regard, Beckett's bilingualism is not an advertisement for European integration and the single market, but signs an act of resistance, a refusal to submit to the totalising logic of history and meaning.[9]

Traces of the specific historical context of the Second World War and especially the Holocaust have been discovered, with more or less justification, throughout Beckett's work. He spent the war in occupied France, was active in the Resistance, saw dear friends vanish into the prisons and camps, and returned to France after the German surrender to help in a hospital for the wounded in bombed-out Saint-Lô. His familiarity with atrocity includes that dreadful knowledge. David Houston Jones stands in the long line of critics, including Leslie Hill, who have turned to Theodor Adorno's praise of Beckett for providing the most appropriate response to the situation of the concentration camps.[10] As Adorno says, Beckett doesn't supply that particular term; but the Irishman's all-embracing account of man's estate, 'how it is', has been adopted by students of the Holocaust to supply models and a language for their own accounts of the degradation of humanity, and the impossibility of bearing witness to it.[11]

The long twentieth century that Beckett lived through presented many variations on the human capacity to impose and endure suffering. A 10-year-old at the time of the Easter Rebellion of 1916, he watched the fires of Dublin with his father from his home suburb of Foxrock; and though his own family environment was a protected one, the bitter fighting for independence, and the accompanying internecine struggles, were the formative context of his adolescent and university years.[12] His writing is crammed with images of Irish men and women cramped out of recognition by the inhumane relationships they were forced into in the Catholic and nationalist Ireland of his youth, in the straitjackets of bourgeois respectability, or on the treadmill of poverty. Maddy Rooney and her husband (*All that Fall*), the old woman of *Not I*, Balfe, the old roadmender, in whom he sees his own reflection (*From an Abandoned Work*), all trudge the impoverished roads of the Irish countryside in the pages of his narratives. In 1930s Paris, he was touched by the ripples of the Spanish Civil War, racism, and the struggle of colonised nations for freedom. These were all mediated through the literary circles he moved in, and his work – which he refused throughout his career to have published or staged under oppressive regimes – was almost his only form of radical action. But David Lloyd, exploring the impact of Irish writing on post-colonial society and culture, has recognised the revolutionary charge of his writing, and its importance for liberation movements, describing it as 'the most exhaustive dismantling we have of the logic of identity that at every level structures and maintains the post-colonial moment'.[13]

Beckett's first-hand and most intense experience of human suffering was at the personal level. It came in the form of his long physical and mental illnesses, from his severe depression in the 1930s to double cataracts, broken ribs, and lung abscess in the 1960s, prostate trouble from the late 1970s, and emphysema in his final years; and through the early, painful deaths, by cancer and stroke, of close family and friends. From these tragedies emerged the images of the human condition by which he is best known: living the space between birth and death, on the edge of the grave, enduring the passing of time that piles up and smothers the body like grains of sand, ears resounding with the screams from the cancer ward. Less well-known, and fewer, are the idyllic moments he charts of long walks across fields, or cycling at speed downhill through city streets or along country lanes, watching and listening to the birds whose lives draw different patterns, in another kind of element.

Images of physical pain also convey the philosophical anguish of the human condition, beginning and ending in the unknown and unknowable, and tormented by the impossible desire for self-knowledge: who, what and where you are, and how it is. Against the pat answers of religious and philosophical traditions, Beckett's work poses the unspeakability of the human subject. He conducts an unremitting attack on language, traditionally claimed to be the distinguishing character of the human. Language, in its multiple forms of inherited social and cultural discourses, is a network of pre-emptive subject positions and styles. Outside language there is nothing; inside language, there is no freedom, only the limits imposed by the authority of others. This is the insight into which Beckett was initiated in interwar Paris, through his association with James Joyce and the Parisian avant-garde, Symbolists, Surrealists and Existentialists. The unending, impossible search for ways of communicating the unsayable, what it is to be human, living and dying, is the theme of all his writing. Alongside his modernist contemporaries, he began his own lifelong experiment in diminishing and dissolving words, using and subverting all the forms that the twentieth century would offer for the inscription of speech: poetry, short story, the novel, stage drama, radio, film, and television.

As the twentieth century moved on, modernism in some circles became old hat – but an old hat, one of Beckett's favourite images, is still of use, as well as ornament. In the post-modernist way of thinking, the attempt to cut off historical antecedents, replacing remembering by forgetting, still provides no answer to questions about identity or freedom. The twenty-first century can still respond to Beckett's rehearsals of the old questions, and his way of dealing with the absence of answers. The riddle of human being loses none of its fascination, and Beckett's writing of it remains inexhaustible: 'I said, with rapture, Here is something I can study all my life, and never understand.'[14]

Everybody's Beckett

Since his death on 22 December 1989, it has become difficult to imagine that time when Samuel Beckett was a complete unknown. Born in 1906 into an unexceptional and obscure childhood in a respectable Dublin suburb, he came late to fame in the early 1950s with *Waiting for Godot*, the work for which he will always be best remembered – and of which, at the end, he was heartily sick ('I'm sick and tired of theatre & of *Godot* in particular. To have to listen to these words day after day has become torture').[15] Since *Godot*, his writing has been translated, published, and staged across countries and continents.[16] Since his death, his work continues to find ever greater favour with the publishing industry on which he originally had to work hard to make an impact. New collections of his works are in production by Faber and Faber and Grove Press; Faber and Faber has a new series of paperback editions of individual texts, and a new annotated collection of all his poetry; and an edited series of his letters is appearing with Cambridge University Press.[17] The landmark biography by James Knowlson that appeared in 1996 brought clearer understanding of the connections of the man and his writing with the movement of his times, with its rich detail on how and where the work was published and produced, insights into the personality of a subject who became a personal friend, and sensitive accounts of Beckett's many close relationships, family and friends.[18] Academic study of Beckett's writing was already taking significant new directions from the late 1970s, engaging with the new perspectives in critical theory coming into the mainstream. In particular, the theorists who drew on the innovative work on philosophy and psychoanalysis undertaken in the 1930s, by Beckett's contemporaries, could cast important light on what Beckett had long been saying on the problematic nature of subject identity, and the operations of language.[19]

The ever-expanding research archives at the Beckett International Foundation at the University of Reading, the Harry Ransom Center at The University of Texas at Austin, Trinity College Dublin, and many other centres, are an invaluable resource for the scholarly study of Beckett's work.[20] There are extensive resources on the internet, consulted by researchers, students, and the general public.[21] The last category has expanded well beyond the Third Programme audience who responded to Beckett's first experiments with modern media. The exhibition 'Fathoms from Anywhere' at the Harry Ransom Center in Austin, Texas, hosts on its website an open blog, featuring a wide range of answers to the question why we should read Beckett. There are many messages from a new generation of Beckett readers, with new perspectives, including one placing Sam Beckett second only to Henry Miller as the most encouraging writer in the world.[22] Video extracts from different productions of the plays figure extensively on YouTube, from performances by the San Quentin Drama Workshop to Sesame Street's offering, 'Waiting for Elmo', which ends abruptly with the irate departure of the famous tree.[23]

The development of electronic recording has given wider access to the plays, though many of them, unfortunately, are still only available to those with deep pockets. CD recordings are widely available of the first BBC radio productions of Beckett's plays, and video and DVD versions are available of stage and television productions, some supervised by Beckett himself.[24]

Even before the internet took off, school syllabuses had taken *Waiting for Godot* to their hearts, and helped produce audiences that understand Beckett much more easily than their predecessors. Peter Hall, the first British director of the play, summed up the sea-change in audiences' ability to relate to what Beckett is saying:

> 'I have been brooding in my bath for the last hour and have come to the conclusion that the success of *Waiting for Godot* means the end of the theatre as we know it.' Robert Morley, the famous character actor, made this prophecy in 1955. His generation – middle-aged – mostly endorsed his gloom. My generation of twentysomethings was glad. [...]
>
> In 1997, I directed *Godot* again at the Old Vic. My 16-year-old daughter was baffled by the programme material detailing the play's controversial history. 'What on earth is there to understand?' she said. 'It's perfectly clear what it is about. You only have to listen.'[25]

Not a year goes by without a new live production of Beckett on stages or in festivals, often graced by celebrity actors, and breaking free, with the permission of the Beckett Estate, from the stricter controls that Beckett tried in his lifetime to exert. A dossier published in *The Observer* in March 2009 offered the percipient comment that *Waiting for Godot* could respond to the needs of very different audiences, especially in times or places under intense pressure.[26] In Sarajevo under siege, in 1993, Haris Pašćovic had expressed his pleasure on hearing that the *Washington Post* had spoken of 'Waiting for Clinton'; while in New Orleans, in 2007, Wendell Pierce starred as Vladimir in the Classical Theatre of Harlem's outdoor production, in the devastated landscape of post-Katrina New Orleans.[27]

Better acquaintance with Beckett's work has been helped by better knowledge of a personality sometimes presented in the press as retired and reclusive. Knowlson's biography includes numerous anecdotes of his generosity with his money and his time, to fellow-artists, scholars, and passers-by in the streets. Those who met him in the flesh spoke warmly of his kindness and charm. The journalist Peter Lennon described their first meeting in January 1961, when as a young Dubliner Lennon had come to work as a freelance in Paris: 'My strongest impression was that I had been with a nice man [...].'[28] He was not, said Lennon, a typical 'McDaid's Irish scribbler'. He was a 'respectable man', 'scholarly', but not a recluse, sociable, and with friends world-wide, who carefully protected his privacy. He was repelled by bad manners, and he told Lennon how Brendan Behan, to his annoyance, had come banging on the door of his Paris flat in the early hours, demanding he come out for a drink. Photographs and sketches, a number reprinted on postcards, have made widely known a face with craggy attractiveness and a penetrating gaze, which Barbara Vine, in one of her popular detective novels, had one of her characters hang on his study wall, out of admiration for his writing.[29]

Ireland's Beckett

There was a time when Beckett, it seemed, appealed to everyone except the Irish, and that the feeling was mutual. Since his death, studies have shown how much of Beckett's writing built out from his affectionate familiarity with the Irish landscape, as well as the patterns and rhythms of Irish language and culture.[30] Any residual resentment at the 'abandonment' of Ireland for Europe by the modernist writers of the 1910s and 1920s must now be deemed at an end, with the delivery to the Irish Naval Service of the first of the Samuel Beckett Class Offshore Patrol Vessels, LÉ *Samuel Beckett* (P61), destined for maritime patrol missions.[31]

Declan Kiberd has argued convincingly for better understanding of the cultural bridges built between Paris and Dublin by the generations of Joyce and Beckett.[32] Today, the Samuel Beckett Bridge commemorates the writer in the heart of Dublin's Docklands. Funded by heritage and development bodies, and by Dublin City Council, it opened to traffic in December 2009, joining the James Joyce Bridge, designed by the same architect (Santiago Calatrava), and the Seán O'Casey footbridge. Beckett's early poems and novels frequently staggered drunkenly across Dublin's historic bridges, and crossings and intersections are fundamental to his drama. The short story 'Ding-Dong' praises a life spent in movement: 'My sometime friend Belacqua enlivened the last phase of his solipsism, before he toed the line and began to relish the world, with the belief that the best thing he had to do was to move constantly from place to place. [...] The simplest form of this exercise was boomerang, out and back.'[33] Belacqua, Beckett's first persona, and the one to which he most frequently returned, was the poet found curled up in the shadow of a rock in Dante's Purgatory, condemned to live forever in Limbo. In 1932, Beckett's Belacqua, born into a more cheerful kind of Purgatory, welcomes readers into his creator's first major work, the *Dream of Fair to Middling Women*, where as a child he hurtles joyfully on his cycle following a horse down a country lane. As a young man, he carouses round Dublin before leaving for Germany and then Paris, to return finally to Dublin, and end up in Ballsbridge with sore feet and violent stomach-ache on the bridge's rain-lashed pavement, being moved on by the Garda.

There was an end to boomerang, and a need for fresh inspiration. The dying Malone, reviewing his resources from his sickbed, notes the diminishing lead in his Venus pencil, and remembers he also has a French one, not as yet much used. Beckett's move to Paris transformed his writing. But whatever pencil he subsequently picked up, Ireland remained the bedrock of his experience, the stone and earth he was forever worming into,[34] or tunnelling out of, and which shaped his experience of the larger European heritage that made him and Ireland both.

Beckett had a knowing way of living his Irishness, according to Peter Lennon. He had a suburban middle-class Dublin accent, with 'a trace of commonness in his vocabulary'.[35] He had a 'preference for idiomatic Dublinese', and loved to make satirical play with cliché, which is 'a very Dublin way of dealing at a tangent with relationships. It is partly a way of displaying your Dublin credentials, sending reassuring signals that you are of the same tribe [...].' He loved the landscapes of Ireland, particularly round the Dublin and Wicklow mountains, and Irish voices. But, to Lennon's surprise, he refused to accept that his novels and plays could be tagged as Irish, preferring to emphasise their universal resonance.

Beckett's early childhood in Ireland was a time he recalled with pleasure. He was born on 13 May 1906 in Foxrock, County Dublin into a prosperous Protestant middle-class family, in a big house (Cooldrinagh) built by his father, William, who was a quantity surveyor.[36] He was very fond of his older brother, Frank, and his mother Maria (May) who was, however, a domineering woman, a strict disciplinarian, and given to violent rages. He adored the company of his father, who fostered his taste for long country walks. His writing evokes a father figure who never manages to communicate with his son, but who once shared the son's longing to cast off on life's open sea, before – like all fathers – he settled, in the image in *Embers*, to sit like a stone on the shore, gazing at the now-forbidden horizon.

Beckett was a sociable, pleasant, and eminently normal child. He was educated at private schools, including the Protestant Portora Royal School, Enniskillen, where he was sent to be out of reach of the Troubles.[37] In the holidays, there were cousins close by, including Peggy Sinclair, his first love, whose blue-green eyes are a recurring motif in his work. He later had a two-year affair with Peggy, whom he followed to Kassel, in Germany, in 1928.

His nemesis was, he said, Trinity College Dublin, where he went in 1923 to read Modern European Literature, specialising in French and Italian, with English literature as a minor subject. Staff and fellow-students struck him as pompous, pedantic, and superficial. He got on well with the Professor of Romance Languages, Thomas Brown Rudmose-Brown, who passed on his enthusiasm for Racine and contemporary French poetry. After graduating in 1927, Beckett began an MA thesis on Pierre Jean Jouve and *Unanimisme*, and in Paris, he was able to meet with Jouve.[38] His Italian professor was far less inspiring, but there was a private tutor, Bianca Esposito, who was responsible for his lifelong love of Dante's *Divina Commedia*.[39]

The time spent at Trinity College was worthwhile because it secured his nomination to Paris as an exchange *lecteur* at the École Normale Supérieure, and through that his introduction to James Joyce. There was a brief return to Dublin to teach French literature, in autumn 1930, which convinced him that the academic life was not for him. 'Brilliant and interesting', 'tall, handsome, mysterious' according to some students, to others he was 'a tall thin streak of misery', 'boring', and 'he despised us'.[40] At the beginning of the summer vacation in 1931, his mother threw him out of the family home, having found, read, and been enraged by some of his writing, carelessly left out in view.[41]

Back in Dublin after travelling in France with his brother Frank, he hung on in his rooms in Trinity College until the end of the year, increasingly miserable, lecturing, writing some poetry and some translation work, taking long walks in the countryside, and continuing to extend his knowledge of Dublin's high and low life, from brothels to the National Gallery. He visited the gallery several times in the second half of 1931 to look at the newly-purchased Perugino *Pietà*, and wrote to his friend Tom MacGreevy deploring its poor restoration and the bad light in which it was hung, but admiring 'a lovely cheery Xist full of sperm, & the woman touching his thighs and mourning his jewels'.[42] He went to Germany for Christmas 1931, and from there sent a letter resigning his post in Trinity College.

He did not however let go of the cultural contacts, and friendships, established during this short period. He had established what would become a lifelong friendship with the painter Jack Butler Yeats, admiring his commitment to the Republic as well as his painting, and visited him regularly in his studio, though not enjoying his Saturday at-homes.[43] He later bought two of Yeats's pictures: just before the war, 'Sligo Morning', and after the war, 'Regatta Evening'.[44] To his aunt, Cissie Sinclair, with whom he shared his interests in painting and literature, he described the 'perception and dispassion' he admired in Yeats's paintings of the relationships between men and woman, in terms which could also be used of his own portraits of all human relationships:

> The way he puts down a man's head & a woman's head side by side, or face to face, is terrifying, two irreducible singlenesses & the impassable immensity between. I suppose that is what gives the stillness to his pictures, as though the convention were suddenly suspended, the convention & performance of love & hate, joy & pain, giving & being given, taking & being taken. A kind of petrified insight into one's ultimate hard irreducible inorganic singleness. All handled with the dispassionate acceptance that is beyond tragedy.[45]

To Tom MacGreevy, he wrote of Yeats's challenge to the romantic fantasy of landscape, and his representation of 'the unalterable alienness' of nature and its human inhabitants, 'the impassable immensity' between them. He adds that: 'God knows it doesn't take much sensitiveness to feel that in Ireland, a nature almost as inhumanly inorganic as a stage set.'[46]

The novelist Francis Stuart remembers being with Beckett in the early 1930s, in the back room at Davy Byrne's, with a bunch of other aspiring writers, and their various friends and acquaintances, some fairly well-off; he picks out especially the poet and painter Cecil Salkeld and the journalist A.J. (Con) Leventhal, who followed Beckett in the lecturer's post at Trinity College.[47] A number of Beckett's poems were published in *The Dublin*

Magazine in the 1930s, through the good offices of its editor, Seumas O'Sullivan.[48] In 1936, O'Sullivan was to offer Beckett the editorship of the *Dublin Magazine*, which he refused.[49] In the early 1930s, the frontiers between avant-garde Dublin and avant-garde Paris were porous; in the summer of 1934, introduced by Tom MacGreevy, Beckett met Brian Coffey and Denis Devlin in Dublin.

Other frontiers were firmly closed. Trinity College, Foxrock, and Beckett's mother, May, had their larger counterpart in the society and politics of an Ireland dominated by the Catholic Church, and an establishment that knew itself to be under siege. Issues of censorship focused the antagonisms. The grip of the Catholic Church on intellectual freedom was strengthened in the mid-1920s by the call for an Irish Ireland, associated with the *Leader* newspaper and the Gaelic League, which argued for a purely Gaelic and Catholic culture, free of the foreign influences that fostered 'the appetite for dirty papers'.[50] In the summer of 1929, a harsh new Censorship of Publications Act became law.

In 1934, under a pseudonym (Andrew Belis), Beckett published an essay on 'Recent Irish Poetry', which is now read as an Irish modernist manifesto.[51] A sharp analysis of the innovatory rewriting of subject identity by Irish modernist poets commended MacGreevy for recognising that 'it is the act and not the object of perception that matters'.[52] This was combined with an even sharper critique of the creative productions of Irish nationalism, the fruits of the Gaelic League. Declan Kiberd has pointed out the political charge underlying this attack on the aesthetics of traditionalism, arguing that the politics of the Gaelic revivalists, focused on the ownership of land, and their alignment with the traditionalist patriarchies of the Irish countryside, go hand in hand with the conservative subject positions asserted in their poetry.[53] Kiberd sees Patrick Kavanagh's *The Great Hunger* as echoing Beckett's argument in 1934: that the refusal of the revival to challenge conventional ideas of the self went hand in hand with their idealisation of rural life.[54]

Beckett was in fact emphasising the importance of something a little different: not simply the imperative of self-exploration, which could, he said, be misdirected into moralising discussion of the collapse of the subject, but the recognition by modern artists of something more terrifying. The nature of perception is no longer to be understood in the same way: the subject must admit that he can have no objective knowledge of the world outside him. Beckett describes

> the new thing that has happened, or the old thing that has happened again, namely the breakdown of the object, whether current, historical, mythical or spook. The thermolaters [...] would no doubt like this amended to breakdown of the subject. It comes to the same thing – rupture of the lines of communication.
>
> The artist who is aware of this may state the space that intervenes between him and the world of objects; he may state it as no-man's-land, Hellespont or vacuum, according as he happens to be feeling resentful, nostalgic or merely depressed. [...] Or he may celebrate the cold comforts of apperception. [...] Those who are not aware of the rupture [...] are the antiquarians, delivering with the altitudinous complacency of the Victorian Gael the Ossianic goods.
>
> Thus contemporary Irish poets may be divided into antiquarians and others, the former in the majority, the latter kindly noticed by Mr W. B. Yeats as 'the fish that lie gasping on the shore', suggesting that they might at least learn to expire with an air.[55]

The antiquarians, initially, triumphed. By the time Beckett finally left Ireland for Paris in October 1937, the censor had suppressed his essay on Marcel Proust (1931), and his short story collection, *More Pricks than Kicks* (1934), both of them for their titles rather than their content. As a result, when he returned in November 1937 to appear as a witness in a libel case brought by his Aunt Cissie's brother-in-law, Harry Sinclair, against Oliver St John Gogarty, he was pilloried by the defence counsel as that 'bawd and blasphemer' from Paris, described by the judge as a witness not to be relied on, and violently attacked in the newspapers.[56] Only much later did fame bring the opportunity to pay back the censors. In 1958, a selection of Beckett's plays was set to appear as part of the Dublin Theatre Festival. The Archbishop of Dublin, Dr John Charles McQuaid, seeing Seán O'Casey's *The Drums of Father Ned* on the programme, notoriously refused a request for a Mass to celebrate the Festival, and Beckett in response refused to allow his own work to be staged.[57]

In the 1970s, Mark Nixon says, with the resurgence of the Troubles, Irish poetry began to create a new place for Samuel Beckett; and the process began when, in 1971, Michael Smith and Trevor Joyce republished in *The*

Lace Curtain Beckett's much-abused essay of 1934.[58] What appealed to the poets of this new moment was the balance Beckett had struck regarding Irish nationalism. Convinced of the need to get the British out of Ireland, a sentiment reinforced for him in Paris in the 1930s by his friend MacGreevy, Beckett was also convinced of the oppressive and reductive effects of nationalism on both individuals and country; and the dead bones of past controversies interested him far less than the humanity of the present. Thinking generally about books on history, he was to write in his German diaries on 15 January 1937 that:

> I am not interested in a 'unification' of the historical chaos any more than I am in the 'clarification' of the individual chaos, and still less in the anthropomorphisation of the inhuman necessities that provoke the chaos. [...] I say the background and the causes are an inhuman and incomprehensible machinery and venture to wonder what kind of appetite it is that can be appeased by the modern animism that consists in rationalising them.[59]

The new generation of Irish poets turned to Beckett's experiences to work through the shifts and contradictions of their own. And at least as important, they looked to his innovative writing for new forms to illuminate that shifting threshold in which historical and individual chaos is framed.

Paul Muldoon, Thomas Kinsella, David Wheatley, and John Montague have all recognised their debt to Beckett, but as Mark Nixon has pointed out, Derek Mahon, more than any other, has taken Beckett's writing into the heart of his own.[60] Mahon's 'An Image from Beckett' is the *locus classicus* for critics looking to illustrate the two writers' consanguinity.[61] The likeness here is not so much one of tone and mood: the flicker of white light that is life, the brief flash between birth and death, which in *Waiting for Godot* provokes Pozzo to furious resentment, is in Mahon's poem a celebration of everything good and lovely in human time. The resemblances are ones of form: their shared predilection for the expression of feeling through landscape, for scenarios which fix time as posthumous expression, for filmic effects, for black and white, and for the sound of the words. Mahon himself has spoken in a review of the filmic nature of many of Beckett's poems, his sharp eye for details of landscape, their vivid visual character, and their musical quality. [62] And as well as the overlap with film and music, there are resonances with Beckett's other work in theatre and radio; for Mahon, the continuity of Beckett's inspiration is striking. Paradoxically, he finds, the persistent, almost physical presence of the poems is indissolubly linked to their celebration of the painful ephemerality of the human. He underlines his insight in the subtitle of his review ('The "brief scattered lights" of Beckett's poems'), which is taken from a line in *Malone Dies.*

Mahon's own poem, 'From "Burbles" (Mirlitonnades)', printed alongside the review, with an epigraph 'After Samuel Beckett', reworks Beckett's characteristic phrases, to capture the rhythm of a vision of being realised in motion, which is simultaneously physical and ephemeral. Mahon situates Beckett's story, and his legacy to writing, at the 'far end of void', in the celebration of that shifting threshold which is that time, gone in no time: 'all in the mind', as 'he strides ahead/ no end in sight'.[63]

NOTES

1 Samuel Beckett, *What Where* (1984); *CDW* 1986.

2 Samuel Beckett, *That Time* (1976); *CDW* 1986, p.388, p.395.

3 Beckett, *That Time*; *CDW* 1986, p.389.

4 Beckett, *That Time*; *CDW* 1986, p.390.

5 Ibid.

6 Derek Mahon, 'Watt is the word. The "brief scattered lights" of Beckett's poems', *TLS*, 5405, (3 November 2006), p.13.

7 Hugh Kenner, 'The Terminator', in *A Colder Eye. The Modern Irish Writers* (Harmondsworth: Penguin Books, 1984), p.329.

8 Karl Ragnar Gierow, 'The Nobel Prize in Literature 1969. Samuel Beckett. Award Ceremony Speech', The Nobel Foundation. (http://www.nobelprize.org/nobel_prizes/literature/laureates/1969/press.html# Consulted 3 December 2012.)

9 Leslie Hill, 'Samuel Beckett (1906–1989)', *Radical Philosophy*, 55 (Summer 1990), p.62.

10 Theodor W. Adorno, *Negative Dialectics* (London: Routledge, 1990), p.380, cit. David Houston Jones, *Samuel Beckett and Testimony* (Houndmills, Basingstoke: Palgrave Macmillan, 2011), p.2.

11 David Houston Jones, *Samuel Beckett and Testimony*, pp.2–4.

12 See for example Lois Gordon, *The World of Samuel Beckett (1906–1946)* (New Haven and London: Yale University Press, 1996), Chapter 1, 'Ireland'.

13 David Lloyd, *Anomalous States: Irish Writing and the Post-Colonial Moment* (Durham, NC: Duke University Press, 1993), p.56.

14 Samuel Beckett, *Molloy* (1955); *Trilogy* 1979, p.156.

15 Letter from Beckett to Alan Schneider, 11 February 1975, in Maurice Harmon (ed.), *No Author Better Served. The Correspondence of Samuel Beckett and Alan Schneider* (Cambridge, Mass.: Harvard University Press, 1998), p.322. This letter, © the Estate of Samuel Beckett, is reproduced by kind permission of the Estate of Samuel Beckett c/o Rosica Colin Limited, London.

16 See Mark Nixon and Matthew Feldman (eds), *The International Reception of Samuel Beckett* (London: Continuum, 2009).

17 See Bibliography for details of the editions used in the present study.

18 James Knowlson, *Damned to Fame. The Life of Samuel Beckett* (London: Bloomsbury Publishing, 1996). The biography by Deirdre Bair, *Samuel Beckett* (London: Jonathan Cape, 1978), did not enjoy the same close collaboration with Beckett, but still has very useful information and perspectives.

19 For extracts from the work of some of the influential writers in this area, see Jennifer Birkett and Kate Ince (eds), *Samuel Beckett* (London and New York: Longman, Longman Critical Readers, 2000).

20 For a recent overview of archive holdings, see Lois More Overbeck, 'Audience of Self/Audience of Reader', *Modernism/modernity*, 18, 4 (November 2011), pp.721–37.

21 See for example The Samuel Beckett On-Line Resources and Links Page (http://www.samuel-beckett.net), The Beckett International Foundation at the University of Reading (http://www.beckettfoundation.org.uk), The Beckett Circle. Official Newsletter of the Samuel Beckett Society (http://www.beckettcircle.org), and The Samuel Beckett Endpage at the University of Antwerp (https://www.uantwerpen.be/en/rg/the-samuel-beckett-endpage).

22 'Fathoms from Anywhere.' A Samuel Beckett Centenary Exhibition, at the Harry Ransom Center at The University of Texas at Austin (http://www.hrc.utexas.edu/exhibitions/web/beckett/share/. Consulted 9 September 2013.)

23 'Waiting for Elmo', Sesame Street – Monsterpiece Theater, Beckett Shorts, YouTube (http://www.youtube.com/playlist?list=PLFA3C073738DAC946. Consulted 9 September 2013.) The tree itself received further internet recognition with its celebration by the sculptor Anthony Gormley. See for example Anthony Gormley, 'Observations: I made a tree because Beckett means a lot to me', *The Independent* (25 August 2012), (http://www.independent.co.uk/arts-entertainment/art/news/observations-i-made-a-tree-because-beckett-means-a-lot-to-me-8076584.html. Consulted 11 November 2011.)

24 See for example *Beckett on Film* (2001), produced by RTE, Channel 4, and the Irish Film Board; *Samuel Beckett: Works for Radio. The Original Broadcasts* (London: British Library Publishing Division, 2006). Everett C. Frost directed

the American project, *The Beckett Festival of Radio Plays*, launched in 1989 (see below, Chapter 7, pp.167ff and p.194n2).

25 Peter Hall, 'Godotmania', *The Guardian* (4 January 2003) (http://www.theguardian.com/stage/2003/jan/04/theatre.beckettat100. Consulted 9 September 2013.)

26 David Smith, Imogen Carter and Ally Carnwath, 'In Godot we trust', *The Observer* (8 March 2009). (http://www.theguardian.com/culture/2009/mar/08/samuel-beckett-waiting-for-godot. Last consulted 11 November 2014.)

27 David Smith et al, 'In Godot we trust'.

28 Peter Lennon, 'Evenings with Sam', *Review Guardian* (25 January 1990), p.23.

29 Barbara Vine, *The Chimney Sweeper's Boy* (London: Viking 1998, Penguin Books, 1998, reissued 2007), p.105.

30 See for example Eoin O'Neill, *The Beckett Country: Samuel Beckett's Ireland* (New York: Arcade Publishing, 1993); C.J. Ackerley and S.E. Gontarski (eds), *The Grove Companion to Samuel Beckett. A Reader's Guide to his Works, Life, and Thought* (New York: Grove Press, 2004); Emilie Morin, *Samuel Beckett and The Problem of Irishness* (London and New York, NY: Palgrave Macmillan, 2009). Seán Kennedy's collection of edited essays, *Beckett and Ireland* (Cambridge: Cambridge University Press, 2010), opens with an essay by Rónán McDonald ('Beckett and Irish Studies', pp.16–30), which traces the treatment, or lack of it, of Beckett's work in academic Irish Studies, and finds some explanation in his origins in the professional Protestant bourgeoisie, and more in his resistance to inclusion in the binaries of any easy narrative of Irish culture which seeks to chart a progressive emergence from tradition into modernity.

31 'Samuel Beckett Class Offshore Patrol Vessels, Ireland', in *naval-technology.com* (http://www.naval-technology.com/projects/samuel-beckett-class-offshore-patrol-vessels-opvs/. Consulted 28 August 2014.) The second OPV is to be named after James Joyce.

32 Declan Kiberd, *Inventing Ireland: The Literature of the Modern Nation* (London: Vintage, 1996).

33 Samuel Beckett, 'Ding-Dong', in *More Pricks than Kicks* (1934); rpt. London: Calder & Boyars, 1973, pp.39–40.

34 See below, Chapter 3, for development of this theme.

35 Lennon, 'Evenings with Sam', p.23.

36 This is the date on his birth certificate, but by reason of some confusion the family always celebrated his birthday on 13 April (Knowlson, *Damned to Fame*, p.1). Biographical detail in this section is from Knowlson's biography, unless otherwise indicated.

37 Interview with Samuel Beckett, in James and Elizabeth Knowlson (eds), *Beckett Remembering/ Remembering Beckett* (London: Bloomsbury, 2006), p.21.

38 Knowlson and Knowlson (eds), *Beckett Remembering*, p.39.
39 Knowlson and Knowlson (eds), *Beckett Remembering*, p.24.
40 Knowlson and Knowlson (eds), *Beckett Remembering*, pp.52–8.
41 Knowlson, *Damned to Fame*, pp.130–31.
42 Letter from Beckett to Thomas MacGreevy, 20 December 1931, in Martha Dow Fehsenfeld, Lois More Overbeck, George Craig and Dan Gunn (eds), *The Letters of Samuel Beckett, Volume I: 1929–1940* (Cambridge and New York: Cambridge University Press, 2009), p.100. Originally known as McGreevy, Thomas adopted the spelling MacGreevy after 1943. This form is used as standard in the present text.
43 Letter from Beckett to Thomas MacGreevy, 4 November [1932], *Letters* I, p.139.
44 Knowlson and Knowlson (eds), *Beckett Remembering*, p.60.
45 Letter from Beckett to Cissie Sinclair, 14 [August 1937], *Letters* I, p.536.
46 Letter from Beckett to Thomas MacGreevy, 14 August 1937, *Letters* I, p.540.
47 Francis Stuart, interview with James Knowlson, in Knowlson and Knowlson (eds), *Beckett Remembering*, p.61.
48 Peter Brooker and Andrew Thacker (eds), *The Oxford Critical and Cultural History of Modernist Magazines. Volume I: Britain and Ireland 1880–1955* (Oxford: Oxford University Press, 2009), p.748, p.711.
49 Knowlson, *Damned to Fame*, p.225.
50 *The Leader*, May 1925, cit. in Brooker and Thacker (eds), *The Oxford Critical and Cultural History of Modernist Magazines*, p.746.
51 Patricia Coughlan, '"The Poetry is Another Pair of Sleeves": Beckett, Ireland and Modernist Lyric Poetry', in Patricia Coughlan and Alex Davis (eds), *Modernism and Ireland: The Poetry of the 1930s* (Cork: Cork University Press, 1995), p.178.
52 Samuel Beckett (pseud. Andrew Belis), 'Recent Irish Poetry', *The Bookman*, August 1934; *Disjecta* 1983, p.74.
53 Declan Kiberd, *Inventing Ireland: The Literature of the Modern Nation* (London: Vintage, 1996), p.476, p.479. The author of *The Unnamable* would have appreciated Kiberd's accounts of the educational and religious systems linked with the anti-modernist mind-set.
54 Kiberd, *Inventing Ireland*, p.478.
55 Samuel Beckett, 'Recent Irish Poetry'; *Disjecta* 1983, p.70.
56 Knowlson, *Damned to Fame*, pp.275–80.
57 C.J. Ackerley and S.E. Gontarski, 'Politics', in *The Grove Companion to Samuel Beckett*, p.449.
58 Mark Nixon, '"A brief glow in the dark": Samuel Beckett's Presence in Modern Irish Poetry', *Yearbook of English Studies 35* (2005), pp.44–5.

59 Samuel Beckett, German Diaries, Notebook 4, 15 January 1937, cit. Knowlson, *Damned to Fame*, p.244.

60 Mark Nixon, '"A brief glow in the dark"', p.56.

61 Derek Mahon, 'An Image from Beckett', *Poems 1962–68* (Oxford and New York: Oxford University Press, 1979), pp.37–8.

62 Mahon, 'Watt is the word'.

63 Derek Mahon, 'Burbles', *The Hudson Letter* (Oldcastle: The Gallery Press, 1995), pp.21–2.

CHAPTER 1

The Long Beginning (1928–46)

Beckett's story is the story of his writing. It properly begins where the writing began, with Beckett crossing the threshold into Paris – the Paris of the expatriates, the heart of modernist Europe – and striding into all the shifts and changes of the years between the wars. David Williams, analysing the attraction of Paris for Peter Brook, places Brook in a tradition of great creative migrants, in which he includes Picasso, Gertrude Stein, James Joyce, and Beckett himself. Paris for them was the space of otherness, a cultural mixing pot, and a transit point, both a second home and the place of the outsider. Both insider and outsider, the artist in Paris could cast an estranging gaze on all things familiar.[1]

Boomeranging between Paris and Dublin, Beckett completed his indenturing and apprenticeship. By the time he made his permanent home in Paris, in 1937, he had come to terms with Ireland, and his family, and he was making a reputation as a writer of both prose and poetry. He began with poetry.

'James Joyce's White Boy'

In autumn 1928, Beckett took up the post of exchange *lecteur* at the École Normale Supérieure, in Paris. He was welcomed by his predecessor, Tom MacGreevy, who in the two years he had already been there had embedded himself deep in French and expatriate modernist circles, and was delighted to introduce Beckett to his many and various friends. Tom MacGreevy, reported Richard Aldington, was a former gunnery officer in the British Expeditionary Force, but he was 'five hundred per cent Irish', and he had formerly held an official post in Ireland, which he had resigned (though himself a Catholic) in protest at Ireland's hostility to Protestants. He was highly knowledgeable about painting, and he wrote decent prose and poetry, though he lacked, said Aldington, the aggressive drive that characterises the true writer; he was however a gifted conversationalist.[2] Aldington also refers to his successor, 'a splendidly mad Irishman who was James Joyce's white boy and wanted to commit suicide, a fate he nearly imposed on half the faculty of the École by playing the flute – an instrument of which he was far from being a master – every night in his room from midnight to dawn'.[3]

MacGreevy introduced Beckett to James Joyce in November 1928. Joyce was at that time engaged on his *Work in Progress* (later *Finnegans Wake*), which was serialised as he wrote it by his friend Eugene Jolas in the little magazine, *transition*. The magazine had been founded by Jolas in the mid-1920s to familiarise European, especially Parisian, readers with new experimental work by a range of international writers.[4] Revolutions in science and philosophy had opened to the imagination new dimensions of time and space, which demanded a corresponding revolution in language: the disintegration and remaking of syntax, and the remaking of worn-out words, of which Joyce, Jolas felt, was the ground-breaking exponent. In the world of *transition*, with its emphasis on multilingualism, translation, and neologism, there was an atmosphere of innovation and heady excitement, far removed from the staid world of Dublin and Trinity College. There the greatest prospect on offer to Beckett had been a career on the academic treadmill. Paris offered a very different kind of society: liberated, international, and devoted to artistic ambition, new thinking and new writing. Beckett enjoyed a privileged entrée into literary history in the making. The American editor and journalist, Samuel Putnam, has described the scene, and the awe he felt when entering the rue de l'Odéon, the quarter of James Joyce and Gertrude Stein, favoured by the *transition* circle (the hard-working Jolas and Elliot Paul) and Joyce's Irish admirers – the latter, he notes dryly, to be seen collected round Beckett and MacGreevy at the École Normale, or lingering in the cafés along the boulevard du Montparnasse.[5]

Beckett had only recently discovered Joyce's work, but he admired it greatly. He came nearly every day to Joyce's flat in the Latin Quarter, read to him, and helped with his research.[6] Like MacGreevy, he was taken into the family. Both were invited to the lunch held on 27 June 1929 by Sylvia Beach and Adrienne Monnier to celebrate the publication of the French translation of *Ulysses*.[7] A month after they met, Joyce suggested to Beckett that he write the critical essay on *Work in Progress* that was published first in *transition* and then in *Our Exagmination Round his Factification for Incamination of 'Work in Progress'*, and suggested to him the approaches his discussion might take.[8]

Beckett soon found he was being considered a potential suitor for Joyce's much-loved and much-spoiled daughter Lucia, then aged 21 (Beckett was 23), who already had a string of admirers.[9] Lucia Joyce had from the age of 15 been familiar with the Surrealists who frequented her father's house, especially André Breton and Philippe Soupault, and she shared their fascination with hysteria, scandal, and sexual licence. She spoke four languages (German, Italian, French, English), she wrote poems, and most famously, she danced. In November 1925, she had joined Margaret Morris's newly-opened school of dance in Paris, and began to pursue what for many women at that time seemed the most promising route into a career in the avant-garde. When she met Beckett, she had already given a number of well-reviewed performances as a member of the group 'Les Six de rhythme et couleur'. In May 1929, she entered her first solo competition at the first international festival of dance at the Bal Bullier in the Latin Quarter. Beckett, along with MacGreevy, was one of Joyce's party, and he kept a photograph of Lucia in her dance costume for the rest of his life. They went out together, on their own and with the family. But Lucia's intensity was not matched by any interest on Beckett's part. He left Paris frequently to go and see Peggy Sinclair in Kassel, and in May 1930, he ended their relationship, telling Lucia he came to the house only to see Joyce.[10] Lucia was heartbroken, and her letters about her unhappiness threw Beckett into confusion. But he wrote to MacGreevy that there was no other solution.[11] Joyce banned both Beckett and MacGreevy from his house, and relations for a while were under strain.

Poetic Beginnings: Translating

In Paris, Beckett had begun to write. After his essay on Joyce, he began work on a translation of part of Joyce's 'Anna Livia Plurabelle', together with his friend Alfred Péron. The two had first met in Trinity College when Péron was an exchange student from the ENS, in 1926–28. Their contribution was later radically revised by Philippe Soupault and others, including Joyce himself, who found it unsatisfactory in both form and content.[12] A short story, 'Assumption', was published in *transition* in June 1929, and in the summer of

1930, Beckett was writing his critical study of the work of Marcel Proust. But poetry was his main preoccupation.

Initially, he was asked to translate poems by others, but he was soon seeing his own work in print.[13] His first publications came through Samuel Putnam, who having moved from Chicago to Paris in 1927 had subsequently became associate editor for *This Quarter*. In 1930, Beckett translated Eugenio Montale's 'Delta' for *This Quarter*.[14] The following year, three of his own poems, including 'Yoke of Liberty' (later entitled 'Moly'), appeared on 13 November 1931 in the first volume of Putnam's planned two-volume collection, *The European Caravan, A Critical Anthology of the New Spirit in European Literature*, where he was praised by Jacob Bronowski as the most interesting of the new Irish poets.[15] Three other poems appeared in Putnam's *The New Review*, 1931–32.[16] Back in 1930, Nancy Cunard's Hours Press had given Beckett another boost with the publication of his poem *Whoroscope*, the prizewinning entry in a competition for the best poem on the subject of time, judged by Cunard and Richard Aldington. At the editors' request, Beckett provided annotations, unpacking references as unfamiliar to most readers as any invoked in T.S. Eliot's poetry, and drawn from a very different area of the cultural heritage: the politics of science and religion in the early Enlightenment.[17] The poem is a narrative, a fairly conventional stream of consciousness, made up of Descartes's fragmentary but vivid recollections of the times of his life, presented in the staccato, snorting and gleeful rhythms of an old man whose memories of past successes and suffering rise up in apparently unbidden but orderly sequence – until time itself, to a body depleted by illness and age, suddenly calls halt. Descartes, tame philosopher at the court of Christina of Sweden, 'the whore of the snows', summoned by the Queen for yet another meeting in the freezing early morning, waits impatiently for his breakfast eggs to mature into the near-addled state he prefers. As he waits, brooding over the entrails of his recalcitrant hens, reverse-haruspicating into his past, he calls up memories of past battles with rivals, scientific and religious, of his father and brother, his dead daughter, his lovers. The eggs ripen as time ticks on, through references to clockwork, the surgeon William Harvey's 'cracked ticker', the 'atomic tempo of species', and the waiting is enlivened by the series of vivid colours and images in which Descartes sees his life run past: splashes of red, scarlet, burning, wine stains, blood, 'a high bright rose', and finally the dripping hands of the violent, high-tempered philosopher-

Queen. Past and present are all he cares for; this is the man who refused to have his birthday horoscope read, for fear of knowing his future death-day. Finally the eggs are ripe, and Descartes prepares himself to enjoy the fruits of time, invoking for the first time in his monologue a future tense where he will feed on his stinking dish, and climb the stairs to his historic meeting with Christina. This future at once vanishes into the past, the stairs have already been climbed, and the speaker, collapsing, is left calling, too late, for Weulles, the Queen's physician, to bleed him and give him a second chance of living the life that refused to contemplate the inevitability of death: 'grant me my second/ starless inscrutable hour.' Beckett's scholarship is clever, but his comic tone undermines all scientific and political pretensions, including those of the rationalist who closes his mind to the greatest of all truths, which is that death comes regardless. These games with time, ripeness and death, bathetically focused on the near-rotten egg, are ones on which Beckett was to play many variations in the future.

Nancy Cunard, rebellious daughter of British upper-class society, disinherited heiress, and ardent campaigner against fascism and racism, became a close friend. Beckett wrote her a poem ('From the only Poet to a Shining Whore'), which was set to music, along with others by Richard Aldington, Walter Lowenfels, and Harold Acton, by Cunard's lover, the pianist Henry Crowder.[18] For her anthology, *Negro* (1934), he translated nineteen items which took him into the Parisian heart of black cultural politics: articles on jazz orchestras, on the culture and politics of Haiti, and a couple of articles by Surrealist writers. The translations included only one poem, Ernst Moerman's 'Armstrong' (in Cunard's collection, 'Louis Armstrong'), which gives an unfavourable impression of Beckett's early translation style. To Moerman's piece, sober in both vocabulary and syntax, Beckett took licence to bring a melodramatic edge, and images considerably more colourful than the original. The seductive glances of the source poem, and the unadorned call of the sea are transformed into the tentacles of decadent femininity, sucking at a victim who in Moerman's image is simply described as walking, eyes closed, into a gulf.

In the early 1930s, Beckett was already becoming familiar with the investigations conducted by the French Symbolists into the mysterious interconnections of language and meaning, and, closer to home, through Joyce and Lucia, by the Surrealists. Their search for new means of expressing the nature of the subject and its relations with the world, and in the case of the Surrealists, their investigations into the nature of the unconscious and its forms, was probably the most powerful influence on Beckett's poetic aesthetic at this time.

In early 1932, Beckett was commissioned to translate Arthur Rimbaud's 'Le Bateau ivre', that famous celebration of the liberation of the senses into new kinds of perception of the world of things, and of the power of poetry's images and rhythms to communicate the freedom that comes from transgressing conventional boundaries. In Rimbaud's poem, the limiters are the canal banks of his homeland, Belgium and Northern France, and the guide-ropes that tie the boat to the workhorses. In Beckett's later writing, their counterpart will be the hedges along country roads or around gardens and parks, or the fences of the racecourse, images drawn from his own home landscapes. Beckett's translation, a poem in its own right, remains this time very close to the original, echoing the force of Rimbaud's images, and the 'rhythmic pulse' of his syntax.[19] In the following lines, mirroring Rimbaud's challenging evocation of the identity of the perceiving subject and his poetic object, Beckett maintains the 'I' at the centre, through all the necessary shifts of syntax and shunts of grammar from an unstressed to stressed language:

> Thenceforward, fused in the poem, milk of stars,
> Of the sea, I coiled through deeps of cloudless green, [...]
>
> [Et dès lors, je me suis baigné dans le poème
> De la mer, infusé d'astres, et lactescent,
> Dévorant les azurs verts ...] [20]

Eschewing Rimbaud's regular end-rhymes, Beckett relies on alliteration and assonance to sustain his meanings. And he discovers a range of ways to echo the coiling syntax of Rimbaud's text, enhancing its dynamism through repetition and inversion, and for nouns and finite verbs substituting present participles, gerunds and gerundives:

> More firmly bland than to children apples' firm pulp,
> Soaked the green water through my hull of pine,
> Scattering helm and grappling and washing me
> Of the stains, the vomitings and blue wine.[21]

[Plus douce qu'aux enfants la chair des pommes sures,
L'eau verte pénétra ma coque de sapin
Et des taches de vins bleus et des vomissures
Me lava, dispersant gouvernail et grappin.]

By an accident of publishing history, Beckett's translation of Rimbaud did not appear until the mid-1970s.[22] But there was no hold-up with the poems by André Breton and Paul Éluard which he translated for the Surrealist Number of *This Quarter*, which appeared in September 1932.[23] His Éluard translations reappeared in 1936 in *Thorns of Thunder*, edited by George Reavey, with a preface by Herbert Read, alongside other translations of Éluard by Reavey, David Gascoyne, Man Ray and Eugene Jolas. This volume, '[o]ne of English Surrealism's most significant publications', introduced Éluard into the English movement, placing Beckett, in consequence, among the important mediators of European Surrealist innovations into English Surrealist coteries, and, through them, into the mainstream of modernist English poetry.[24] Beckett expressed considerable enthusiasm for Éluard's form, very different from Rimbaud's in its simplicity and directness, and tending to an abstraction that Beckett admired but could not always copy. In 'Lady Love', for example, Éluard's evocation of a beloved who has the 'shape' of his hands is rendered as 'She has the body of my hand', a stronger and more physical image.[25] Even so, Éluard's poetry and his aesthetic have striking resonances in Beckett's later work. The opening image of Éluard's 'L'Invention', the hand winnowing the sand, which expresses faith in the transformative power of poetry to release the potential of the most recalcitrant material, is in strong contrast to the more familiar images of sand in Beckett, which represent the monotonous fall of identical sterile moments of time. But in the same poem, Éluard's commitment to clarity of perception, the materiality of vision and its object, and the formation of vision in the rhythm of contraries, is one which Beckett unreservedly shared: 'Clear with my two eyes/ As water and fire.'[26]

Coming into His Own

In the first half of 1932, Beckett was still in Paris, working on his first novel, the *Dream of Fair to Middling Women*. He moved to London at the start of the summer, reading in the British Museum, seeing the sights, and trying, without success, to find a publisher for his novel.[27] By the end of August, extreme poverty had forced him back home to Dublin, where he had initially a warm welcome from his long-suffering family.

Throughout the following year, his physical and mental health deteriorated, and there were tragic blows to bear. In May, Peggy Sinclair died in Germany, of tuberculosis. His quarrels with his mother grew more frequent and intense. He drew closer to his father, and when William died in June from a heart attack, after a week's illness during which Beckett and his mother nursed him together, the shock was unbearable. 'I can't write about him', he told Tom MacGreevy, 'I can only walk the fields and climb the ditches after him'.[28]

After Christmas 1933, he settled in London, and for two years he followed an intensive course of psychotherapy with Wilfred Ruprecht Bion at the Tavistock Clinic, paid for by his mother; to Bion, he reported suffering severe anxiety, heart problems, night sweats and panics, and sometimes complete paralysis.[29] He got on well with Bion, whose treatment, he felt, involving the search for the origins of his symptoms in the past, was at worst likely to make his life more bearable; and Bion enabled him to see that his self-imposed isolation and misery, his sneers at others, the physical problems he had been experiencing, were all part of a morbid condition 'that began in a time which I could not remember, in my "pre-history"'.[30] He read up on psychology and psychoanalysis.

London's museums and galleries continued to supply diversion and inspiration, confirming his developing insights into the nature of artistic understanding. He saw Cézanne's Mont Sainte-Victoire at the National Gallery, and praised Cézanne as he had praised Jack Yeats for his understanding of landscape as 'something by definition unapproachably alien, unintelligible arrangement of atoms', concluding:

> Perhaps it is the one bright spot in a mechanistic age – the deanthropomorphisations of the artist. Even the portrait beginning to be dehumanised as the individual feels himself more & more hermetic and alone & his neighbour a coagulum as alien as a protoplast or God, incapable of loving or hating anyone but himself or of being loved or hated by anyone but himself.[31]

Throughout this time, he continued to work on short stories, translations, and, especially, poems. In 1935, George Reavey's recently-established Europa

Press, based in Paris and London, accepted a selection of the poems Beckett had been writing since 1931. *Echo's Bones and Other Precipitates* was published in November, as the first of a series of important first collections by Irish poets. By then, Reavey had become Beckett's first literary agent. Between 1935 and 1939, Europa Press published the first volumes of poetry by Brian Coffey and Denis Devlin, as well as by Paul Éluard and Reavey himself.[32] Sales of Beckett's book were poor, but it elicited a fairly favourable review from the *Dublin Magazine*.[33]

The Western poetic tradition, from ancient to modernist, provides the scaffolding of a collection which celebrates the dissolving of the old into the matter of the new. The poems play games with the familiar lyric of Provençal romance, with titles that point to the troubadour forms of dawn song, or aubade ('Alba'), evening song ('Serena'), and complaint ('Enueg'), in which the troubadours sang of the body erotic. Epic names and places familiar from Homer and Virgil are invoked to rewrite the landscapes of Dublin, and run an ironic counterpoint to the disease, dissolution, and death which are the lot of a lover who is not founding empires but tearing them down. In the opening poem, 'The Vulture', the voracious eye that flies over the urban spaces of Dublin, Paris, and London, dissolving the familiar boundaries of mind and body, and self and world, animating the inanimate, is there to take what it sees into 'the sky of my skull' and turn it into 'offal'.[34] The voice that closes the collection speaks of trampling underfoot the revellers in the asylum, as flesh falls, words and meaning break into wind, and finally the maggots take them all, for 'what they are' ('Echo's Bones').[35] What they are is decaying matter, but matter devoured by the poet is the makings of something new: Beckett's modernist voice privileges 'the act rather than the object of perception'.[36] Beckett's act of perception is Baudelairean, and the transmutation of material decay into artistic form echoes the French poet's epic of modern Paris, *Les Fleurs du mal* [Flowers of Evil], not least 'Une Charogne', where the worms and the flies devour the imagined carcass of the loved and hated mistress, and the poet turns his lost love into rhythm, colour and line: 'J'ai gardé la forme et l'essence divine de mes amours décomposés.' [I have preserved the form and the divine essence of my decayed loves.][37]

Beckett's poetry, like Baudelaire's, evokes his complex love and hatred of the places and people he has been set among, and is couched as bitter satire and raging despair. In this early work, there is no attempt to imitate the dehumanisation of form that he had admired in the work of Yeats and

Cézanne. The poetry starts with the streets of Dublin, modelling the different rhythms in which the poet is living his life. In 'Enueg I', the poet, spat out of the Portobello Nursing Home, trundles along the corpse-pale canal with its 'dying barge', and crosses Parnell Bridge into a Homericised Chapelizod, through the gathering wind, dark and storm, constantly changing his angle of vision, but always pursued by fungus, toadstool and pestilence. Even the wind turns stinking 'in my skull'; and the poem concludes with a flourish, brandishing 'the banner of meat bleeding': all flesh, damsels and heroes, is neither grass, nor dust, but matter for maggots.[38] 'Sanies I' goes at a different pace, charting the nostos of a hero with a tiger in his heart, making his epic journey back home on his bicycle, pedalling and freewheeling from Portrane on the seashore, accompanied by echoes of Horace ('atra cura [black care] on the step'), popular song ('home [...] where I was born'), and strings of popular clichés, all levels of culture compounded into a single long sentence which finally brakes to a halt, pulled up short by the loved one and the dismal constraints of grammar: 'I see main verb at last/ her whom alone in the accusative/ I have dismounted to love.'[39] The comedy of the poem belies the ugly title (sanies: a running sore) – but the rhythm of the bicycle, not the image, is the important thing. The same paradoxical performance appears in 'Sanies II', where the poetic voice, complaining of his piles, fresh from the bath but his clothes still stinking, celebrates the grotesque ugliness of revelry. From the American Bar in the rue Mouffetard to Becky's brothel in Dublin, haunt of pimps and a fat-bottomed barmaid, he beats out the end to the ideal love of Dante and Beatrice: ('Alighieri has got off, au revoir to all that').[40] There are echoes everywhere of the old faith in things of the spirit, pagan and Christian, empty words now, all held up to ridicule. London, in 'Serena I', is a place of fraught, intense experiences, where the highest achievements of the human intellect jostle with the lowest manifestations of animality and the mob: 'all things full of gods/ pressed down and bleeding'.[41] In vivid contrasts of colour, blood-scarlet and dead white, and sharp detail, the eye of the poet–tourist records the sights, from the grandiose British Museum to the imprisoned and humiliated creatures in Regent's Park Zoo, Crystal Palace, the heights of St Paul's, and finally the thickets of Ken Wood, spying on lovers in the bushes. This unsavoury creature is an 'I' who corrodes and decomposes what he sees as he speaks it, and in the end shares his eye with his disease-ridden brother, the fly. He too stands lightly, pivots on his many legs, delights in the many planes of his vision, and is tormented by the divided loyalties of his brief moment: 'he could not serve typhoid and mammon'.[42] Spreading the news of collective sickness, as Beckett was finding, does not make for a lucrative career.

The satirical bitterness disappears at the end of the collection, with the poems on the death of the poet's father ('Malacoda'). There is still mockery for the rites and rituals of established religion, figured in the bowler-hatted undertaker's man who farts his way down the garden path to measure the father's corpse. But what the poet believes, and what he knows his mother needs to believe, are different things. He deploys all his poetic skills to keep her attention on the weeds in the garden, until the hammering that closes up the coffin cannot be ignored, and the loss must be acknowledged of something for which there is no longer any word, be it spirit or husk, neither 'it' nor 'he'. The traditional image of the ship of souls, summoning the departed, begins to take shape, only to be confronted by the son's final nay-saying to religious consolation. In the next poem, a quatrain, 'Da Tagte Es', the motif of the ship is completely reworked. There is no more to be said of dying and decay, and nothing either of what will be seen beyond death, since there is nothing. The ship is unspoken, but there is the rhythm of the rope running free in 'your' hand, there are no more goodbyes, no more land, and there is only seeing, through a clear glass, 'your eyes' – the closing words.[43] All that is left of a lost love is what can be glimpsed in the form of art, the hand and eye that evoke the living body of the departing other, reflected in the vision and the speech of the one left alone.

Living in London, and visiting Bion twice a week, gradually helped Beckett's depression to lift, and contributed some new images for his developing sense of who and what he was. 'I think it all helped me to understand a bit better what I was doing and what I was feeling. I certainly came up with some extraordinary memories of being in the womb, intra-uterine memories. I remember feeling trapped, being imprisoned and unable to escape, of crying to be let out, but no one could hear, no one was listening.'[44] His longstanding dependency on his mother, and his struggles to break free of her, were being identified as the problem. He wrote more poetry, and short stories, and worked on his comic novel, *Murphy*. He went back to Ireland before Christmas 1935, to stay in the family home.

At the end of September 1936, he left for Germany, for a tour that had more low spots than highs, and was punctuated by letters from his agent about the string of rejections that were coming for *Murphy*. But the trip added importantly to his already considerable knowledge and understanding of European painting traditions, and his hostility to many of them, and brought a new dimension to his understanding of the fate of the resistant artist. In Hamburg, he decided that the most interesting German painting was by the moderns, whose work had already by then gone underground, and could only be seen in the private collections to which he was given access. The campaign against 'Art-Bolschevism' was just beginning; museums and galleries were being stripped, and exhibiting and selling contemporary work was dangerous, if not impossible.[45] He became friendly with the members of a group that had been broken up in 1933, including Willem Grimm and the Swiss Karl Ballmer, whose work he compared to the later Picasso, 'metaphysical concrete'.[46] Elsewhere in Germany, there was even less left to see. But in Brunswick, he found Giorgione's self-portrait in the Herzog-Anton-Ulrich Museum gallery, and began his long imaginative obsession with the head emerging from a dark background, noting the intense contrasts of its expression of patient suffering, and describing it as 'an antithesis of mind and sense'.[47] In Berlin, Weimar, Leipzig, Dresden and Munich, he toured more galleries, mostly to little purpose. In the Kaiser Friedrich Museum in Berlin (now the Bode Museum), he enjoyed the Italian Renaissance and Flemish collections, but discovered how much he disliked what seemed to him the bullying, blindingly obvious productions of Rembrandt, Titian and Rubens.[48]

In Dresden, he met an art historian, Will Grohmann, who had been stripped of his teaching post in 1933. Grohmann knew all the great moderns, owned Picassos, Klees, Kandinskys and Mondrians, and helped Beckett gain entrance to the Ida Bienert collection of modern art, which to Beckett's delight included Cézanne, Léger, Munch, as well as all the other familiar names, and the best surprise of all, a portrait of Nancy Cunard, painted in Paris by Oskar Kokoschka, in 1924.[49] In Dresden, he also found Caspar David Friedrich's 'Two Men Observing the Moon', which would later help shape the stage image of *Waiting for Godot*.[50] He flew home on 1 April 1937, with his German much improved, some important new images lodged in his head, and aware of the war hysteria building behind him.[51]

The best times of his last year in Ireland had been spent in discussing painting with Jack Yeats, reading Schopenhauer on women,[52] and collecting notes for a play on the relationship of Dr Samuel Johnson and Mrs Thrale, for a play he never completed.[53] But there was no end to the conflicts with his mother, who was driven to fury by his wild living and lack of success. In the middle of October, he went to settle finally in Paris.

He took up again with old friends and publishing connections, including the Joyces. He became friendly with the painter Geer van Velde and his wife, Elisabeth, who were to introduce him to Geer's brother, the painter Bram van Velde.[54] He later praised Bram as presenting the most significant of contemporary refusals of expressive art; and his own renunciation of the image owes much to Bram's example.[55] Life was increasingly exciting. On 5 January 1938, he wrote to Tom MacGreevy of meeting up with Peggy Guggenheim, and with a Mrs Bethell, who came from Dublin, both of whom he already knew, and with whom he was to begin simultaneous affairs.[56] On the evening of the following day, he was stabbed by a beggar while walking home with friends from a café. Friends and family, including his mother, flocked to his bedside in the Hôpital Broussais, but the damage, widely reported and exaggerated in the Dublin press, was less serious than it might have been.[57]

Murphy was finally accepted for publication, and Alfred Péron asked to translate it. Beckett received an offer from Jack Kahane to translate a new edition of the Marquis de Sade's novel *Les 120 Journées de Sodome* [The 120 Days of Sodom] into English, which he decided he could accept on condition he could write a preface explaining why he admired the work. Despite the surface obscenity, he thought, it was not pornographic, the composition was 'extraordinary, as rigorous as Dante's', it was puritanical in its dispassionate tone, and it filled him 'with a kind of metaphysical ecstasy'.[58] He intended to sign his name to the translation, despite the possible adverse effect on his own writing career. The contract however never arrived. He published further translations in *transition*, signed and unsigned, of French poets such as Henri Michaux, Stéphane Mallarmé, Éluard, René Char, Jacques Prévert, many of them on painters, in whom he recognised the aims of his own work.[59]

The Writer in Wartime

In September, he wrote to George Reavey of hearing Hitler's broadcast on Czechoslovakia, and watching the newly-mobilised soldiers leaving in requisitioned transport; he himself was staying in Paris, and had promised Alfred Péron to evacuate his family when the need arose.[60] For a while, it was business as usual. In April of the following year, he told Tom MacGreevy he had met a French girl, of whom he was 'dispassionately' fond, though neither of them had any sense of where the relationship might end.[61] This was Suzanne Deschevaux-Dumesnil, a pianist, who had visited him a few times in hospital after his stabbing. Before long, she took over for him the practical side of living, including pressing his work with publishers, and they settled into a lifelong partnership.[62]

In August 1939, while Beckett was visiting Dublin, Germany and the USSR signed a Treaty of Non-Aggression, and on 1 September Hitler invaded Poland. France and Britain declared war on Germany; Ireland remained neutral. Beckett went back to Paris on 4 September. He wrote to George Reavey with news of friends and fellow-writers. The Joyces had gone to La Baule. Alfred Péron had been called up, and Beckett himself was waiting to hear about an application he had made to serve France. Paul Nizan had resigned from the Communist Party, and Jean Giono had been arrested; he had no news of Jean-Paul Sartre.[63] Germany invaded France on 12 May 1940. Beckett stayed in Paris, translating *Murphy*, and writing poems. He left, with Suzanne, on 12 June, two days before the Germans marched into the capital. His papers were not in order, as a result of the slowness of wartime bureaucracy, and he had no money, but with the help of friends he and Suzanne reached Arcachon.[64]

The couple eventually returned to Paris in mid-September, just before the German occupiers began their programme of anti-Jewish legislation and action. In May 1941, the first of three mass round-ups of Jews took place in Paris, conducted by the French police. Some of Beckett's Jewish friends were arrested, and other Jews were executed. His friend Paul Léon was arrested in the second round-up, in August. On 1 September, Beckett joined Jeannine Picabia's Resistance cell, 'Gloria SMH', an information-collecting network, which was part of the British Special Operations Executive.[65] Beckett typed and translated information reports about German military movements. The group was betrayed in August 1942 by a Catholic priest and double agent, Robert Alesch, and more than fifty members were arrested and deported, many ending up in concentration camps, including Alfred Péron.

A telegram from Péron's wife warned Beckett, and he and Suzanne fled just before the Gestapo arrived. They were hidden for a few days in Paris by Suzanne's Communist friends, then by Nathalie Sarraute in a village just outside Paris, and finally, with forged passports, they were smuggled into the free zone. They had been in flight for six weeks. In the remote village of Roussillon d'Apt, in the Vaucluse, they rented a little house, and Beckett found work on a local farm. Eventually he began writing again, returning to his novel *Watt*, which he had begun in Paris. He rejoined the Forces Françaises de l'Intérieur in May 1944, the month in which Paris was liberated, and he worked from time to time with the local Resistance. In August, the first American soldiers entered Roussillon.

With the war over, he was determined to get back to Paris as soon as possible, but it was April 1945 before it was possible for the two of them to leave, and even then, there were difficulties with his papers on the days-long journey towards the capital. There were repeated checks, and although his Irish passport was in order he still had to explain each time where he had been for the past two years, and why he had lost contact with the Irish Legation. Eventually, he decided it would be easier to travel separately, and Suzanne went to their flat in Paris, in the rue des Favorites, while he made his way to Ireland, through England.[66]

In Ireland, distressed by the contrast between the austere conditions of France and the comfortable circumstances in which Irish friends and family had spent the war, he had difficulty remaking old contacts. He stayed with his mother, now 74, who was in the first stages of Parkinson's, and living in a small bungalow in Foxrock.[67] He told James Knowlson that it was in his mother's room that he experienced the revelation of what was to be the distinctive mark of his work,[68] together with the recognition of his own inadequacy. Years later, describing for Knowlson the difference he had felt he needed to establish between Joyce's work, focused on control and amplification, and his own, he was precise: 'my own way was in impoverishment, in lack of knowledge, and in taking away [...].'[69] In future, he would look to his inner world for his subjects, give up quoting or alluding to the common cultural heritage, and focus on themes of poverty, failure and loss.[70] None of these so-called revelations was really new to him, as Knowlson points out, but the sense of having reached a watershed was important.

He had a long struggle to return to France, in the face of new regulations about money and property ownership, but with the help of a friend he got a job in Normandy in August 1945 with the Red Cross as 'Quartermaster/ Interpreter', helping to rebuild the hospital in St-Lô, a town flattened by the bombing. From there, he was able to return legally to Paris in October, and eventually settle down again in the flat in the rue des Favorites, much changed by his wartime experiences, and ready to resume writing.[71]

Scraping a living from translating and teaching, he was writing furiously from February 1946 onwards, in French, and by the end of the year had published, in journals, the short stories that were eventually to go into *Nouvelles et Textes pour rien* (1955).[72]

The Poetry of the Subject: Lost in Time

After the war, publishing opportunities began to appear again, and Beckett's pre-war work finally saw the light of day. *Poèmes '38-39* first appeared in November 1946 in Jean-Paul Sartre's *Les Temps modernes.*[73] The themes are love, experienced as loss, but also as erotic pleasure, and the interplay of subjectivity and time. The style is reminiscent of Éluard in its directness and the powerful simplicity of its images, and its movement through contraries, but it is Beckett's own play with varied syntax and rhythm that drives the collection, and gives it its distinctive edge. Beginning very often with a simple preposition or adverb, the poems are built of phrases, two or three to a line, which swing in a regular rhythm to a long-delayed climax, ending usually on a falling note. 'Ainsi a-t-on beau' is a sonnet of two sentences, eleven and three lines respectively, which evokes the futility of the human condition, where the individual is locked in his own experience, and the experience of his species, and all are devoured by time. The three-line sequences, echoing and reflecting one another, that open and close this poem, lock in those aeons of geological time which make nonsense of the short interval that is human history and of human intellectual pretensions, in all their inhumanity (Kant, the rationalist, coldly ponders the smoking ruins of Lisbon after the great earthquake). 'Arènes de Lutèce', exploring the multiple splitting of self in the processes of perceiving, remembering and creating, starts with a couple sitting together in Paris, high up in the ruins of the arena. The man, speaking in the first person, watches another couple, who may be themselves, a past memory or an intimation of the future, or, as the poem draws to a close, may be another couple of lovers, walking towards them over the sands of the arena, through a fast-moving series of verbs, all in the present tense. The subject comes back to himself with a shiver, which marks the uncanny experience of self-displacement and self-recognition; and now he sees with different eyes the landscape round about him, and the sad face beside him. Here again is the paradox: the living movement which is human subjectivity, fixed inside the ruins of human time. Written in both French and English, the four lines of 'Dieppe', in contrast, renouncing verbs, use juxtaposed nouns to present an idea of living fixed in amber. The limits to the time of human life are evoked in the images of place which reverberate through all Beckett's later work: the dead shingle on the beach, and the ebbing tide. The sense of ending, age and death, is contradicted by adverbs which suggest a cycle of repetition which could be renewal; but though the preposition in the final line suggests forward movement, there is nothing to see ahead but the 'lights of old'.[74]

Other poems Beckett wrote in French include the three poems published in *Transition* in the summer of 1948, with French and English versions on facing pages.[75] Like 'Dieppe', they encapsulate the themes of Beckett's later work on the paradoxical relationships of time, the subject, and the external world, and exploit familiar motifs: the moving sand, the threshold and the space of a door, the deadlight through which the subject searches for another, the silence and the dying murmurs.

He carried on writing and translating his own poetry throughout his life, increasingly blurring the boundaries between poetry and prose. Short prose pieces such as those in *Fizzles*, which explore the conundrum of being and consciousness, first published in English in 1976, are most rewarding when studied not only for their ideas but as prose poems.[76] But there are later poems which Beckett himself termed poems, and in some cases attributed to known forms, such as roundelays, or rondeaux. And there are the 'mirlitonnades', bits of doggerel, mostly written in the first half of 1977,[77] short *pièces de circonstance*, often simply exploiting word-echoes; these are the 'Burbles' in which Derek Mahon found an inspiration of his own. Last of all, as Beckett's own death drew nearer, there is his last written work, 'what is the word', celebrating and deprecating his lifelong need for others to recognise his claim, or desire, 'to seem to glimpse afaint afar away over there/ what - '; that is, nothing namable, but the question mark that for all poets hovers over all words: 'what is the word'.[78]

NOTES

1 David Williams, '"Towards an art of memory": Peter Brook, a foreigner in Paris', in David Bradby and Maria M. Delgado (eds), *The Paris Jigsaw. Internationalism and the City's Stages* (Manchester: Manchester University Press, 2002), p.38. Williams refers to Salman Rushdie's analysis of the migrant/ outsider, in *Imaginary Homelands* (London: Granta Books, 1991).

2 See Richard Aldington, *Life for Life's Sake* (1940; rpt. London: Cassell, 1968), pp.312–19. In 1950, MacGreevy's knowledge of painting would secure his appointment as Director of the National Gallery of Ireland.

3 Aldington, *Life for Life's Sake*, p.319. According to Beckett, his instrument was a tin whistle (see interview with James Knowlson, in Knowlson and Knowlson (eds), *Beckett Remembering*, p.41).

4 See for example Craig Monk, 'Eugene Jolas and the translation policies of *transition*', *Mosaic: a Journal for the Interdisciplinary Study of Literature*, 32, 4 (December 1999), pp.17–34.

5 Samuel Putnam, *Paris Was Our Mistress. Memoirs of a Lost and Found Generation* (1947; rpt. Carbondale IL: Southern Illinois University Press, Arcturus Books Edition, 1970), p.97.

6 Bair, *Samuel Beckett*, pp.67–73.

7 Carol Loeb Shloss, *Lucia Joyce. To Dance in the Wake* (London: Bloomsbury Publishing Plc, 2005), p.177.

8 Bair, *Samuel Beckett*, pp.75–6.

9 The account given here of the relationship between Beckett and Lucia Joyce draws on Loeb Shloss, *Lucia Joyce*, pp.173–7.

10 Knowlson, *Damned to Fame*, p.105.

11 Letter from Beckett to Thomas MacGreevy [? 17 July 1930], *Letters* I, p.27. The letters between Lucia Joyce and Beckett are no longer extant. Stephen Joyce destroyed his aunt's letters and persuaded Beckett to do the same (Loeb Shloss, *Lucia Joyce*, p.27).

12 Knowlson, *Damned to Fame*, p.128.

13 See Sinéad Mooney, *A Tongue Not Mine: Beckett and Translation* (Oxford: Oxford University Press, 2011), for discussion of the links between Beckett's translations of others, his self-translation, and his work overall.

14 *This Quarter*, 2, 4 (April-May-June 1930); see *CP* 2012, p.356.

15 See Seán Lawlor, '"That's how it was and them were the days": Beckett's early publications with Samuel Putnam and Nancy Cunard', in Mark Nixon (ed.), *Publishing Samuel Beckett* (London: The British Library Publishing Division, 2011), p.25.

16 Seán Lawlor, '"That's how it was and them were the days"', p.26.

17 For an extensive discussion of the references, see Lawrence E. Harvey, *Samuel Beckett*, pp.13–33. For the text of *Whoroscope* quoted here, see *CP* 2012, pp.40–3.

18 See Hugh Ford, Introduction to *Negro. An Anthology* (1934), collected and edited by Nancy Cunard, ed. and abridged with an introduction by Hugh Ford (New York and London: Continuum, 2002), p.249.

19 Jennifer Higgins, *English Responses to French Poetry 1880–1940. Translation and Mediation* (Oxford: Legenda, 2011), p.126. See also James Knowlson and Felix Leakey (eds), *Samuel Beckett 'Drunken Boat': A Translation of Arthur Rimbaud's poem 'Le*

Bateau ivre' (Reading: Whiteknights Press, 1976); Gerald M. Macklin, '"Drunken Boat": Samuel Beckett's Translation of Arthur Rimbaud's "Le Bateau ivre"', *Studies in 20th-Century Literature*, 27, 1 (January 2003) (http://dx.doi.org/10.4148/2334-4415.1549. Consulted 22 October 2014.)

20 Samuel Beckett, 'Drunken Boat', in *CP* 2012, p.64; Arthur Rimbaud, 'Le Bateau ivre', in Paterne Berrichon (ed.), *Oeuvres de Arthur Rimbaud: Vers et proses*, (Paris: Mercure de France, 1912).

21 Samuel Beckett, 'Drunken Boat', in *CP* 2012, p.64.

22 See *CP* 2012, pp.358–9.

23 See *CP* 2012, p.361.

24 Higgins, *English Responses*, p.114.

25 Samuel Beckett, 'Lady Love', in *CP* 2012, p.72.

26 Samuel Beckett, 'The Invention', in *CP* 2012, p.75.

27 Knowlson, *Damned to Fame*, pp.160–1.

28 Letter from Beckett to Thomas MacGreevy, 2 July 1933, *Letters* I, p.165.

29 Knowlson, *Damned to Fame*, pp.174–6. See also for example letter from Beckett to Morris Sinclair, 27 January [1934], and letter from Beckett to Thomas MacGreevy, 10 March [1935], *Letters* I, p.179, p.258.

30 Letter from Beckett to Thomas MacGreevy, 10 March [1935], *Letters* I, pp.258–9.

31 Letter from Beckett to Thomas MacGreevy, 8 September 1934, *Letters* I, p.223.

32 Mark Nixon, 'George Reavey – Beckett's first literary agent', in Mark Nixon (ed.), *Publishing Samuel Beckett*, p.43.

33 See *CP* 2012, p.260.

34 Samuel Beckett, 'The Vulture', in *CP* 2012, p.5.

35 Samuel Beckett, 'Echo's Bones', in *CP* 2012, p.23.

36 Patricia Coughlan here echoes Beckett's essay on 'Recent Irish Poetry'; Patricia Coughlan, '"The Poetry is Another Pair of Sleeves": Beckett, Ireland and Modernist Lyric Poetry', p.181.

37 Charles Baudelaire, 'Une Charogne', *Les Fleurs du mal* (Paris: Poulet-Malassis et de Broise, 1857). My translation.

38 Samuel Beckett, 'Enueg I', in *CP* 2012, p.7; p.8.

39 Samuel Beckett, 'Sanies I', in *CP* 2012, p.12; p.13.

40 Samuel Beckett, 'Sanies II', in *CP* 2012, p.14.

41 Samuel Beckett, 'Serena I', in *CP* 2012, p.16.

42 Samuel Beckett, 'Serena I', in *CP* 2012, p.17.

43 Samuel Beckett, 'Da Tagte Es', in *CP* 2012, p.22.

44 Samuel Beckett, in Knowlson and Knowlson (eds), *Beckett Remembering*, p.68.

45 James Knowlson's readings in Beckett's German Diaries first illuminated this little-known area of Beckett's experience (Knowlson, *Damned to Fame*, pp.237–9),

to which can now be added Beckett's own letters (see for example, letter from Beckett to Thomas MacGreevy, 28 November [1936], *Letters* I, pp.386–90, where Beckett refers to the campaign, and uses the term 'Art-Bolschevism').

46 Letter from Beckett to Thomas MacGreevy, 28 November [1936], *Letters* I, p.387.

47 Samuel Beckett, German Diaries, Notebook 2, 9 Dec 1936, cit. Knowlson, *Damned to Fame*, p.241.

48 Letter from Beckett to Thomas MacGreevy, 18 January 1937, *Letters* I, p.430.

49 Letter from Beckett to Thomas MacGreevy, 16 February 1937, *Letters* I, p.436.

50 Knowlson, *Damned to Fame*, p.254.

51 Knowlson, *Damned to Fame*, pp.260–1.

52 Letter from Beckett to Joseph Hone, 3 July 1937, *Letters* I, p.507.

53 Only one fragment was written up; see *Human Wishes* (1937), in *Disjecta* 1983, pp.155–66. See the detailed account of the project, and Johnson's appeal for Beckett, in Bair, *Samuel Beckett*, pp.253–7.

54 Knowlson, *Damned to Fame*, p.275.

55 See Beckett's *Three Dialogues: Samuel Beckett & Georges Duthuit* (London: John Calder, 1965, collected with Beckett's *Proust*), first published in *transition 49*.

56 Letter from Beckett to Thomas MacGreevy, 12 January 1938, *Letters* I, p.583.

57 Letter from Beckett to Thomas MacGreevy, 5 January 1938, *Letters* I, p.580.

58 Letter from Beckett to Thomas MacGreevy, 21 February 1938, *Letters* I, p.607.

59 After the war, Beckett published in the last issue of the new series of *Transition* (April–May 1938), his translation of 'Zone', Guillaume Apollinaire's great hymn to modernity (*CP* 2012, pp.414–16).

60 Letter from Beckett to George Reavey, 27 September 1938, *Letters* I, p.642.

61 Letter from Beckett to Thomas MacGreevy, 18 April 1939, *Letters* I, p.657.

62 Knowlson, *Damned to Fame*, p.288.

63 Letter from Beckett to George Reavey, 26 September 1939, *Letters* I, pp.667–8.

64 Knowlson, *Damned to Fame*, pp.300–301. Deirdre Bair (*Samuel Beckett*, pp.306–7), does not mention that Suzanne was with him.

65 This section draws on Knowlson (*Damned to Fame*, Chapter 12), who uses interviews with the members of Gloria SMH and Beckett himself, and Bair, *Samuel Beckett*, Chapters 13 and 14.

66 Bair, *Samuel Beckett*, p.335; Knowlson, *Damned to Fame*, p.340 and p.769 n.1, says both of them travelled to Paris before Beckett returned alone to Ireland.

67 Bair, *Samuel Beckett*, pp.337–40.

68 Undated interview with Beckett (c. 1987), in Knowlson, p.352 and p.772 n.55.

69 Interview with Beckett by James Knowlson, 27 October 1989, cit. Knowlson, *Damned to Fame*, p.352 and p.772 n.57.

70 Knowlson, *Damned to Fame*, pp.352–3.

71 Bair, *Samuel Beckett*, pp.342–5.

72 Collected in *No's Knife: Collected Shorter Prose, 1945–66* (London: John Calder, 1967), and *Stories and Texts for Nothing* (New York: Grove Press, 1967).

73 'Poèmes '38-39', *Les Temps modernes* II (November 1946), pp.288–93. The collection did not include 'Dieppe'. See *CP* 2012, p.372.

74 Samuel Beckett, 'Dieppe', in *CP* 2012, p.99.

75 *Transition*, 48.2 (June 1948), 96–7; *CP* 2012, pp.401–2.

76 See below, pp.99-100.

77 *CP* 2012, p.447. A 'mirliton' or onion flute, is a sixteenth-century instrument closed at the top by a membrane. When the player sings into the tube, the vibrations transform his voice.

78 Samuel Beckett, 'what is the word' (1989); *CP* 2012, p.229.

CHAPTER 2

Beginning with Prose

The Apprentice

Beckett's vision in his mother's house in Foxrock, after the end of the war, marked his awareness that he was embarking on a route that would take him far away from James Joyce, the writer who had dominated the previous modernist generation. But in the landscape of pre-war Paris, where his career began, there was no escaping the shadow of Joyce, and alongside it, that other great writer of modernist prose and co-founder of modernist epic: Marcel Proust. Between the two of them, Beckett found his models for writing the new ideas about language and the human subject, and its situation in time and space, that were the foundations of the modern(ist) world. The history of the development of his prose writing is a history of how he learned his trade from the masters: and then made it new, all over again.

In his essay 'Dante ... Bruno. Vico ... Joyce',[1] what Beckett had to say about Joyce's work is less important than his unpicking of the influential concepts that he (with Joyce's help) identified in the work of the earlier writers. These ideas on the form of the world, man's material place in it, the movement of history, and the nature of writing – specifically, the identity of form and content – became part of Beckett's thinking, and the principles by which he shaped his own work.

Giambattista Vico's theory of contraries, the idea that history moves by opposites, underlies the structure of many of Beckett's narratives, from *Molloy* onwards, where from section to section the narrator switches to fresh starts on contrary paths. Vico's insistence on the interdependence of the individual and the universal, and his associated refusal to see History as the result of either Fate or Chance, feeds into Beckett's understanding of the material base that generates individual identity and common cultural history, including the language of cultures; this understanding is to be worked out in depth in *The Unnamable*. The Italian's identification of the three phases of human development, Birth, Maturity, Corruption, is a classification which, Beckett notes, Joyce has adopted as 'a structural convenience', and he explains how this works in Joyce's writing: 'By structural I do not only mean a bold outward division, a bare skeleton for the housing of material. I mean the endless substantial variations on these three beats, and interior intertwining of these three themes into a decoration of arabesques – decoration and more than decoration.'[2] This combination of a strict overarching sequence of themes, three beats, which then becomes filled up with the interweaving play of variations, is a form Beckett finds highly effective to, as he put it, accommodate the mess which is human experience. Quoting Joyce, he speaks of 'Vico's insistence on the inevitable character of every progression, or retrogression: "The Vico road goes round to meet where terms begin."'[3] The cycles of history, individual and universal, are a key structuring image for Beckett's own work. They appear in the comic form of the bicycle, from the first poems through to the first novels, often ironically breaking down and leaving their riders in the ditch (*Molloy*). In more serious mode, the return to the beginning is one of Beckett's preferred themes. The journey in search of new horizons, out of the house, or the village, or the town, and returning home, is there throughout his work, in, for instance, the *Dream of Fair to Middling Women*, *Mercier and Camier*, and the second part of *Molloy*.

Vico's treatment of the natural origin and growth of language, which was created, he argues, by the poetic, myth-making power of human imagination, provokes Beckett to lengthy comment. This dynamic making of language, through signs where form and content are one, is the impulse Beckett will strive to emulate in his own work.[4] It is, he says, what drives every true artist, and he finds it in both Dante and Joyce. Of Joyce, he says:

> You complain that this stuff is not written in English. It is not written at all. It is not to be read – or rather it is not only to be read. It is to be looked at and listened to. His writing is not *about* something; *it is that something itself.* [...] This writing that you find so obscure is a quintessential abstraction of language and painting and gesture, with

> all the inevitable clarity of the old inarticulation. Here is the savage economy of hieroglyphics.[5]

In the same issue of *transition* as Beckett's essay, Eugene Jolas published 'The Revolution of the Word', his first statement of the principles of the magazine. Beckett, it appears, may not have much liked Jolas, or appreciated much of what went on in the *transition* camp;[6] but the manifesto resonates with the ideas Beckett's study had emphasised.[7] Jolas's main theme was the subjective nature of poetic creation, which produces its own version of material reality. Pure poetry is 'a lyrical absolute that seeks an a priori reality within ourselves alone' and narrative is not merely anecdote, but 'the projection of a metamorphosis of reality'. Language creates poetic reality: 'The expression of these concepts can be achieved only through the rhythmic "hallucination of the word"'. The reader must share in the act of creation: 'The writer expresses. He does not communicate' and 'The plain reader be damned.' Jolas admired Joyce's work as the model of these principles, and saw him as engaging in a renascence of language as great as any in the Western past. Whatever Beckett's personal feelings about Jolas, the hothouse of *transition* fostered that renascence, and the fortunes of Joyce; and between the two, Beckett's own creativity found fertile ground for development.

The other half of Beckett's induction into modernist prose writing came through the work of Marcel Proust, who created for his Paris the language of its distinctively modern experience, as Joyce created the language of his Dublin. Proust wrote the discourse of the monied aristocratic circles of Paris, springing from their closed and exclusive salons; Joyce recreated that of the inhabitants of the impoverished underside of modernity, situated in the equally closed world of Dublin streets and pubs. In both cases, the view was mediated through the Jewish outsider, Swann or Leopold Bloom, who figures as the crossing-point of two cultures, and the bearer of disruptive change who longs for incorporation. Beckett, another kind of outsider, may have noticed the points of contact between the three of them, but he says nothing of that.

Both Joyce and Proust provided models of innovation in form, as well as in themes. In the case of Joyce, Beckett took direction from the man himself, and in working closely alongside him on his 'Work in Progress', researching, reading and taking notes, he learned how a text comes together in terms of language and form. With Proust, he had his own confrontation with the text as a reader, and he seems to have found Proust's themes – his explorations of time, memory, and habit – more interesting than his forms.

Beckett had applied to write a doctoral thesis for the University of Paris on Joyce and Proust, but the topic was refused.[8] Instead, he found himself reading the sixteen volumes of *A la recherche du temps perdu*, for the first time, in the summer of 1929, in preparation for a study Tom MacGreevy suggested he undertake, and that Aldington, and Chatto & Windus (cautiously) encouraged.[9] He wrote to Tom MacGreevy of his response to the first volume, *Du côté de chez Swann*, disappointed by a style he decided swerved between the artificial and dishonest and the dazzling, sometimes heavy-footed and sometimes achieving a light, subtle equilibrium. Slave to his form, Proust at his worst was over-loquacious, his writing 'a maudlin false teeth gobble-gobble discharge from a colic-afflicted belly. I think he drank too much tilleul.'[10] Having read all sixteen volumes by the following summer, he then started reading them again, before writing what threatened to be a harsh critique: 'I am looking forward to pulling the balls off the critical and poetical Proustian cock.'[11] It was very heavy going, he complained; but there seems to have been some consolation in the fact that Proust too liked Schopenhauer, and Beckett was currently reading Proust's favourite texts, especially Schopenhauer's aphorisms on *The Wisdom of Life*, and his chapter on music in *Will and Representation.*[12] He handed over his text to Chatto & Windus in September, where it was received with flattering comments, published promptly in their Dolphin Series (March 1931) and sold reasonably well.[13]

Beckett opened his essay with a discussion of Proust's preoccupation with Time. One of Jolas's manifesto principles had been that Time was a tyranny and should be abolished. Proust understood Time as not merely a tyranny, but a matrix to be explored and reconceptualised. Beckett was impressed by Proust's determination

> 'to stamp [my work] with the seal of that Time, now so forcibly present to my mind, and in it [...] describe men, even at the risk of giving them the appearance of monstrous beings, as occupying in Time a much greater place than that so sparingly conceded to them in Space, a place indeed extended beyond measure, because, like giants plunged in the years, they touch at once those periods of their lives – separated by so many days – so far apart in Time.'[14]

Beckett dwells on an insight that will underpin his own explorations of the human subject and subject–object relations. Individual personality is the site of 'a constant process of decantation' between future and past, recognisable only as 'a retrospective hypothesis'.[15] This mobile subject, he says, in perpetual flux, 'infects' perceived objects with its own mobility; so that between two human subjects, 'two separate and immanent dynamisms related by no system of synchronisation' (the terms he would soon be using to praise the subjects presented by Cézanne and Jack B. Yeats), there can be no question of mutual knowing or communication.[16]

Habit, which in *Waiting for Godot* is 'a great deadener',[17] is for Proust the second nature by which the painful, terrifying strangeness of reality, the flux of self and being, is held by most men at a bearable distance. Habit, according to Beckett, generates Boredom, and occludes Suffering, the two terms between which human experience oscillates. Pain and Suffering are the price the artist pays for recognizing the flux that is the real, and having the temerity to try to communicate it.[18]

In the impossible work of poetry, memory is key. This is not, to use Proust's term, voluntary memory: the willed so-called recovery of time past, which fails to recognize that all that is ever recovered is fiction, a construct shaped by the perceptions of the subject seeking to remember. Beckett wholeheartedly agrees and adds his own excoriation of a kind of remembering which is nothing but 'the plagiarism of oneself', adding that 'if Habit is the Goddess of Dullness, voluntary memory is Shadwell, and of Irish extraction'.[19] The highest form of remembering is what Proust called involuntary memory, the unbidden, accidental, and explosive irruption of the real, in all its sharpness and colour, which restores not an object in itself but the process of its perception, giving new life to both object and perceiver: 'not merely the past object, but the Lazarus that it charmed or tortured'.[20] There are, in Beckett's exposition, deep-stored memories we do not know we have, items registered without our knowing it, which are 'the essence of ourselves, the best of our many selves and their concretions'.[21] Later in his essay, Beckett argues that the selection and storage of those deep-stored memories, of thrilling objects and sensations, is determined by the presence in them of some mysterious element which cannot be captured in the logical nets of Habit, the deadener. Retrieved by some gratuitous analogy – say, a sound, colour or perfume which is similar to one that, all unnoticed, was part of the original experience, the original thrill returns in all its original power: 'the total past sensation, not its echo, nor its copy, but the sensation itself, annihilating every spatial and temporal restriction, comes in a rush to engulf the subject in all the beauty of its infallible proportion.'[22] The thrill of seeing, not the object seen, is the element that resists the prison of conventional sense: 'and we breathe the true air of Paradise, of the only Paradise that is not the dream of a madman, the Paradise that has been lost.'[23] Remembering is not renewal of time past, but a celebration of time present. 'Time is not recovered', Beckett comments of the Proustian Paradise, 'it is obliterated.'[24]

In this light, Beckett's recognition, through Proust, of the relationship of remembered past to present is a warning against any critical attempt to make too much of the autobiographical reference of his own writing. What matters, as he explains (though in much less detail than he explores Proust's theses on time, habit and memory), are the processes of Proustian language, the artist's attempt to create a world through form. He picks out the disjointed structure of Proust's narratives which disregard conventional chronology, the role of music which marks the moments of privileged perception, and the central significance of metaphor, perception in transformation, which is the artist's mode of apprehending the real: 'The rhetorical equivalent of the Proustian real is the chain-figure of the metaphor.'[25]

Proust's cult of the image, expressed in the chain-figure of the metaphor, is not one that Beckett could follow for long, as subsequent chapters will show; and even in its earlier stages, Beckett's pursuit of the image was in pared-down terms, far removed from Proust's loquacious accounts. The passing of time and the inevitability of death remain the dark ground of Beckett's writing. It can be no accident that John Calder's edition of *Proust* was printed together with Beckett's *Three Dialogues* with Georges Duthuit, which denounce 'an art weary of pretending to be able', and prefer: 'The expression that there is nothing to express, nothing with which to express, nothing from which to express, no power to express, no desire to express, together with the obligation to express.'[26]

The study was perhaps hard to write because of the need to address Proust's homosexuality. He complained to MacGreevy, in a jokey throwaway remark, that he didn't know where to start: 'should the Proustian arse-hole be considered as entrée or sortie – libre in either case.'[27] He restricted himself in the event to the comment that in Proust there is no question of right and wrong, and homosexuality is never called a vice. Unlike Proust, Beckett entered belatedly into the exploration of gender constructions of identity, and gendered perceptions of the world.[28] In *Whoroscope* and *Dream of Fair to Middling Women,* there is a robustly heterosexual misogyny, calculated to entertain and shock the reader, and very much of its artistic moment. By the time he writes *Molloy,* Beckett takes more interest in the games people play with gender. When Molloy wakes up to find he is wearing someone else's pink nightdress, this need not, according to some critics, be seen as posing '[a] threat of emasculation to the heroic athletics of patriarchal masculinity', and Molloy's exchanges with Sucky Moll will soon show that heroic athletics are still very much on his agenda.[29] In *Malone Dies,* Malone, planning his four stories, each on a different theme, thinks first of having separate stories about a man and about a woman, and then thinks he may put them in the same one: 'there is so little difference between a man and a woman, between mine I mean'.[30] In later work, Beckett will have more to say about the fundamental uncertainty of gender orientation. The narcissism of the mirror-stage, in, for instance, *How It Is,* and the violence practised on Pim, the first double, are not so much intimations of homosexual desire or its repression, as evocations of the ambivalence of desire in every subject-in-formation.[31] The male couples of the first plays (*Waiting for Godot* and *Endgame*) are shaped within the power relationships embedded in capital and class, without reference to gender.

Beckett's first prose fictions notoriously show signs of Joyce's influence in their interest in what Hélène Cixous praised as Joyce's feminine mode of writing; like Eugene Jolas, Cixous admired Joyce's exuberant play with words and discourses, mixing high and low registers, piling on sophisticated and scholarly references, flaunting demotic idioms, and speaking many tongues. In an essay of 1976, Cixous picks out the cowrymaid of *Finnegans Wake,* the feminine body who springs into being simultaneously, and apparently spontaneously, with the language of Western rationalism, and describes the proliferation of discourses and figures for which she is the catalyst.[32] In the polemic binaries of feminist theories of language, as developed in the 1970s and 1980s, the pared-down approach adopted by Beckett, by contrast with Joyce's mode, might be termed a masculine one. But Cixous avoids that temptation in her essay of 1976, 'Une Passion: l'un peu moins que rien',[33] as does Julia Kristeva in 'The Father, Love, and Banishment', writing on Beckett's short story, 'First Love'. For Kristeva, Beckett's masculinity recognises itself with regret as the product of the world of limits and loss created by the Fathers, and his writing works to rediscover the babble lost to repression.[34]

The Journeyman

With so much weighty intellectual baggage piling up about the fledgling writer, the chances of his producing a readable work of fiction might seem much reduced. But along with his fascination with the operations of writing, Beckett had a gift for storytelling and image-making, and a talent for comedy; all these fed into his full-length novel, *Dream of Fair to Middling Women*, which he wrote in Paris in 1931–1932.[35] This is Beckett's first attempt at telling the story of the disruption of story, in a brilliantly funny, ground-clearing satire on the discourses of the European cultural tradition which takes Jolas's *transition* project out of theory, and into a new kind of writing practice.

From the start, theory has its place in the text, in an account of how artistic inspiration works, coming unbidden, and making its own spontaneous form

> from a labour and a weariness of deep castings that brook no schema. The mind suddenly entombed, then active in an anger and a rhapsody of energy, in a scurrying and plunging towards exitus, such is the ultimate mode and factor of the creative integrity, its proton, incommunicable; but there, insistent, invisible rat, fidgeting behind the astral incoherence of the art surface.[36]

The rhetoric delights in its own pretentiousness. But it also has its own seriousness, and this image of the animal activity of creation, where thought burrows out through intense feeling, towards a light never reached, is one to which Beckett constantly returns. The self-deprecating rat is also the rabid, disease-carrying vermin, brother to the plague-bearing fly of 'Serena I', itching to break through the reverential language of high art. The art surface of this work is a star-studded mixture of parody, satire and caricature, which takes on all the great models of narrative, from Chaucerian romance to Balzacian realism, not forgetting a side-swipe at its most recent exponent, Joyce himself.[37]

The West's coming to self-knowledge has been chiefly told in the forms of erotic sensibility, so Chaucer's *Legend of Good Women* provides Beckett with an appropriate epigraph for his hero, Belacqua, to embark on his own journey of self-discovery through all the pleasures and pains of love. Tennyson's *A Dream of Fair Women* lurks inside Beckett's title, and the twentieth century supplies its twist towards the 'middling'. Cultural forms are parasites on one another; and the heritage depreciates. Belacqua, too lazy to repent and be saved, reappears in the streets of Dublin, to relive the cycle of his creator's own adventures in Ireland, Paris, and Austria. Still the expert in minimal and middling effort, he finally returns to Dublin, and the cold pavement of Ballsbridge.

The romance of Dante and Beatrice is brutally updated, and carnality, to the point of obscenity, leaves no place for platonic desire. The space of action is the Irish equivalent of the bar in the rue Mouffetard, in 'Sanies II', where Dante had at last got off with his Beatrice, so Belacqua too can say farewell to all that. The Muse of this modern dreamer is threefold. The Smeraldina-Rima is based on Peggy Sinclair, Beckett's cousin and first love. In the name of his love for Smerry, Belacqua virtuously shuns brothels ('such excellent institutions of pleasure and hygiene')[38] and instead gives himself over to masturbation, and the 'purity' of his own imagination. He tires of her eventually, as he does of the Syra-Cusa, a vicious figuration of Lucia Joyce, as vain, 'lascivious and lickerish', and 'a cursed nuisance'.[39] The Alba (Ethna MacCarthy, a close friend from university days) is the dream-woman who endures, drinking vast quantities of brandy, exercising a serpentine fascination, memorable for her magnificent eyes, 'black as sloes'.[40]

Oblivious of the pains to come, the narrator courses in these three names through a highly pleasurable wet dream of sweet sentimentality and black obscenity. His lifelong situation is drawn in that opening image of an overfed child-Belacqua peddling at speed through country lanes in the wake of a horse, enveloped in the scent of hawthorn (a nod, perhaps, to Proust) and horseshit. The reader who travels through Beckett's pages, pursuing with him 'the memory of an unspeakable trajectory', is carried on a similar vehicle, described precisely by its author: 'If ever I do drop a book, which God forbid, trade being what it is, it will be a ramshackle, tumbledown, a bone-shaker, held together with bits of twine, and at the same time as innocent of the slightest velleity of coming unstuck as Mr Wright's original flying machine that could never be persuaded to leave the ground.'[41]

This bone-shaker is a challenge thrown down to the great Realists, Balzac (on whom Beckett had lectured at Trinity College), Stendhal, Dostoevsky, and Austen. 'To read Balzac', this third-person narrator says, in authoritative Balzacian style, 'is to receive the impression of a chloroformed world';[42] and Balzac's techniques are mercilessly pillaged and parodied. Beckett's characters refuse to fit into the Balzacian categories and types that celebrate scientific reason, and none of them strikes the single clear note that feeds into the harmony that is realism, that 'lovely Pythagorean chain-chant solo of cause and effect'.[43] Instead, this book holds together in the mode of the music of early Beethoven, 'a punctuation of dehiscence', ripening seeds bursting out in all directions, and its only unity is an 'involuntary' one.[44] There are leitmotifs that the reader addicted to unity can pursue, but they are of no conventional kind: recurring images of hands, feet (and boots), spit, diarrhoea, rain and mizzle, evoke the characteristic mood of Dublin's space. Time follows no conventional realist order; it rattles along in a semblance of chronological progression, but takes great leaps across and within chapters of wildly different lengths, and disappears in long plunges into the stream of the Belacquian unconscious. The layers of cultural time buried beneath the present are brought to the surface in surroundings described in realist detail, precise and selective, through the eye of an artist who marries scientific observation to awareness of the transformations of matter, so-called reality, which are operated by changing aesthetic perceptions. The slow mood of Dublin in October, rewritten, like the poems Beckett was writing at this time, under the signs of Ronsard, Homer and Malory, moves into the modern with popular consumerism, under the Bovril sign that dances above College Green, to the Queens theatre, the Fire Station, and Merrion Row, all of them linked by the narrator's wandering fancy and the trams moaning up and down the avenue of a degenerated heritage.

The Dublin vernacular, in its registers high and low, has its own place in the modern cultural mix. There are the vivid altercations between the Professor (the Polar Bear, Beckett's mentor, Rudmose-Brown) and the constable, and the tram conductor whose slow rhythms are mimicked in the third person narrative ('the conductor was slow, he was Irish, his name was Hudson, he had not the Cockney gift of repartee').[45] Alongside that are the other layers of discourse created by the high culture of modernism, the Joycean stream of plurilingual consciousness, a riot of puns and neologisms, which Beckett also parodies. Beyond all this, the writer yearns for something better, a different kind of model, out of which Beckett/Belacqua could build a language of his own:

> the writing of, say, Racine or Malherbe, perpendicular, diamanté, is pitted, is it not, and sprigged with sparkles; the flints and pebbles are there, no end of humble tags and commonplaces. They have no style, they write without style, do they not, they give you the phrase, the sparkle, the precious margaret. Perhaps only the French can do it. Perhaps only the French language can give you the thing you want.[46]

Beckett's attempts to find a publisher for the book in London in 1932 came to nothing, and much of the material was plundered for the short stories published in the Paris review *This Quarter*, and collected in *More Pricks than Kicks* (1934), which gained some attention, not always favourable.[47] It could have been much worse. A story written at the publisher's request to fill out the volume was rejected on submission, as something the public would not understand or tolerate. 'Echo's Bones' resurrects Belacqua, who had been killed off in the penultimate story, in a torrent of obscenities and improprieties of language and situations, a narrative where logical structure has been joyfully abandoned, a lot of good jokes, and an overwhelming cloud of allusions.[48]

Beckett was more successful in challenging moral and stylistic orthodoxies with his next full-length fiction, *Murphy*, written out of his experiences in London, while he was in therapy with Wilfred Bion. The book was finally accepted by Routledge and published in March 1938.

The dustjacket praised the novel for its excellent comic scenes and ironic situations that only an Irish writer could imagine,[49] and Beckett wrote to Tom MacGreevy expressing pleasure at Routledge's effort 'to make an Irishman of me'.[50] Ireland itself was less welcoming. An unsigned review in the *Dublin Magazine* found the book strange and unpleasant, and over-clever.[51] Alex Glendinning's review in the *Times Literary Supplement* was much more positive, appreciating what he saw as a comic narrative style in the tradition of Rabelaisian parody and burlesque; the humour was lodged in the language, witty, violent, and immensely learned, which created a world that echoed that of the conventionally real but was distinctively Beckett's own.[52]

Other friendly reviews included those by the novelist Kate O'Brien, in the *Spectator*, and Dylan Thomas in the *New English Weekly*,[53] and one by Brian Coffey. Coffey was close to Beckett during the last stages of the writing of *Murphy*, and Beckett later gave him the manuscript of his novel. He had pressed Beckett into reading Descartes's follower, the Belgian, Arnold Geulincx, by whom Beckett became fascinated. Coffey drafted an erudite and abstruse review, completed in March 1938, and never accepted for publication. It completely ignored the comedy, but, according to J.C.C. Mays, it was the only response to address Beckett's novel in its own philosophical terms.[54] Anthony Cronin surmised much later that it was the book's sophistication that led it to be so easily overlooked and so long lost from sight.[55]

When he began writing, in August 1935, Beckett had been living in London for almost a year. He was working over the poems to be published in *Echo's Bones and Other Precipitates*, while waiting for proofs, and admiring the intense, obsessive commitment of the old men flying kites at the Round Pond in Kensington, telling Tom MacGreevy that 'My next old man, or old young man, not of the big world but of the little world, must be a kite-flyer. So absolutely disinterested, like a poem [...].'[56] In *Murphy*, Beckett's own obsessive commitment is to the portrayal of a paradox: a character who is seeking to retreat into solipsism, but who craves the company of others like himself. This was not far off Beckett's own situation, but he made a point of distancing himself from a character who, he told MacGreevy, he did not want to take too seriously, showing him throughout sympathy as well as mockery, but in the end pointedly losing patience with him.[57] Chapter 6, a statement of 'the mind of Murphy', a carrot dangled before the reader from the start of the book, finally arrives with apologies from the narrator, and is mercifully short. Feeling himself split in two, a body and a mind, with no understanding of how they interconnect, Murphy finds that the less attention he pays to the body the more he can withdraw into his mind, and within the mind he finds three zones, differently illuminated. One, brightly-lit, deals in fantasy, playing with the familiar forms of the world; in another, half-lit, 'the Belacqua bliss', he contemplates, unmoving and unmoved, the familiar forms; in the third, all dark, is a flux of forms in becoming, in constant movement, unconditioned by any principles, 'a tumult of non-Newtonian motion'; in the third, he increasingly spends his time, motionless, without will, feeling himself 'not free, but a mote in the dark of absolute freedom'.[58] His duty accomplished (and a clear distinction drawn between the confessed idleness of a Belacqua, and the uncommunicable state of human being which it is now Beckett's project to communicate), the narrator promises no further bulletins. The storyline is restored, to chart the view from the outside of a Murphy disappearing into his own dream, while the rest of the world loses itself flying its own kites.

A parody of realist narrative, the book wraps all the trappings of the form around its portrait of a life lived against the grain of the conventional real. In the process, it generates a world of strange edges and angles. The action is set with geographical precision, in the 'real' world of Murphy's London, and the Dublin he has left behind him. Murphy moves from a street of condemned houses in West Brompton to a flat found by his lover, Celia, situated between Pentonville Prison and the Metropolitan Meat Market. Place, a juxtaposition of discrete landscapes, is, like Murphy, not to be taken too seriously. Nor is plot, whose rambling absurdities, narrated, like *Dream of Fair to Middling Women*, in that third person mode which for the realist is the guarantee of objective truth, are a major source of comedy. Murphy's story, despite his efforts at isolation, is interwoven with the tales of many others: Celia, who works as a prostitute to make up for his not working at all, his many friends and acquaintances in Dublin, who have erotic and murderous intentions towards him of which he never becomes aware, and the patients in the sanatorium where he eventually winds up as a keeper, playing long, obsessive chess with the paranoid Mr Endon. In Mr Endon, listed by the authorities as a potential suicide, Murphy finds his long-desired mirror-image, and in their chess game he has the longed-for world of logical structures in which to lose himself.

The book opens with Murphy alone in his room, strapped into his rocking chair, naked, pleasuring his body and freeing his mind, listening out for his landlady, and working towards a state of mind variously described as Apmonia, Isonomy, or the Attunement. The condition and its names were disclosed to him by Neary, formerly a fellow-student in Cork and now a philosopher and bigamist, living in Dublin. Neary loves Miss Counihan, who loves Murphy, and says she can never love another while he lives; so Neary sends a hitman to London, to find and kill his rival. Murphy never finds out about the plot. Wandering round London in the Kings Cross area, pretending to look for work at Celia's command, he meets up with the poet Austin Ticklepenny (a cruel caricature of Austin Clarke), and takes over his job as a nurse in the Magdalen Mental Mercyseat. The patients here, he feels, who are unable to fit into everyday reality, are his kind of people; they return the compliment. This brief period of ideal community ends when Murphy accidentally blows himself up with the Heath Robinson arrangement of pipes he puts together to transfer gas from the lavatory to heat his attic room. All his former friends, from the everyday world of prostitution and murder, come together in the morgue at the sanatorium for the coroner's investigation. Murphy is cremated according to his expressed wish, and as he also wished, his ashes are packed up to be flushed down the toilets in the Abbey Theatre in Dublin. The hitman is entrusted with the packet, but in a drunken rage he throws it at a man in a London street; it bursts, and passers-by kick it to bits. The narrative ends at the Round Pond in Kensington Gardens, where the old men and a young boy are flying their kites, and Celia, back with her clients, gets on with normal business.

Murphy's story is spun out in a mode of surrealist black humour well-established in France, but whose time in London and Dublin was yet to come. The Pythagorean solo of realist cause and effect, already the butt of ironic praise in *Dream of Fair to Middling Women*, runs its course, and no one caught inside it challenges the irrationality of its logic. Two-dimensional characters play out conventional games of passion, jealousy, anxiety and frustration, with a deadpan seriousness that generates its own comedy, and compels from the reader some sort of interest and affection. This kind of story, though, is a kite that will no longer fly on its own, and Beckett and the reader must move on. Belacqua ended cold and shivering in Ballsbridge. Murphy has exploded. The next delegate, Watt, has a different fate.

Begun in Paris, in English, in February 1941, interrupted by the German invasion of Paris, taken up again in March 1943, in the safety and privations of Roussillon,[59] *Watt* was finished in December 1944. Another comic novel, *Watt* is far more disruptive of conventional form, more biting in its satire of the rationalist mindset,[60] and more precise and analytical in its account of the creative process – the relation between the writer, his material, and the words and forms which are his means of expression and inscription. Watt, who will soon also appear as a character in *Mercier and Camier*, will there justifiably declare himself to be the only begetter of Beckett's delegates, past and future.

The world according to Watt is an expansion of the game of chess Murphy played with Mr Endon. It operates within a strictly limited field of play (Mr Knott's house, for the most part), and exhausts a long series of variations, in accordance with strict but arbitrary rules. As the narrative develops, again in the third person, its relation to conventional reality is increasingly tangential. The opening frame of Part I, set at a tram stop, figures recognisable characters from the well-policed world of the respectable middle classes, whose 'normality' is quickly established before the layers of their strangeness, perversity, and violence begin to emerge, in a procedure reminiscent of Ionesco's plays. Mr Hackett, a hunchback, is furiously obsessed by the usurpation of his bench at the tram stop by a courting couple, and he summons a policeman to stop what he calls the obscenity of their embraces. Hackett's conversation with the next arrivals, Mr and Mrs Nixon, Goff and Tetty, is a startling mixture of polite and unconventional exchanges. He reads out an obscene poem to 'Nelly', written, he says, by a prisoner, and Mrs Nixon replies with the anecdote of how she gave birth unobserved during a dinner party. Thoughts normally repressed are presented as if spoken out loud, thanks to a novel policy on grammar. A note at the beginning explains that 'the plethoric reflexive pronoun after *say*' has been left out, to save time and space.[61] In such society, Watt is one oddity among many, his oddest feature perhaps being his intellectual curiosity, which replaces almost all his erotic impulses; and Mr Nixon tells Hackett that each of them reminds him of the other, though he can't think why.

When Watt makes his first appearance, getting off the tram across the road in order to walk to the station, he strikes Hackett as an object of curiosity and wonder, and yet to all appearances, nothing out of the ordinary. He is not clearly visible or audible to the three watchers in the gathering darkness. Nixon tells his friends that he has a big red nose, owes Nixon five shillings, has no fixed abode, and is an experienced traveller. Watt, the modern pilgrim progressing, with no visible means of support, is a horrifyingly plausible Everyman for modern times.

The narrative abandons Hackett and his friends, and the account, still delivered in the third person, turns into a mixture of Watt's perceptions and considerations and (as we later discover in Part III) those of Sam, whose little house and garden are adjacent to Watt's own, situated in the same great park into which Watt, along with the whole range of his fellows, occasionally issues. All the author's creations, including the author himself, inhabit the same space, and exist at the same level of being. Sam, telling a story told him by Watt, tells the reader he can only tell it as Watt told it to him, doing his best to illuminate the darkness. Sam can only follow Watt in his sense of how narrative should proceed, that is, with jumps and skips of time and space, forward, back, and in cycles of repetition. Things will happen, but clarity will be slow in coming.

A second reading of the novel, with the hindsight granted by Part III, will produce a very different experience of the shape and purpose of the narrative. But first time through, the reader must live with mystery and conjecture. Lost in the murmuring voices in his own head, Watt emerges erratically and spasmodically into awareness of where he is on his journey, where he is going, and who he is with, a procedure which can only irritate all right-thinking people, Watt's fellows and Sam's readers. Leaving the train at the station by the racecourse, with his peculiar jerky, hopping walk and swivelling head, Watt provokes the sudden brief appearance of a furious Lady McCann, who throws a stone at him.

The narrative has a semblance of plot. Watt's journey has an aim, which is to reach Mr Knott's house. With some difficulty, he does so, and with even more difficulty, and much repetition and ratiocination, he gets in. This – the house, repetition, and ratiocination – is the site of the main narrative action. In this space, Watt, the homeless traveller, with no resources of his own, has a function, and a reason to be. He is to replace Arsene, his predecessor in line of a sequence of servants, some big and bony and others small and fat, the two contrasting types who appear to be strangely drawn to Mr Knott. Arsene, in a twenty-page monologue packed with repetitions, lists, and digressions, explains, inter alia, Mr Knott's simple and pleasingly symmetrical system for organising his household, based on pairs of servants, downstairs and upstairs, working to a strict pattern. Having set out the system, Arsene leaves. The whole night has passed in the delivery of his monologue, which was presumably its point. This is all that language does in the house of Western reason, as Vladimir and Estragon will soon point out: it passes the time, but the time would have passed anyway.

In Part II, Watt works on the ground floor of this house constructed on the binary oppositions of Western rationalism (Vico's contraries, by any other name), with only brief glimpses of Mr Knott, who chose to give it this particular form. He is puzzled by most of what he sees, and increasingly questions his situation. He is tormented by his inability to distinguish reality from his fantasies. He wants to find some significance to the incidents he finds himself confronted with:

> Watt could not accept them for what they perhaps were, the simple games that time plays with space, now with these toys and now with those, but was obliged, because of his peculiar character, to enquire into what they meant, oh not into what they really meant, his character was not so peculiar as all that, but into what they

> might be induced to mean, with the help of a little patience, a little ingenuity.[62]

He wants words for the things around him, and his situation, but words in this house are slippery and empty, and things, and his own situation, resist being named. More worrying, he has discovered that he can no longer speak of himself with any certainty.[63] The text progresses by means of Watt's attempts to invent significance inside Knott's arbitrary order, creating his own version of Arsene's monologue, to pass the time. Time escapes him: episodes are stretched or compacted with no apparent rationale. Information accumulates to no purpose: lists, tables, enumerations, figures, statistics, and calculations. The statistics on the Lynch family, who for five generations have lived on Mr Knott's charity, are presented with a footnote explaining that the figures on its members being incorrect, calculations based on them will be doubly so.[64] But the stories of the Lynch family and others in similar situations to Watt are diverting, and there are other interesting encounters to be had under Mr Knott's roof – with the old fishwoman, for example, Mrs Gorman, who calls every Thursday except when she doesn't. They kiss and cuddle in the kitchen, but nothing more: 'For Watt had not the strength, and Mrs Gorman had not the time.'[65] A world where Mr Knott is proprietor and paymaster offers an infinite variety of distractions, and a secure living; but incoherence, irrationality, and error appear to be its markers, and Watt is unlikely to stay here long, despite being erotically drawn to the smell of fish.

At the end of Part II, with the arrival of Arthur, Watt is promoted to the first floor, and hopes he may at last discover more about Mr Knott's person and activities. He doesn't: there is apparently little material for him to go on, and his senses are becoming numbed. Mr Knott lived, it turns out, 'in empty hush, in airless gloom', and took this atmosphere with him wherever he went, 'dimming all, dulling all, stilling all, numbing all, where he passed'.[66] But before the narrative line gets to that discovery, Part III begins, and leaps to the description of how Sam and Watt discovered one another in the park. This new space puts Watt in a very different situation, so that he becomes not merely the subject of reason but also (like Sam) the object of writing. As well as a satirical critique of reason, the novel is now also an account of how the creative imagination works. The situations of Sam and Watt are almost mirror images, but not quite. Watt's side of the fence that divides their particular spaces is also occupied by the other denizens of Mr Knott's house. Beckett the creator, unlike his creations, can now distinguish within himself the teller, the telling, and what is told. Across a breach in the fence, Watt tells Sam his story in fragments, inverting sounds, syntactical ordering, and the order of the letters in his words. Sam retells the information Watt has given to make it intelligible. In terms of the splitting of authorial identity that will be explored in later work (*Rough for Radio* is especially clear), Sam is the Listener and the Transcriber of the material presented by Watt. Watt is the nothing of human reality in action, the sound of the rat scrabbling under the surface, the formlessness of an idea that prompted Sam to produce a shape. By this point, the reader is glimpsing the shape coming through, and can begin to enjoy participating in its production, released from ploughing through the still-accumulating 'facts' Mr Knott's servant doggedly persists in enumerating, numbing all. Sam pokes fun at the 'attentive' reader, who struggles on to make sense of a long divagation on Mr Knott's nightshirt, offering him, for his guidance, a note containing another lengthy, equally opaque, account of what the nightshirt might signify.[67] Only a fool, or a pedant, or a critic, expects any help from footnotes. Plodding through to unearth the author's meaning is no way to read, as the last line of the Appendix points out: 'no symbols where none intended'.[68] The reader who has been interacting with the disruptions of the story, not just trying to make sense of the story itself, will make the intuitive leap, and grasp the heart of the matter: these are the games people play with time and space. There is nothing to discover about Mr Knott, or his house. As Watt probably knew from the start, Mr Knott's house, the space of (so-called) rationalist logic and order, was just a place to pass through.[69]

The time is ripe (Part IV) for Micks to arrive, and it is Watt's turn to pack his bags, put on his overcoat and hat, and abandon the house where the storyteller has blown his cover, the games are up, and there is no option but to depart into the night, back down to the station, to wait for the next train. There is nothing left for Watt to do but enjoy the smell of his own slow farts until dawn comes, and finally disappear from Beckett's pages in a flurry of gaps in the manuscript, swamped by an invasion of new characters, all horrified by his filthy state, and covered in fresh abuse from Lady McCann. A bucket of cold water is thrown on him, together with the bucket, and with blood trickling from the wound on his head he buys a ticket for the end of the line, and disappears from everyone's sight. A travelling signifier, with no fixed abode, this particular figment of Sam's imagination ('the long wet dream with the hat and bags')[70] has had, metaphorically speaking, the shit beaten out of it, and the comedy is over.

All that remains is an Appendix – a marker, like footnotes, of a well-researched and truthful text – which the reader is exhorted to read, because, according to another footnote, it contains, in fragments, all the material Sam was too exhausted or fed up to put into his account. This, readers are asked to believe, is the clearest guide to what Sam thinks he has done with his novel. Here is no allegory, only a frank and unvarnished account of the modern human condition (after Dante, 'parole non ci appulcro' – there will be no dressing up of words), which is an image of what humanity, and human culture, has made of the human: 'Watt looking as though nearing end of course of injections of sterile pus.'[71] And 'for all the good that frequent departures out of Ireland had done him, he might just as well have stayed there'.[72] Whether 'he' is Watt or Beckett must remain unclear.

For the time being, he (Beckett) might indeed have felt that leaving Ireland had made no difference. Offered the novel at the end of the war, publishers in England turned it down, beginning with Routledge, who had published *Murphy* in 1938, but found this novel incomprehensible.[73] Only in the summer of 1953, in interesting circumstances, did it find a publisher in Maurice Girodias's Merlin Press.[74]

Girodias, who in 1946 had provided the funding for Georges Bataille's important new magazine, *Critique*, had been approached by the group of young writers and poets who had just launched the new little magazine, *Merlin* (Austryn Wainhouse, Alex Trocchi, Richard Seaver, Christopher Logue, Patrick Bowles), and were keen to help Beckett publish *Watt*. Girodias notes in his memoirs that the first issue of *Merlin* was entirely devoted to Joyce's generation, and included especially pieces by Beckett, whom Wainhouse and Trocchi admired as continuing Joyce's work.[75]

Girodias had inaugurated his Olympia Press in June 1953 with the simultaneous publication of Arthur Miller's *Plexus*, Sade's *Philosopher in the Bedroom*, Georges Bataille's *A Tale of Satisfied Desire*, and Richard Seaver's translation of Apollinaire's *Memoirs of a Young Rakehell*. Through the Merlin group, he signed up Genet's *The Thief's Journal*, translated by Bernard Frechtman, and Beckett's *Watt*.[76] He liked *Watt*, which he much preferred to

Molloy. In *Watt*, he thought, Beckett wrote with his native Irish inflections, while *Molloy* was too reminiscent of Kafka.[77]

Beckett found himself part of a star-studded project including Georges Bataille, Henry Miller, and the marquis de Sade, which aimed to break down the barriers within erotic writing, and, according to Girodias, end the hypocritical distinction between high art and crude pornography.[78] It was a useful market for Beckett to break into. Girodias sent information about his new departure to the list of private clients he had acquired from Jack Kahane's Obelisk Press, and his own core of bookshop contacts in Paris, the Côte d'Azur, and various other centres outside France. In due course, *Watt* appeared in the Traveller's Companion series, one of the 'greenbacks', snapped up avidly by GIs and the Sixth Fleet on shore leave.

Some of Girodias's readers, expecting pornography rather than high art, sometimes felt disappointed and complained vigorously. This was the case, Girodias noted, with the translations of Beckett's texts. He thought everyone still had their money's worth, because the work would certainly keep its resale value.[79] It can be conjectured that Beckett himself would have been very satisfied with the fixed sum payment of eight hundred dollars for the first print run.

Mercier et Camier, begun in July 1946 and completed at the beginning of October, was to be another publishing disappointment. Pierre Bordas had signed a contract with Beckett at the end of October for Beckett's translation of *Murphy*, and all his future work in both French and English.[80] Beckett sent him *Mercier et Camier*, and not long after received an advance; and then the sales of *Murphy* were poor, and Bordas refused Beckett's next two novels.[81] Jérôme Lindon, preparing to publish *Watt* (in Beckett's French translation) in the Editions de Minuit, asked for *Mercier et Camier*, but Beckett refused, saying it could appear after he was dead, with all his other false starts, in a volume of *Posthumous Droppings*.[82] It was finally published by the Editions de Minuit in 1970,[83] as one of a group of early works which, one reviewer suggested, Beckett had perhaps not published earlier because he felt (in the reviewer's view, wrongly) that *Waiting for Godot*, and the novel 'trilogy', had produced more satisfactory metaphors of existence.[84] Certainly, the two old men in the rejected novel, 'one tall, one short, on a bridge', rejoicing in 'our blessed sense of nothing, nothing to be done, nothing to be said',[85] who repeatedly separate and come together again, irritating and consoling each other in equal proportions, live a narrative very much their own. They mark out their own space in Dublin's streets and suburbs, and for once, theirs is a fairly happy ending.

Whatever Beckett thought of his novel, it has distinctive charm, a witty turn of comic language, and sharp, fast-moving comic sequences, as well as some formal innovations that go much further than any in *Murphy*. This is Beckett's last sustained confrontation with the conventions of the realist novel. The first-person narrative voice who tells the journey of Mercier and Camier identifies and caricatures the familiar tricks of realism, noting the 'stink of artifice', or marking an 'End of descriptive passage',[86] and underlining the constructed nature of the plot by providing a summary of events after every two chapters. The narrative avoids anything that might develop into clear plotlines or characterisation. Names are attributed belatedly, and then changed. The story moves at the rambling pace of a journey that has no objective, and is in no haste to conclude: '[L]et our watchword be [...] lente, lente, and circumspection, with deviations to right and left and sudden reversals of course. Nor let us hesitate to halt, for days and even weeks on end. We have all life before us, all the fag end that is.'[87]

The novel satirises the current condition of Ireland, and the mood of everyday Irishness, with the cruel affection that had become Beckett's trademark. It is easy to see why in 1954, with the success of *Waiting for Godot* at last winning hearts and minds, Beckett might have decided against publication of a savage critique which would have provided an unwelcome diversion. These two old men, journeying within the strict limits of home territory, move between town and country, cutting cudgels as they walk the country roads, encountering nothing new, and discovering nothing about themselves. Men of modest but sufficient means, as adapted to the prevailing weather as 'the average native fittingly clad and shod',[88] they are Beckett's version of the *homme moyen sensible* – far removed, though, from their vigorous predecessor in Dublin's streets, Leopold Bloom, or their French counterparts of the previous century, those would-be scientific observers, Flaubert's Bouvard and Pécuchet, with whom they have been compared. They have none of the received ideas which characterise the French couple or indeed any ideas at all. They have things, which for Beckett's characters are as good as ideas, if not better: a raincoat, an umbrella, a sack, and eventually a bicycle, most of which are lost as the journey progresses. Losing things, after starting out, is the next stage on the journey. Making its first appearance in Beckett's prose, though *Molloy* beat it into print, the bicycle is a woman's model, with no free wheel: an early indication of Beckett's awareness of the difference of the feminine situation.

The average Irishman, in this version, lacks the power and drive of the poet who twenty years before freewheeled through Dublin with a tiger in his heart. Their friend Helen refuses to have sex with either of them, but she lets them shelter in her house, and on their second visit, returns their umbrella, which she has mended. There all three, to pass the time, 'manstuprated mildly, without fatigue [...] while the rain beat on the panes'.[89] That same evening, they go to a bar in search of a different route to oblivion, because 'it is in bars that the Merciers of this world, and the Camiers, find it least tedious to await the dark'.[90] They live in the embrace of the urban crowd, to a slow beating rhythm like that of the falling rain, that carries them along to the canal, or the slow train, surrounded by vague ghosts that suddenly leap into threatening focus. In the park, there was a drunken old woman with her skirts lifted high, the menacing park ranger in top hat and frock-coat, and two children in black oilskins, who address Mercier as Papa and have to be frightened off; there is an episode with a fat woman in a car accident, and a confrontation with a policeman who is beaten to death. This Irish journey is the journey of modern humanity, where force of circumstance, in the shape of the unending rain, sees desire, repressed to near-extinction, always on the point of turning to rage and frustration. Violence is close to the surface of the blandness, waiting to erupt, pointlessly, at a scratch. On the horizon, there are energies that might once have been directed to a purpose, but the couple have no way, or wish, to tap into them. Crossing the moorland, they glimpse a distant cross, marking the grave of the Irish nationalist, Masse or Massey; they say they have forgotten his name, but they knew it once. They set out to find his gravestone, but they never get there, and the impulse is forgotten.

The pattern of their journey, within the larger circle of setting out and coming back home, is one of separations and coming together. In the final chapter, having sworn to part company this time for ever, the couple are reunited in a public house by Watt, a huge figure, squalid and stinking, old and unwashed, who forces them back onto speaking terms, and lifts the narrative onto a level where it begins to fold round and speak of itself, and its own performance. Watt is a delegate of the author, the Third, the Observer, who makes explicit the created nature of the aesthetic object. Mercier has for some time suspected his existence: 'Like the presence of a third party. Enveloping us. I have felt it from the start.'[91] Watt reminds Mercier of Murphy, who died ten years ago, and who Watt claims was his dream. Watt, like the couple he has joined, is also, he claims, a seeking subject; with the difference that he thought he had an aim. He prophesies other would-be subjects to come, with other aims: 'One shall be born, said Watt, one is born of us, who having nothing will wish for nothing, except to be left the nothing he hath.'[92] Leaving Watt to his drunken stupor, and his gnomic visions of Beckett's next delegates, Mercier and Camier slip out of the pub to return home, deciding that their journey has been a failure. They had no aim at the beginning, so failure is hardly an appropriate word, but the meeting with Watt seems to have shown up something that was missing in their particular performance: the self-awareness, and the realisation what it was all about, that can only come with hindsight, after a project is over.

> Looking back on it, said Camier, we heard ourselves speaking of everything but ourselves.
>
> We didn't bring it off, said Mercier, I grant you that.[93]

At the end, his interlocutor gone home, Mercier is left alone on the bridge, a motionless subject-position, dwindled to a single point of perception, staring at a mysterious outside world which, for the day's wanderings through his local landscape, is now a richer mystery. He watches the dark deepen, 'And in the dark he could hear better too, he could hear the sounds the long day had kept from him, human murmurs for example, and the rain on the water.'[94]

The 'failure' of Mercier and Camier, wandering aimlessly in the world outside them, together with that of Watt, the subject enclosed in rationalist assumptions, explores two routes which by themselves lead nowhere, but, looking back, are searches which throw up, as Watt says, the prospect of more to come – and the more subjects that come, the more combinations there are to explore. The human murmurs Mercier hears on his bridge are the echoes created in the text in the confrontation between the couple and Watt, which repeat and illuminate the confrontation in *Watt* between the different aspects of Beckett's creative persona. In such interactions, the nothing that passes the time takes shape, and will now project itself into an infinite future. In Mercier's lonely darkness, there is an implicit tomorrow, where the birth of nothing, prophesied by Watt, is on its way.

NOTES

1 Samuel Beckett, 'Dante ... Bruno. Vico ... Joyce', first published in *transition* 16/17 (June 1929); collected in Samuel Beckett and others, *Our Exagmination Round His Factification for Incamination of Work in Progress* (Paris: Shakespeare & Company, 1929). Page references are to the reprint in *Disjecta* 1983.

2 Beckett, 'Dante ...'; *Disjecta* 1983, p.22.

3 Beckett, 'Dante ...'; *Disjecta* 1983, p.23.

4 Beckett, 'Dante ...'; *Disjecta* 1983, p.25.

5 Beckett, 'Dante ...'; *Disjecta* 1983, pp.27–8.

6 John Pilling and Seán Lawlor, 'Beckett in Transition', in Mark Nixon, *Beckett and Publishing*, pp.83–96.

7 Manifesto for 'The Revolution of the Word', *transition* No. 16–17 (June 1929). Signed by Kay Boyle, Whit Burnett, Hart Crane, Caresse Crosby, Harry Crosby, Martha Foley, Stuart Gilbert, A.L. Gillespie, Leigh Hoffman, Eugene Jolas, Elliot Paul, Douglas Rigby, Theo Rutra, Robert Sage, Harold J. Salemson, Laurence Vail. On Jolas's project, see Craig Monk, 'Eugene Jolas'.

8 Letter from Beckett to Ernest Vessiot, 10 April 1929, *Letters* I, p.9 and p.10 n.3.

9 Knowlson, *Damned to Fame*, p.113.

10 Letter from Beckett to Thomas MacGreevy [?summer 1929], *Letters* I, p.12.

11 Letter from Beckett to Thomas MacGreevy [before 5 August 1930], *Letters* I, p.36.

12 Letter from Beckett to Thomas MacGreevy, 25 August [1930], *Letters* I, p.43.

13 Letter from Beckett to Charles Prentice, 15 September 1930 (*Letters* 1, p.48 and p.48 n.1).

14 Marcel Proust, cit. Samuel Beckett, *Proust* (1931); rpt. in Samuel Beckett, *Proust and 'Three Dialogues: Samuel Beckett & Georges Duthuit'* (London: John Calder, 1965), p.12.

15 Beckett, *Proust*, p.15.

16 Beckett, *Proust*, p.17.

17 Beckett, *Waiting for Godot* (1954); *CDW* 1986, p.83.

18 Beckett, *Proust*, p.28.

19 Beckett, *Proust*, p.33.

20 Ibid.

21 Beckett, *Proust*, p.31.

22 Beckett, *Proust*, pp.72–3.

23 Beckett, *Proust*, p.74.

24 Beckett, *Proust*, p.75.

25 Beckett, *Proust*, p.88.

26 Samuel Beckett and Georges Duthuit, *Three Dialogues* (1949); rpt. in Samuel Beckett, *Proust and 'Three Dialogues: Samuel Beckett & Georges Duthuit'*, p.103.

27 Letter from Beckett to Thomas MacGreevy, 25 August [1930], *Letters* I, p.43.

28 Mary Bryden, in *Women in Samuel Beckett's Prose and Drama. Her Own Other* (Houndmills, Basingstoke: The Macmillan Press, and Lanham: Barnes & Noble, 1993), records a progression in Beckett's writing from conventional oppositional presentations of gender to a free, open, and expansive vision of the instability of the concept. See especially Chapter 2, 'Beckett/ Deleuze/ Guattari: Gender in Process', pp.58–69.

29 Berthold Schoene, 'The Union and Jack: British Masculinities, Pomophobia, and the Post-nation', Glenda Norquay and Gerry Smith (eds), *Across the Margins: Cultural Identity and Change in the Atlantic Archipelago* (New York: Palgrave Macmillan, 2002), p. 86; cit. Jennifer M. Jeffers, 'Deviant Masculinity and Deleuzian Difference in Proust and Beckett', in Bryden, Mary and Topping, Margaret (eds), *Beckett's Proust/ Deleuze's Proust* (Houndmills, Basingstoke and New York: Palgrave Macmillan, 2009), p.177.

30 Samuel Beckett, *Malone Dies* (1956); *Trilogy* 1979, p.166.

31 See below, Chapter 4, p.94.

32 Hélène Cixous, 'La Missexualité: où jouis-je?' *Poétique* 26 (1976); rpt. in *Entre l'écriture* (Paris: éditions des femmes, 1986), p.80.

33 Hélène Cixous, 'Une Passion: l'un peu moins que rien', in Tom Bishop and Raymond Federman (eds), *Samuel Beckett, Cahiers de l'Herne*, Special Issue, 31, 1976, pp.326–35.

34 Julia Kristeva, 'Le Père, l'amour, l'exil', in Tom Bishop and Raymond Federman (eds), *Samuel Beckett, Cahiers de l'Herne*, Special Issue, 31, 1976, pp.246–52; 'The Father, Love and Banishment', in Leon S. Roudiez (ed.), *Desire in Language: A Semiotic Approach to Literature and Arts*, trans. Thomas Gora, Alice Jardine, Leon S. Roudiez (New York: Columbia UP; Oxford: Basil Blackwell, 1980), pp.148–58.

35 Samuel Beckett, *Dream of Fair to Middling Women*, Eoin O'Brien and Edith Fournier (eds) (Dublin: The Black Cat Press, 1992).

36 Beckett, *Dream*, pp.16–17.

37 For the many texts and authors invoked in the novel, from Richard Burton to Mario Praz, see John Pilling, 'Guesses and Recesses: Notes on, in and towards *Dream of Fair to Middling Women*', in Marius Buning, Danielle de Ruyter, Matthijs Engelberts and Sjef Houppermans (eds), *Beckett versus Beckett, Samuel Beckett Today/ Aujourd'hui* (Amsterdam-Atlanta, GA: Rodopi, 1998), pp.13–23.

38 Beckett, *Dream*, p.38.

39 Beckett, *Dream*, pp.50–1.

40 Beckett, *Dream*, p.174.

41 Beckett, *Dream*, p.137, p.139.

42 Beckett, *Dream*, p.119.

43 Beckett, *Dream*, p.10.

44 Beckett, *Dream*, p.138, p.132.

45 Beckett, *Dream*, p.158.

46 Beckett, *Dream*, p.48.

47 The *TLS* reviewer was interested by the satirical effect created by presenting the everyday through a mass of observed detail, cross-cut with unexpected and unsettling terseness; he also pointed to Beckett's links with Joyce, and the dangers of Joyce's example (Alex Glendinning, '*More Pricks than Kicks*', *TLS*, 1695 (26 July 1934), p.526.

48 The story has finally been published in an annotated edition by Mark Nixon (New York: Grove Press/ Atlantic Monthly Press, 2014). See the review by Nicholas Lezard, 'People will shudder …', Review Supplement, *The Saturday Guardian* (10 May 2014), p.20.

49 Dustjacket for Samuel Beckett, *Murphy* (London: Routledge and Sons, 1938), cit. *Letters* I, p.611 n.1.

50 Letter from Beckett to Thomas MacGreevy, 8 March 1938, *Letters* I, p.611 n.1.

51 Anon, [Review of *Murphy*], *Dublin Magazine*, 14.2 (April–June 1939), p.98, cit. *Letters* I, p.640 n.4.

52 Alex Glendinning, 'The New Novels', *TLS*, Spring Books Number, 1884 (12 March 1938), p.172.

53 Kate O'Brien, 'Fiction. *Murphy*. By Samuel Beckett', *The Spectator* (25 March 1938), p.50 (http://archive.spectator.co.uk/article/25th-march-1938/50/fiction. Consulted 27 August 2013); Dylan Thomas, 'Recent Novels', *New English Weekly*, 12 (17 March 1938), pp.454–5.

54 J.C.C. Mays, 'Brian Coffey's Review of Beckett's *Murphy*: "Take Warning while you praise"', in Benjamin Keatinge and Aengus Woods (eds), *Other Edens. The Life and Work of Brian Coffey* (Irish Academic Press: Dublin and Portland, Oregon, 2010), pp.82–100. Mays's essay includes the text of Coffey's review (pp.86–90). On Beckett and Geulincx, see David Tucker, *Samuel Beckett and Arnold Geulincx. Tracing 'a Literary Fantasia'* (Continuum: London and New York, 2012).

55 Anthony Cronin, 'A Vote for the Little World. *Watt* by Samuel Beckett', *TLS*, 3231 (30 January 1964), p.81.

56 Letter from Beckett to Thomas MacGreevy, 8 September [1935], *Letters* I, p.274.

57 Letter from Beckett to Thomas MacGreevy, 7 July 1936, *Letters* I, p.350.

58 Samuel Beckett, *Murphy* (1938), *Grove* 2006, p. 69 and p.70. P.J. Murphy reports that Chapter 6 draws heavily on Beckett's close reading of Spinoza, which, he proposes, also underlies all the other philosophical references in the novel ('Beckett and the Philosophers', in John Pilling [ed.], *The Cambridge Companion to Beckett* [Cambridge: Cambridge University Press, 1994], pp.225–9).

59 Knowlson, *Damned to Fame*, p.333.

60 P.J. Murphy argues that *Watt* is a Kantian novel (Murphy, 'Beckett and the Philosophers', pp.229–35).

61 Samuel Beckett, *Watt* (1953); *Grove* 2006, p.172n.

62 Beckett, *Watt*; *Grove* 2006, p.227.

63 Beckett, *Watt*; *Grove* 2006, pp.232–3.

64 Beckett, *Watt*; *Grove* 2006, p.250. See for a discussion of these games John J. Mood, 'The Personal System – Samuel Beckett's *Watt*', *PMLA*, 86, 2 (March 1971), pp.255–65.

65 Beckett, *Watt*; *Grove* 2006, p.283.

66 Beckett, *Watt*; *Grove* 2006, p.332.

67 Beckett, *Watt*; *Grove* 2006, p.342.

68 Beckett, *Watt*; *Grove* 2006, p.379.

69 Beckett, *Watt*; *Grove* 2006, p.233n.

70 Beckett, *Watt*; *Grove* 2006, p.371.

71 Beckett, *Watt*; *Grove* 2006, p.378.

72 Beckett, *Watt*; *Grove* 2006, p.374.

73 Letter from T.M. Ragg to Beckett, 6 June 1945, *Letters* I, 25, n.1. Routledge were also disappointed by the sales of *Murphy*; only half the first 1500 print run had been sold, and the rest, to Beckett's fury, were remaindered (Bair, *Samuel Beckett*, p.336).

74 See Knowlson, *Damned to Fame*, pp.393–7.

75 Maurice Girodias, *Une Journée sur la terre. II Les Jardins d'Eros* (Paris: Editions de la Différence, 1990), p.224.

76 Girodias, *Une Journée sur la terre. II*, pp.233–5.

77 Girodias, *Une Journée sur la terre. II*, p.226. The Editions de Minuit had just published *Molloy* in French.

78 Girodias, *Une Journée sur la terre. II*, p.282.

79 Girodias, *Une Journée sur la terre. II*, p.284.

80 Letter from Beckett to Pierre Bordas, 30 October 1946, *Letters* II, p.45.

81 Knowlson, *Damned to Fame*, p.376.

82 Letter from Beckett to Jérôme Lindon, 20 January 1954, *Letters* II, p.446.

83 The author's translation into English, with a quarter of the text cut, was published by Calder & Boyars in 1974.

84 Charles H. Peake, 'In pursuit of failure', *TLS*, 3589 (11 December 1970), p.1442.

85 Samuel Beckett, *Mercier and Camier* (1974); *Grove* 2006, p.476, p.449.

86 Beckett, *Mercier and Camier*; *Grove* 2006, p.384, p.460.

87 Beckett, *Mercier and Camier*; *Grove* 2006, p.431.

88 Beckett, *Mercier and Camier*; *Grove* 2006, p.383.

89 Beckett, *Mercier and Camier*; *Grove* 2006, pp.435–6.

90 Beckett, *Mercier and Camier*, *Grove* 2006, p.436.
91 Beckett, *Mercier and Camier*, *Grove* 2006, p.461.
92 Beckett, *Mercier and Camier*, *Grove* 2006, p.471.
93 Beckett, *Mercier and Camier*, *Grove* 2006, p.475.
94 Beckett, *Mercier and Camier*, *Grove* 2006, p.478.

CHAPTER 3

Refusing Mastery

Consuming, Composting, Composing

Beckett's next three major texts dig deeper into the question of the subject and the external world, expanding the search for ways of expressing the ever-changing embedding of the perceiving subject in its landscape; an earth that simultaneously confines, limits, and nourishes. In the process, they discover more about the nature of the subject who searches. At the end of the journey, after all the frenzy, anguish, and rejoicing, all the subject can know is that there is nothing to know – except, as Mercier has discovered, caught in the silence between the dark enclosing sky and its reflection in the dark running river of time, the longing to find the calm, unembellished expression of that nothing.[1]

The embedding of the subject in the landscapes of its creation is a familiar concept in modernism. Beckett knew it from personal experience, as well as through Joyce and Jolas, right from the start of his writing career. Luke Gibbons, exploring the interactions of culture, history, and Irish identity in the Introduction to his *Transformations in Irish Culture* (1996), makes the point when he challenges the conventional view that writers such as Joyce and Beckett abandoned Irish culture for the excitement of the Parisian avant-garde. Rather, he argues, their insertion into European culture was all the more fruitful for the formative experience they brought with them of the violence and turmoil of Irish history and politics.[2]

By the time Beckett was composing his three interlinked novels, *Molloy, Malone Dies,* and *The Unnamable,* written in French between May 1947 and January 1950,[3] he had become deeply familiar with the complexities of the landscapes, Irish and European, in which he and his contemporaries were situated, physically and psychologically, and the layers of language and culture out of which they and it were constantly constructed and reconstructed, in the performance of identities of others' choosing.[4] These three texts model his struggle with that double heritage, in search of the language that will express the nothing that underlies all its forms: Nothing, or the infinite chaos of possibilities through which the human subject is forever tunnelling in the impossible attempt to create a form for its expression.

In *Molloy*, the urgency of reworking the discursive context is graphically conveyed in the blackly comic description of the constricted, impoverished landscape which is Molloy country. In the narrow domains of Ballybaba, around the market-town of Bally, the view of the 'strangled creek' which the inhabitants are given to admire fixes their imaginations on greyness and repetition. The land, meadows, grass and trees are turned over to the grotesque cultural products of religion and capital ('amulets, paper-knives, napkin-rings, rosaries and other knick-knacks'), and only 'the ass, the goat and the black sheep' can use the poisonous weeds that remain for nourishment.[5] Beckett and his readers, the scapegoats and outcasts, are those who have learned to consume, digest and decompose the poisonous material their culture gives them to graze.

The three novels take to a new level Beckett's exploration of the processes of story-making. To have lived stories is not enough; they have to be talked about, and in the talking, taken apart. This is work that attacks the linguistic practices that underpin the deadening everyday lives, and the deadened imaginations, of the subjects of Western culture, Irish and European alike: the attachment to inherited ways of telling the story, fixed images, and the drumbeat of rigid grammar and syntax. The body of human culture is the space of composition; and in that same body, Beckett seeks the means of decomposition.

Beckett's world is now no longer simply a prison-house of language, where words and concepts are the bars of a cage that stands separate from the wild creature it contains. The image of the rat, scrabbling under the surface of the artwork, has been displaced.[6] In the fantasy formulation that best satisfies the narrative voice of *The Unnamable*, Beckett's world is a pit in the depths, of which the inhabitant is physically part, separated from the rest by the thinnest of membranes, absorbing its nourishment bodily, directly from the material about it. Words are a part of that material, and this particular creation knows itself, and its other, in the terms in which it dwells: 'an outside and an inside and me in the middle, perhaps that's what I am, the thing that divides the world in two [...], perhaps that's what I feel, myself vibrating, I'm the tympanum, on the one hand the mind, on the other the world, I don't belong to either'.[7]

The rat, gnawing at the outside, is replaced by Worm, absorbing and vibrating, the feeling of living the in-between, which comes closest to knowing the Nothing. This is, as Molloy had already realised, 'the period I'm worming into now'.[8]

Every period, in both senses of that word, is a language-production. History, like all story, is produced in images, as the early Beckett had understood, but also in the order of syntax, and the rhythms by which syntax moves. A change in the dynamic of story and history, like the cultural watershed marked by *transition,* requires a change in syntactical rhythm. Each of the three novels experiments with ways of changing the period – the moment and the sentence – of its inheritance into something different, trying to disrupt and displace the authoritative accounts of objects, places and persons. The images that we put together to designate ourselves a place within the 'silence', which is Beckett's other term for the Nothing, and the designations we give to the fantasy image that is inscribed as 'self', 'I', 'me', can only fix the silence. Fixing reinforces the old poisons, and marks acceptance of the limits to understanding and invention. But the rhythms by which we live, the syntax through which the images are linked in experience and memory, are in movement, and in them lies the chance of generating another kind of syntax, open not to order but to disruption, distortion and displacement. In *The Unnamable*, the breakthrough is achieved, with the production not of a new kind of image but of a new syntactical rhythm. In place of the familiar classical period, that tool of scientific analysis which was elaborated through the long history of the rhetorical tradition, the voice of this text breaks out in the vibrations of breath and the beating of the heart, the 'fundamental sounds' of Beckett's form, which, he said, were all he took responsibility for.[9]

Decomposition is the best word for the process at work along the length of the trilogy. Studies of Beckett's writing in terms of 'exhaustion' have been productive, but the term has a negative dimension that leaves the tale half told.[10] Beckett's near-exhaustive demolition of the conventional forms of discourse empties out the fixed forms of 'literature' only to fill its space with movement.[11] Nor can Beckett's attempt to write towards 'lessness' be fully understood in the terms he famously used in a letter of 1937: a matter of trying to drill holes into language, until whatever meaning, or absence of meaning, that lies beneath, slowly emerges.[12] In *The Unnamable*, he makes comic play with the concept of amplification ('dilation', he calls it), best instanced in Joyce's preference for writing more, which in Beckett's view is a failed machine when it comes to making transformations in language. Beckett's form of reduction is that of the soup-maker in his kitchen ('that's a darling dream I've been having, a broth of a dream')[13] or the chemist in his laboratory. The point is to break down conventional discourse into its basic elements, and then to remake them into a more condensed form of energy, creating a dynamic in which words expand and dissolve into new connections and connotations. What's left is not merely less, but an intense reduction, a more flavoursome stock, with the potential to produce more and better creations. The old question of subject identity, in particular, here shifts into motion, and becomes the new concept of the subject identifying; and in the process, it opens the door to a new understanding of the collective and contextual nature of subjectivity.

For Paul Kelley, this rewriting of subjectivity is the main goal of the literature of exhaustion. He argues that Beckett first achieves it in *Company*, where the first-person subject no longer has a role in the narrative, and its place is filled by the exploration of intersubjectivity.[14] But this particular form of play, the rhythmic repositioning of individual to others, is already in operation in the closing pages of *The Unnamable*, in the dance of the pronouns, 'I', 'they', 'me', 'it', 'you'. The bees' dance in *Molloy* foreshadows it in non-human form, in the collective movement of the return to the hive, where identity and difference are performed in 'a great variety of figures and rhythms' and 'very different hums', a production of movement and sound that fascinates Moran with its mysterious complexity.[15]

The discussion in this chapter pursues the metaphorical thinking associated with Beckett's images of 'ground', 'Worm' and 'worming', to show how Beckett models the decomposition of the body of conventional discourse, engaged in its landscape, into the rhythm of a new dance. There are two issues to be explored. First, there is Beckett's systematic evocation across all three texts of the simplifying binaries which are key markers of that discourse – Vico's contraries, yet again – those patterns of understanding which writer and reader have in common and without which, it would seem, no communication is possible. This is the 'yes-no' structure, which is re-enacted throughout human experience, down to the bodily rhythms of human consumption (ingestion–elimination, filling–emptying, composition–decomposition). In *The Unnamable*, as will be explored below, the couple Mahood–Worm figures the binary. Secondly, there is the way the text works to dissolve and remake that structure of oppositions, and the role played in that process by the image of Worm, in its various manifestations. Principally, I shall be concerned with the turning of that image, and its transformation from Worm to worming. The finite object becomes open-ended action, as noun turns to gerund, the verbal noun which puts the image into motion. With the turning of Worm, Beckett's transformation of the period begins.

Impasse: The Rhythm of Contradiction

Reading the three books in sequence is the best way to perceive the structure of Beckett's project. There is an obvious difference between *The Unnamable* and its two predecessors. All three texts acknowledge that in themselves inherited discourses are irrefutable, the material within whose limits any given speaking subject is constructed, and so the only language it can ever deploy. *The Unnamable* makes the point best, in a ruefully comic tone: 'There's no getting rid of them without naming them and their contraptions'.[16] And it's *The Unnamable* that has the best shot at getting rid of them.

The first two books set out, in different ways, the operations of familiar narrative forms, written to order, which perpetually reinscribe in writers and readers the allegiance of the Western self to the discursive orders of Western culture. In both novels, the reader, like the characters, is called to fall into line, and addressed as a passive consumer of narrative form, not a participant in its creation.

The 'I' of *Molloy* is writing pages of what seems to be a memoir, that are collected weekly and returned to him weekly in the form of what seem to be proofs. In the second part of the book, Moran is instructed to write a report on Molloy, who has managed to disappear, and in the process, bring him home – that is, back into the fold. The narrative structures are those of traditional realism. Both parts open with clear statements of the situation, time and place of the narrative subject, who is an unambiguous 'I', and both end in closure. In between, the realist illusion is maintained by ample use of external detail, and obsessive registration of things, people, and places. *Molloy* is based on a double quest: Molloy is in search of his mother, Moran and his son go in search of Molloy. Both journeys are variations on the epic nostos – the long return home – and both take place within the ambit of some overarching, well-policed authority. They are differently situated in the ground of gender: Molloy inhabits the mother's room; Moran, the father's house (his own). But gender makes no real difference here. Both speak the same language of rationally and syntactically coherent statements, obeying the formal constraints of grammar.

The end of Moran's narrative seems to be on the threshold of some new form of perception, recognising the possibility of some different relationship between Moran and the world of objects. Back in his home, free of his son, Moran finds his house is empty, and his hens and his bees are dead. The wild birds, however, have survived, and Moran declares that he hears beyond their language snatches of a new voice and a new language.[17] There is not much to support his belief. The old realities of space and time are unchanged (he returns one year later, and the house and garden are still there), and so is his own language. His dream of difference is expressed simply by breaking his sentences in two, and his language is still incapable of embracing that of the birds. The text ends in ambivalence. Moran's final 'report' challenges reality but submits to the order of language, and is no more than a contradiction in terms, which confirms the fundamental structure of 'yes-no': 'I [...] wrote, It is midnight. The rain is beating on the windows. It was not midnight. It was not raining.'[18] It is however a start; and Beckett's later prose will find ways of restating the language of contradiction in ways that turn flat statement into oscillation, bringing words into movement.

Malone Dies declares its closed position from the start. Its end is in its beginning; it starts and ends on the narrator's own deathbed. This time, the form slated for reconstruction is not the epic but the short story (Malone plans four, and then, with comic practicality, reduces the scheme to three, in view of his deteriorating condition), to be followed by an inventory of his possessions. 'Things' are always a good resource. These stories are only drafts, never satisfactory, none of them completed, but none rejected either; together they constitute the sheaf of failed projects which constitutes Malone. They are stories in realist mode, expressed in third person or dialogue form (Malone is satisfied with neither), presenting characters in a landscape, interacting, relating, full of passion and emotion, whose merely fictive nature is regularly disclosed by a puncturing absurdity. Action and characters are grotesque and exaggerated, both melodramatic and banal. Lambert the pig-sticker buries his mule, the rabbit dies of fright on its way to the pot, hens run round with their heads cut off, pigeons struggle as they're strangled, Mrs Lambert bad-temperedly sorts lentils, brother Edmund masturbates, and incest is in the air. 'What tedium', the narrator comments.[19]

In May, the narrator himself is invaded by a 'sensation of dilation' which engages his whole body, starting with the feet, and promises the longed-for transformation of landscape. Even the air, he claims, and with it the syntax of the language, have changed, splitting apart subject, verb, and object.[20] This is not the case. Most of Malone's sentences are still complex classical periods, constructed in familiar rhetorical forms, and their significance is clear, even when accompanied by the speaker's comments on the flow of his own voice and his complaint that the noises of world outside have turned into nonsense: 'one vast continuous buzzing'.[21]

Malone, at ease in his own sense of himself, telling his tale to, of and for himself, thinks he is in full possession of his own space: 'This room seems to be mine.'[22] But the exercise in possessive individualism which is his life is written down in the child's exercise book which is Malone's equivalent of Moran's report to the masters.[23] And the room, like his life, is not his own. He writes in a hospital bed (brought there, like Molloy, by the hospital ambulance), between ruled lines, with his two branded pencils, one a little Venus, and another made in France. Despite his efforts, he cannot hide his book from the monitor who comes into his room at the end, and takes it. This book ends in no fantasy of a freer voice, but in irretrievable decomposition, a bleak representation of the panting, frustrated rhythms of dying breath, with meaning dribbling, shapeless, into the blankness of the borrowed page.

The Unnamable, in contrast to its predecessors, opens not with statements to situate the place and time of the narrative voice, or its purposes, but with question forms, which themselves are open to question ('Questions, hypotheses, call them that'), and a lunge at stating some kind of intention which also immediately undercuts itself with the recognition that its status is purely declarative: 'Keep going, going on, call that going, call that on.'[24] In this cloud of meaningless words, the narrator's voice flutters and turns like a wild bird in the air, unthinkingly supported by the words as the bird is supported by the air, unthinkingly scattering its productions, prompted only by gleeful delight in its own being: 'Can one be ephectic otherwise than unawares? I don't know. With the yesses and noes it is different, they will come back to me as I go along and now, like a bird, to shit on them all without exception.' [25] Here is the scaffolding of conventional sentence forms – question, answer, statement – but inside it, meaning is decomposing into overlapping rhyme and rhythm ('otherwise'/ 'unawares'; 'unawares'/ 'yesses'/ 'noes'; 'know'/ 'noes'/ 'now'); and on 'now', with a sudden twist of syntax, the subject pronouns 'they' and 'I' topple into confusion, swooping unexpectedly into a vigorous imperative, in the form of a triumphant subject-free infinitive. This is the early bird that stands the best chance of getting the worm. Here is the first draft, in miniature, of the repeated process of composition and decomposition of which the rest of the text is made, with the crucial difference that by the final page all has changed, the word for the bird has been consumed along with the rest, the simile has gone, along with all the other images that imprison desire, and what remains is the long vibration of process without end.

There is shape to this narrative, but it is reduced to the minimum necessary for keeping going, and it is fluid; system and logic have no place here.[26] The voice speaks of a preamble and a statement, but the difference between them is only a matter of labelling.[27] The statement is a series of gestures towards themes and forms already explored in Beckett's earlier fictions, all of which here become games played inside the forms of story: description, digression and meditation, all instruments to recapitulate the operations of language, to shit out 'their' sense, and to invoke the beat of a different dance. These sequences are, increasingly, musical variations, of which the closing movement, beginning 'Enormous prison', is composed of two great sentences, which retain of the classical period only the minimum: the capital letter and the full stop.[28] Between those two limits, the complexity of clauses and subclauses has dissolved away.

Juliette Taylor-Batty has studied Beckett's systematic review in *The Unnamable* of the forms of traditional grammar, as taught by rote in schools.[29] She shows how readers are made aware in the novel of the linguistic patterns that internalise authoritarian order; and she cites Émile Benveniste's contention that the concept of subjectivity, established in language, is what creates the category of 'person', both inside and outside the linguistic field.[30] Beckett's aim in *The Unnamable*, she argues, is to produce a critique of the way grammatical form works to impose order:

> Beckett's bewildering manipulation of linguistic form in *L'Innommable* thus both provides a critique of the ordering and defining impulse of form and itself constitutes a form which might well be seen to '[accommodate] the mess' (Driver 23). In *L'Innommable*, grammar is thus exposed as a mask, and an ineffective one at that: grammar not only attempts to mask the chaos, it actually ends up producing chaos.[31]

Grammar, by Beckett's showing, is a very effective instrument for the subject-forms that 'they' find it profitable to impose. The long Indian file of the masters departs at the end of many of *The Unnamable*'s stories, but it always returns. If all the third text can generate is a form that accommodates the mess, then it has produced yet another cage. So the final movement of *The Unnamable* moves to a new tune: a song where the words carry traces of what they were, but only enough to make a melody, which turns into notes carried on a radically different rhythm. The end movement abandons all semblance of story, and becomes a prose poem whose deepest rhythms are breathing and heartbeat, the simple ticking alternation of systole-diastole, short phrases which create continuity by internal echoes and repetitions, and mirror-reversals: 'if I gave up, if only I could give up, before beginning, before beginning again, what breathlessness, that's right, ejaculations'.[32] The rhythm decomposes articulate speech, and reduces language to the simplest of oppositions, murmurs and cries, the edge of silence from which sound vibrates back into existence.[33] The rhythm builds up to a throbbing climax of suspense, a rocking cradle of sound where themes, ideas, and textual leitmotivs, summoned for one last project, play against one another in mutual decomposition. Tenses, like pronouns, disappear into one another, not into buzzing and gibberish, but into the turning point where 'I' suddenly swoops through the medium of words into a new form of being, recognising selfhood as identity with the other and the silence:

> you must say words, as long as there are any, until they find me, until they say me, strange pain, strange sin, you must go on, perhaps it's done already, perhaps they have said me already, perhaps they have carried me to the threshold of my story, before the door that opens on my own story, that would surprise me, if it opens, it will be I, it will be the silence, where I am, I don't know, I'll never know, in the silence you don't know, you must go on, I can't go on, I'll go on.[34]

This is not, as Paul Kelley terms it, an abrupt ending, but a long-prepared, reverberating climax. For its making, it requires the reader's patient attention, and a willingness to be drawn into those beating rhythms where grammar works differently, and its workings themselves become meaning, and where the cumulative reduction of the human dictionary to its keywords – words, story, door, threshold, silence – ends with all energy investing itself in a model of a continuous present, forcing its way into being. The first-person subject merges with the third, and the larger silence, and then, in the last line, all nouns and pronouns are subordinated to the echoing tick of verb and preposition: ('go on' [...] 'go on' [...] 'go on'). Here there is no closure, but the urge to endless replay, with the engaged reader pushed by the echoes and the leitmotifs to turn back to the beginning, and seek out all the threads afresh. This is not an unreadable text, but one that constantly demands fresh reading, requiring the reader's return, like the narrator's, to the inexhaustible ground of language, to begin again. This is the period of Worm's making.

Another Way Through: The Turning of Worm

Within *The Unnamable*, the last and best figuration of Vico's rhythm of contradiction, which runs through all three novels, is the couple Mahood–Worm. The novel was originally titled Mahood, and the character of Mahood appears in the text as yet another in the series of Beckett's 'delegates'. Progressively stripped of clothes and limbs, a speechless head on a trunk stuck in a deep jar, eyes streaming with tears, reduced further than any other of the narrator's dream-delegates, Mahood has a tantalising resemblance to Worm.[35] But locked like his predecessors into the old ways of telling, by the simple fact of starting out human, Mahood, for all his abnormality, is the property of the authorities. Mahood's natural rhythms, his processes of nutrition and elimination, are trapped in a system that actively contributes to the nourishment of 'their' order. Fed by the woman from the restaurant across the street on her rubbish, his composted excrement goes into her kitchen-garden, and her clients, at a short remove, thrive on his shit. Her menu, with its list of commodities and prices, hangs on his jar. But coupled with Worm, the image of Mahood stands a chance of feeding into something different: a moment of turning. The narrator sets out the project, acknowledging its obscene absurdity: '[L]et me complete my views, before I shit on them. For if I am Mahood, I am Worm too, plop. Or if I am not yet Worm, I shall be when I cease to be Mahood, plop.'[36]

Worm might easily be only one more of Beckett's delegates, and eventually, like the rest of them, he accepts the conventional attributes 'they' require, and takes shape as yet another disappointment to his progenitor. The figuration of Worm is however best read as one of Beckett's better fails, probably the best, not only as good as it gets, but as good as it needs to get. A complete and irreducible image of difference would be a contradiction in terms, yet another dead end for narrator, reader and text, and an untruth that could only close down the process of collective (de)composition to which *The Unnamable* is committed. In his essay of 1999, Michael Billington expressed admiration for Beckett's early theatre, from *Waiting for Godot* to *Happy Days*, and his ability to construct images of human tragedy, cut down to the bone; but that, he went on, was a disadvantage in his later drama, where the images become too precise.[37] But in some of that later drama, which is a theatre of perception, the point is to generate models of the limited, and limiting, nature of precise ways of seeing. In *The Unnamable*, there is the clearly critical image of the devastating fixity of vision which is the mark of owl-eyed wisdom, the motionless gaze, tears streaming from unblinking eyes.[38] Linked with Mahood, that other unmoving image of wholeness, Worm is the desire for an image with a difference, which absorbs into itself the material of the text, and is itself absorbed as the new rhythms reach towards their own conclusion. Worm is the bait that draws readers onto the double hook of a text that will not let them rest in fixity, and engages them in the wrestling match with language that is the human condition.

In the context of Worm, the narrative voice makes its clearest statement of textual purpose, which is to represent the movement which is the essence of being human: 'The essential is never to arrive anywhere, never to be anywhere, neither where Mahood is, nor where Worm is, nor where I am, it little matters thanks to what dispensation. The essential is to go on squirming forever at the end of the line.'[39] As the sentence writhes on, the bait and the fish, narrating voice and the material of the narrative, merge into a single performance, the nothing that is to be done, and that goes on forever: 'I've swallowed three hooks and am still hungry.'

The appearance of Worm intensifies the rhythms of displacement that break down the familiar elements of the text. In the image that immediately suggests itself to the reader, Worm is a figure with the rhythms of displacement established in and through its centre, a tube that couples ingestion and excretion, making and communicating significance, and a gesture towards the narrator's dream of existence as a vibrating tympanum. Worm, the figure of the process of changing, is also an agent of change.[40] Once the language of authority has been through Worm, it can never be the same again. The fixed subject is churned into movement, to create a truer representation of reality: 'As for the squirming, nothing doing.'[41] The much-neglected gerund is the centre of this text, evoking the process of worming and squirming.

Intimations of worming go back to the first text of the trilogy, where Beckett is already unobtrusively engaged in composing and decomposing. Molloy, in his first attempts to investigate his identity, burrowing back to recreate his earliest memories of his mother, had spoken of 'the period I'm worming into now'.[42] Not long after, burying Lousse's dog, he consigns to the worms the Cartesian image of God the watchmaker.[43] After that, the word 'worm' goes underground, while the texts experiment with different ways of teasing it out again, into new forms of textual movement.

In *The Unnamable*, the first break with the straight line of the classical period comes in the form of one-legged Mahood and his enforced experiments with new forms of physical locomotion. Mahood's thrusting, jerky advance, propelled by the thrust of his crutches, is a clumsy parody of the lively squirming of the living worm. His well-ordered syntax evokes movements that curl and spiral, but stay on the surface of his landscape, the island and its bogs, and get nowhere new; as he says ruefully at the end: 'No good wriggling, I'm a mine of useless knowledge.'[44]

The true Worm, when he appears, is distinguished from all Beckett's other delegates, by his origins in sound, as a murmur whose resonances, the narrator now asserts, have been running below the surface of all earlier drafts.[45] Sound, fundamental to the world of human discourse, functions differently with Worm, who, unspeaking, has a different relationship to words, experiencing them not as meaning but movement:

> These millions of different sounds, always the same, recurring without pause [...]. Yes, I know they are words [...].Two holes and me in the middle, slightly choked. Or a single one, entrance and exit, where the words swarm and jostle like ants, hasty, indifferent, bringing nothing, taking nothing away, too light to leave a mark.[46]

In yet another turning of the text, the elimination of words ('it's like shit, there we have it at last, there it is at last, the right word [...] it's a question of elimination')[47] is redefined as not an ending, just a process of passing through, which is the same as being passed through. The subject and its environment, words and their speaker, are two aspects of the same thing, incessantly rehearsed, with variations.[48] In that process, there is the hope that in the shit might be found the words that really matter: 'Perhaps they are somewhere there, the words that count'.[49]

The words that really count are the words beating out the right rhythms, just the sounds. All the rest must be eliminated, and that includes the image of Worm. That warning is there from the beginning. The injunction 'Worm to play, his lead'[50] triggers a lengthy sequence of squirming, writhing and convoluted sentences built of short phrases, a series of negations of what Worm is, ignorant and voiceless, structured by echoes that foreground the rhythm of his creation, but in the end, nothing but a bad joke: 'being conceived, if only by the beer.'[51] Worm is the drunken dream of his creator, not the I-in-itself, the unnamable subject, for which Beckett was fishing – without, as yet, realising the futility of his enterprise. So Worm himself must be eliminated, in the moment of his invention, like all Beckett's projects, only a passing thing.[52]

But the time of his invention is the place of creative origins, where narratives and narrators merge and meld, and 'I' comes at last under suspicion. The narrative voice asks what 'I', Mahood and Worm are doing in each other's stories; and this is the point where the text reassigns to itself the negative attributes of Worm (no mouth, no head, no ear), and designates itself as resonance and murmur, a vibrating tympanum,[53] surrounded and invaded by words, and buried deep in the landscapes of time: 'it piles up all about you, instant on instant, on all sides, deeper and deeper, thicker and thicker, your time, other's time, the time of the ancient dead and the dead yet unborn'.[54] 'I the orator'[55] stands at the centre of a sequence that rehearses yet once more the old categories, the old tales, and the old jokes. Then a final mention of Worm, coupled with his contrary, Mahood, introduces a final overview of all the material the text has processed: the landscape ('old slush to be churned everlastingly') and the language ('it's the fault of the pronouns, there is no name, for me, no pronoun for me, all the trouble comes from that, that, it's a kind of pronoun too, it isn't that either').[56] The final gesture of displacement dissolves all the fixed images and opens them up to movement: 'I must have forgotten them, I must have mixed them up, these nameless images I have, these imageless names, these windows I should perhaps rather call doors'.[57]

Words are not places to be in, or to look through, but to go through. The immense prison which is living is challenged: 'how false this space is'.[58] The challenge generates the last long unending squirming which is 'my turn of the lifescrew', worming out the unnamable space of the knowing subject, between 'I' and 'it':

> I hear everything, what difference does it make, the moment it's not my turn, my turn to understand, my turn to live, my turn of the lifescrew, it calls that living, the space of the way from here to the door [...][59]

NOTES

1 Writing to Georges Duthuit, Beckett set out the pattern and goal of his writing: 'Il faut crier, murmurer, exulter, insensément, en attendant de trouver le langage calme sans doute du non sans plus, ou avec si peu en plus' (Letter from Beckett to Georges Duthuit, 11 August 1948, cit. *Letters* II, p.96).

2 Luke Gibbons, *Transformations in Irish Culture* (Notre Dame, Ind.: University of Notre Dame Press, in association with Field Day, 1996).

3 Knowlson, *Damned to Fame*, p.371. *Molloy* and *Malone Dies* were first published in French in 1951 and *L'Innommable* in 1952 (Paris: Les Editions de Minuit). The English translation of *Molloy* by Patrick Bowles in collaboration with Beckett was published in 1955 (Paris: Olympia Press). Beckett's translation of *Malone meurt* appeared in 1956 (New York: Grove; London: John Calder, 1958) and his translation of *L'Innommable* in 1958 (New York: Grove). The three novels were published together in 1959 by Grove in the US (*Three Novels*), and by John Calder in London (*The Beckett Trilogy. Molloy, Malone Dies, The Unnamable)*.

4 In 'The Trilogy Translated', *Beckett's Fiction: In Different Words* (Cambridge: Cambridge University Press, 1990), Chapter 3, Leslie Hill explores the 'hybrid status' of the three texts, written in French, with gestures towards Anglo-Irish language and culture, and then translated by the author into his own English.

5 Beckett, *Molloy*; *Trilogy* 1979, pp.123–4.

6 Beckett, *Dream*, pp.16–17.

7 Beckett, *The Unnamable*; *Trilogy* 1979, p.352.

8 Beckett, *Molloy*; *Trilogy* 1979, p.18.

9 Letter from Beckett to Alan Schneider, 29 December 1957, in Maurice Harmon (ed.), *No Author Better Served*, p.24. Letter © the Estate of Samuel Beckett, reproduced by kind permission of the Estate of Samuel Beckett c/o Rosica Colin Limited, London.

10 For the literature of exhaustion, Beckett is frequently a point of reference: see for example John Barth's essay on 'The Literature of Exhaustion' (*Atlantic Monthly*, 220, 33 [August 1967], pp.29–34), and Gilles Deleuze's essay 'L'Épuisé', in Samuel Beckett, *'Quad' et autres pièces pour la télévision, suivi de 'L'Épuisé' par Gilles Deleuze* (Paris: Editions de Minuit, 1992).

11 Paul Kelley, *Stories for Nothing: Samuel Beckett's Narrative Poetics* (New York, Bern, and Frankfurt am Main: Peter Lang, 2002), p.4.

12 Letter from Beckett to Axel Kaun, 9 July 1937, *Letters* I, p.518.

13 *The Unnamable*; *Trilogy* 1979, p.348.

14 Kelley, *Stories for Nothing*, p.6.

15 Beckett, *Molloy*; *Trilogy* 1979, p.156.

16 Beckett, *The Unnamable*; *Trilogy* 1979, p.299.

17 Beckett, *Molloy*; *Trilogy* 1979, p.162.

18 Ibid.

19 Beckett, *Malone Dies*; *Trilogy* 1979, p.198.

20 Beckett, *Malone Dies*; *Trilogy* 1979, p.215.

21 Beckett, *Malone Dies*; *Trilogy* 1979, p.190.

22 Beckett, *Malone Dies*; *Trilogy* 1979, p.168.

23 Beckett, *Malone Dies*; *Trilogy* 1979, p.252.

24 Beckett, *The Unnamable*; *Trilogy* 1979, p.267.

25 Ibid.

26 Beckett, *The Unnamable*; *Trilogy* 1979, p.268.

27 Beckett, *The Unnamable*; *Trilogy* 1979, p.277.

28 Beckett, *The Unnamable*; *Trilogy* 1979, pp.377–82.

29 Juliette Taylor-Batty, 'Imperfect Mastery: The Failure of Grammar in Beckett's *L'Innommable*', *Journal of Modern Literature* 30, 2 (2007), pp.163–179.

30 Emile Benveniste, *Problèmes de linguistique générale*, 1966, trans. Mary Elizabeth Meek, *Problems in General Linguistics* (Coral Gables: University of Miami Press, 1981), p.277, cit. Taylor-Batty, 'Imperfect Mastery', p.167.

31 Taylor-Batty, 'Imperfect Mastery', p.177. The reference is to Tom Driver's article, 'Beckett by the Madeleine', *Columbia University Forum* 4, 3 (1961), pp.21–5.

32 Beckett, *The Unnamable*; *Trilogy* 1979, p.377.

33 Beckett, *The Unnamable*; *Trilogy* 1979, p.381.

34 Beckett, *The Unnamable*; *Trilogy* 1979, pp.381–2.

35 Beckett, *The Unnamable*; *Trilogy* 1979, pp.300–7.

36 Beckett, *The Unnamable*; *Trilogy* 1979, p.310.
37 Michael Billington, 'Plays for Today. Beckett wrote four masterpieces. The rest will soon be forgotten', *The Guardian* (1 September 1999) (https://archive.today/TxK4. Consulted 24 October 2013.)
38 Beckett, *The Unnamable; Trilogy* 1979, p.269.
39 Beckett, *The Unnamable*; *Trilogy* 1979, p.311.
40 Beckett, *The Unnamable*; *Trilogy* 1979, pp.317–18.
41 Beckett, *The Unnamable*; *Trilogy* 1979, p.337.
42 Beckett, *Molloy*; *Trilogy* 1979, p.18.
43 Beckett, *The Unnamable*; *Trilogy* 1979, p.35.
44 Beckett, *The Unnamable*; *Trilogy* 1979, p.290.
45 Beckett, *The Unnamable*; *Trilogy* 1979, p.310.
46 Beckett, *The Unnamable*; *Trilogy* 1979, pp.325–6.
47 Beckett, *The Unnamable*; *Trilogy* 1979, p.336.
48 Beckett, *The Unnamable*; *Trilogy* 1979, p.340.
49 Beckett, *The Unnamable*; *Trilogy* 1979, p.340.
50 Beckett, *The Unnamable*; *Trilogy* 1979, p.318.
51 Beckett, *The Unnamable*; *Trilogy* 1979, p.318. The joke is not there in the original French (*L'Innommable* [Paris: Les Editions de Minuit, 1953], pp.99–100).
52 Beckett, *The Unnamable*; *Trilogy* 1979, p.342.
53 Beckett, *The Unnamable*; *Trilogy* 1979, p.352.
54 Beckett, *The Unnamable*; *Trilogy* 1979, p.358.
55 Beckett, *The Unnamable*; *Trilogy* 1979, p.361.
56 Beckett, *The Unnamable*; *Trilogy* 1979, p.371, p.372.
57 Beckett, *The Unnamable*; *Trilogy* 1979, p.375.
58 Beckett, *The Unnamable*; *Trilogy* 1979, p.377.
59 Beckett, *The Unnamable*; *Trilogy* 1979, p.379.

CHAPTER 4

The Shorter Prose – False Starts, Fresh Ends

In 1950, Suzanne and devoted friends hawked the three novels around publishing houses, while Beckett made what income he could from translation – a translation for UNESCO of an *Anthology of Modern Poetry*, edited by Octavio Paz (Paz had chosen him to do the work), book translations for Bordas and Georges Duthuit, and texts for Duthuit's new series of *Transition*.[1] At the end of the year, Beckett wrote to George Reavey that he had a contract with Jérôme Lindon's Editions de Minuit for all work, and specifically the three novels.[2] There were protests from Pierre Bordas, but as Beckett pointed out to him, politely but very firmly, he had failed in his contractual promise to publish any of Beckett's work since *Murphy*, and his position was not tenable.[3]

The success of *Waiting for Godot* was to change many things for Beckett, not least the projects he now undertook. For the next decade, plays engrossed his attention (see next chapter), offering the challenge of different forms and technologies of expression, and also, perhaps, being easier for the public to understand. Translating the plays and the novels, or overseeing their translation, as European and international markets opened up, took considerable time and effort. In 1954, in answer to a complaint from Beckett about his difficulty in pursuing new writing, Barney Rosset suggested sympathetically that translations, though a useful source of income, must be getting in the way. Beckett replied that, apart from his own translation of *Godot*, he made no money from his work revising others' efforts, but did it because he felt protective towards his texts.[4] A German version of *Molloy*, he thought, had been generally well done, but was full of mistakes and had 'an irritating way of turning the unusual into the usual so that it won't read like a translation!', while the Spanish version of *Godot* had been 'awful'.[5]

In any case, it seemed his triumphant reverberating finish to *The Unnamable* had brought him to a dead end. A fairly fallow prose period followed, lasting ten years, producing only *Texts for Nothing*, written in French between December 1950 and December 1951, with its image of the plough turning at the end of a furrow, and after that, the last few extended texts written in the 1960s and 1970s.

Mark Nixon, in the Preface to his edition of Beckett's shorter prose pieces, speaks of Beckett's own feeling that these texts were all false starts: 'texts which no sooner begun ended in abandonment, or were discarded after a long struggle to find the path to a satisfactory conclusion.'[6] And he reports Beckett telling a friend in that period that he enjoyed two aspects of creative writing: beginning a text, and throwing it into the waste-paper basket.

Beckett's dissatisfaction with his work was perennial, and it cannot always be taken at face value. All his texts are false starts, in the sense that all starts, he came to realise, always have to be done again; and it might be argued that the shorter post-1950 pieces accept this as a given of artistic making: 'nothing like breathing your last to put new life in you'.[7] Equally, what Beckett might have understood as a satisfactory conclusion is never certain. The apparently categorical assertion in *Texts for Nothing* ('it's the end gives meaning to words')[8] is undermined by the double meaning of 'end'. *The Unnamable* certainly closes on a high note, with its reverberation that resists silence, and as the three beats of *That Time* come to an end, the presiding face opens its eyes and breaks into a smile – these at least might seem satisfactory in the generally accepted sense. In contrast, *Words and Music* ends with Croak, the Opener, shuffling out in displeasure, and his instruments in disarray.

Texts for Nothing: 'Under a Different Glass'

Beckett's letter to Barney Rosset of February 1954 also referred to a little book he was putting together for Jérôme Lindon; it would include three long short stories and 'the thirteen or fourteen very short abortive texts (Textes pour Rien) that express the failure to implement the last words of L'Innommable'.[9] The *Textes pour rien* had been on the boil by then for over two years. It was described by Beckett to Mania Péron as 'quelques petites merdes' which answered the question of how to go on after *L'Innommable*, and also, more positively, as attempts to see if he couldn't invent something else ('des petites texts-sondes pour tâter la possibilité d'autre chose').[10]

The first of the *Texts for Nothing* begins by contradicting the confident closing phrases of *The Unnamable*: 'Suddenly, no, at last, long last, I couldn't any more, I couldn't go on.'[11] The rhythm of expansion has gone, to be replaced by short gasps and stutters, alliterating hard, choking 'g' and 'c'. All 'I' can do is breathe in and out, and see what happens. There has been a change, the authorial voice notes, a high point has been reached, and in the next text, the voice is now trapped in a new, experimental place: 'Here you are under a different glass, not long habitable either, it's time to leave it. [...] Go then, no, better stay, for where would you go, now that you know?'[12]

The first texts of the sequence get into gear by making an inventory of what their author now knows, reviewing the same old mutterings and stories, and the same old questions and answers, trying everything, establishing the devastating falseness of all the principles on which the old world was built, and recognising that there are no truths to replace them. The concept of place has dissolved. The speaker imagines he is caught in a trough, the centuries-old peaty quagmire, full of mist and rain, on top of the wild, flat hill to which he has finally struggled (Text I), or he is on a cliff edge, or on a journey out from home and back, from the turn of a furrow (Text II) – none of these old scenarios are true, and none of them can satisfy. There is no 'where' to go to. The words for time have dissolved into those of space: 'by before I mean elsewhere, time has turned into space, and there will be no more time, till I get out of here.'[13] Time is paused, and the mind is slow, words are slow, and both mind and words are moving to a stop (Text II). This is still better than the fluent language of the old life, which snuffed out all truth. Words like evening, night, and morning, are now treated as rhetorical instruments for the creation of those false scenarios from the past in which the voice still indulges itself. The concept of memory has lost all conviction, gone along with time. Text II invents 'one last memory' as a pretext to create a shambolic story, full of hesitations and contradictions, of the return home from the turn of the plough in the furrow, to a warm red glow. There is even a full stop, which is certainly an ending of a kind ('I end there'), though the text hobbles on for a few more short sentences. In Text III, words keep coming, and they have to be uttered, but all concerned agree they are failing and false: 'let us be dupes,

dupes of every time and tense, until it's done'.[14] Voice is a fiction, without life, and the body is a textual construct – still a necessary invention; but its gender doesn't matter, just 'feel between your legs'.[15] For all the emptiness of words, Beckett retains his gift for creating the vivid illusion of the real, in direct, sensuous detail.

Grammar, strangled by a syntax that reverberates in all directions, confesses the true mystery of the human situation, in the dance of the pronouns ('he', 'me' and 'I'), which performs the incapacity of the subject to exist, except as its own object: 'It's the same old stranger as ever, for whom alone accusative I exist, in the pit of my inexistence.'[16] In Text V, 'I' stands ready for interrogation in the dock, the multifunctional subject: 'I' am my own accused, clerk, and scribe. Story is still a productive concept, though whether storytelling negates life or makes it is still under discussion. Life, in Text IV, exists between speech and silence: 'There's my life [...]. There has to be one, it seems, once there is speech, no need of a story, a story is not compulsory, just a life, that's the mistake I made, one of the mistakes, to have wanted a story for myself, whereas life alone is enough.'[17] What gets in the way of life is the fascination of the old stories, the rhythms which lull the speaker and keep him company. In Text I, there is the adventure of Joe Breen, the lighthouse keeper's son, a story told many times by the father to the son on his knee, which the speaker now tells to himself, rocking himself to sleep in a familiar, consoling, and illusory closure – one kind of satisfactory conclusion. As the sequence develops, the storylines break up, to give way to short anecdotes framed in inconsequential speech, and finally, in the last of the *Texts for Nothing* (XIII), the babbling of a weakening voice. This dying voice is reduced to functioning on the basics: a structure of contraries, and a will to self-empowerment. The text drives determinedly towards an intense climax, and in place of the consolations of sleep presents an inextricable tangle of contradictions, the figure of the inexpressible Nothing that is being in action. Future, past and present, silence and speech, all merge, as the point of origins becomes the point of ending:

> And were there one day to be here, where there are no days, which is no place, born of the impossible voice the unmakable being, and a gleam of light, still all would be silent and empty and dark, as now, as soon now, when all will be ended, all said, it says, it murmurs.[18]

The Unnamable ended in expansion. This text turns in on itself, in its incantatory rhythms, and multiple echoes.

Texts for Nothing expresses the hope that the author may yet write the true story, with truthful words, that will set out what his life is. One thing is clear enough, as always, that his life is words: 'I give you my word.'[19] But there is a new variant on the question of who I am. Text VI asks who and where am I when I am not writing, and performing a conscious act of self-mirroring? The answer to this one must await fuller expansion until the end of the decade, when Beckett undertakes to tell *How It Is.* This future text may well be the narrative that he glimpsed as the *Texts for Nothing* were first taking shape, telling Barney Rosset that 'At the moment I have a "man" crawling along a corridor in the rock in the dark, but he's due to vanish any day now'.[20]

The 1950s were a roller coaster for Beckett, in terms of his career and his personal life. The year 1954 was marked by the successful production in Paris of *Waiting for Godot,* and by Beckett's first meeting, in September, with the American Pamela Mitchell, a representative of the publishing house Harold Oram Incorporated, who came to Paris to enquire about the English language rights of his play. They enjoyed pleasant evenings together, eating and drinking, and wandering through the streets of Paris, and that, he wrote to her, was a good way to do business.[21] This was the start of a brief but intense affair, which resolved into a long-lasting friendship. But the decade began with his mother's death, on 25 August 1950.[22] At the end of May 1954, news came that Beckett's brother Frank had been diagnosed with terminal lung cancer. Beckett spent the next three and a half months with his brother and his family in Killiney, until Frank's death in September.[23] In November 1958, he flew to Ireland again to see Ethna MacCarthy, who was in the terminal stages of throat cancer; she died in May of the following year.[24]

How It Is

Beckett began a new prose text, *Comment c'est* (provisionally entitled *Pim*), in December 1958, and spent the next eighteen months in writing and revision. French publication was in 1961. The final translation into English, *How It Is,* begun in September 1960, appeared in the spring of 1964.[25]

The text revisits the drama of being and knowing that was acted out in the pit of *The Unnamable,* and then again in the trough on the plateau of *Texts for Nothing*. This time there are no delegates, those third-person projections or sounding boards ('he') by which the subject registers its existence. This time, the dark is inhabited by a self-identifying point of origin, into which is folded back the capacity for voice which the point, once it begins its journey into self-determination, will only find at the end. Only with hindsight can the subject know and speak itself. The images and the structural syntax of this new text, from the journey that is its storyline through to the games it plays with time and space, are organised into a dynamic model which gets as close to showing how it is to be human as any of Beckett's models have so far managed to do.

The point is embedded in a material landscape (mud and dark) and soundscape (the rhythms of its own breathing). Beckett told Donald McWhinnie, in a letter of April 1960: 'A "man" is lying panting in the mud and dark murmuring his "life" as he hears it obscurely uttered by a voice inside him.'[26] There is a new dimension to this turn of the textual plough. Self-knowing is generated through sense-perceptions. The question to be explored here (or rather, for the writer, to be put into imaginative form) is how perception enters into the process of identity formation.

As Beckett explained to McWhinnie, the text is conceived in three parts, all expressed in the present tense. The first part consists of the 'man's' solitary journey through the dark towards the discovery of Pim, his mirror-other. The second, the two of them together, ends with the departure of Pim, leaving the man alone but with the new dimension to being which is body-awareness. The third part is the point of origin of the voice the 'man' hears inside him in Part I, which displaces the panting. The emergence of the voice in that final part is the emergence of the 'I'. The present tense is only appropriate for this part. The first two parts must already have been completed for the voice to emerge, but without the voice the journey could not have been narrated. Time must be folded back, and what is represented is the illusory present in which all subject being is lived.[27]

How it is, then – becoming a speaking subject, and knowing what it is to be a speaking subject – is a process which is only graspable in retrospect, and in terms which are all fictions. The first and second parts of the text are written in the present, but the 'man' could not have articulated them in that present, which is a fiction, and the words in which they are present-ed can only themselves be fictions. These temporal and spatial stages of knowing are all fictions, a scaffold whose function is to communicate different aspects of subjectivity. The subject who speaks an experience is not the same as the subject/object spoken of, and neither aspect can exist until that difference is realised. In this fiction, the difference is made real in the language of body-experience (in the section where Pim is 'discovered'), and in the language of intellectual understanding (in the third section, the place of voice). This realisation involves a third aspect, an observer-function within the self, who recognises the identity of body and voice, perceiver and perceived. There is one more aspect to it all, in which the observer also operates as scribe, the function within the subject who has developed the techniques and tools capable of communicating these insights to others, in the form of this particular written text.

As the voice of the text drives forward, in its panting, then its murmurs, and its repetitions, it enacts as best it can how 'it' is, that is, my life. My life is a continual, always imperfect attempt to give form to my life, using my words to evoke its origins in the formless and the unspeakable: 'my life last state last version ill-said ill-heard ill-recaptured ill-murmured in the mud brief movements of the lower face losses everywhere'.[28] Two impulses make up this text: a celebration of the materiality of being – the location of the body in its earthy environment – and a pervasive anxiety about the possibility of finding an adequate way of speaking being in the language of materiality. The text hovers between two forms of utterance: panting, which is the immediate, unconscious production of the animal body, and telling, the production of the conscious human subject ('when the panting stops scraps of an ancient voice').[29]

The account underlines its untrustworthiness. This is only one version of me among many ('it's the beginning of my life present formulation').[30] There have been other formulations, with different elements: more characters ('no callers this time no stories but mine'), and using the concept of memories ('I haven't been given memories this time').[31] Memories, which, however fragmentary, are developed narratives of past experience, are inappropriate forms for a point that can only receive sense-impressions. Instead, images from 'life in the light'[32] flicker into the darkness of the text, themselves more developed and coherent than the context should allow, pointing up the necessarily retrospective and fictive nature of the voicing of the simplest sense-experience. The images disappear in the third part, after the meeting with Pim, with the subject's recognition of itself as whole body in the mirror of the other, and with the realisation that how it is, the nature of my life, is the process by which I come to say that my own voice speaks, through my own body. My life is an unending search through a story that slips through unending versions, never to rest in any final time or place.

In the beginning is the warm dark and the primeval mud, foul, abject, but also cocooning and thirst-quenching, the elemental support of life, through which 'I' advances by slow push and pull; and the voice, inside, outside, and everywhere. Things are the next material stimuli to bring subject-knowledge closer. The damp old coal sack with tins in it, and the tin-opener, are markers of place for the moving point, as well as a comic promise of survival, beyond the mud. Like the images, they come in a form already processed and pre-empted. When the transitional object that is the sack is lost, the body of Pim takes its place. Before Pim, there were only fragmentary self-perceptions, of hand, fingers, face, eyes, lips, right leg, and right arm, and those simple oppositional movements of push and pull. With Pim comes the great discovery, as the subject recognises himself in the mirror of his own other ('I see me').[33] There is now exploratory touching and feeling over Pim's flesh, establishing the presence of buttock, fork, spine, ribs, head, testicle, and skull, with old man's white hair. With the discovery of Pim's heavy watch, time enters the equation. Pim can be made to scream, sing, and speak, by scratching, thumping, and – a novel adaptation of the materials serendipitously given – stabbing in the buttocks with the tin-opener. Finally, there is now script, something to write on, and to write about. This newly self-aware subject carves Pim's name, with his nails, on Pim's back, and then carves 'YOUR LIFE',[34] recognising that a life in the first person cannot be written, except in objectified form. This inscription on flesh is a new kind of writing, a poetry of shockingly raw materiality, intuitive and sensuous, which opens up a new perspective onto human time, all falling back into indeterminacy, just as it is beginning to take shape:

> unbroken no paragraphs no commas not a second for reflection with the nail of the index until it falls and the worn back bleeding passim it was near the end like yesterday vast stretch of time.[35]

In the final part, after that first self-knowing through Pim, the same violent scenario of discovery and enforced speech is repeated, with Prim, Bom, and Kram. The making of words which is my life, and yet is not my life, is repeated ad infinitum. There is nothing new to be said, only the repeated acknowledgement that this is how it was and how it is, with the same images and stories of the same self proliferating to infinity, more or less the same words, and the same old phrases, all created in the same rhythms of contradiction, push and pull, dark and light, tormentor and victim, voice and mud. The figures are all interchangeable, and there are millions of them: 'so eternally I quote on'.[36] The text builds to a closing climax in a chaos of words that complements the chaos that was the originary mud and dark. The mud, dark, and me, alone there with my voice, forever quoting myself, are the only truths. There is no answer to the questions of how it was, and who I was, even when howled in upper case, except the acknowledgement, again, that 'THAT'S MY LIFE HERE'.[37] To the question whether things may change, there is only the growing realisation that the ultimate knowledge of 'I' is death ('I MAY DIE [...] I SHALL DIE'); the text ends immediately, and quietly: 'good good end at last of part three and last that's how it was end of quotation after Pim how it is'.[38] With the discovery of the body, the tablet on which all experience is written, comes the discovery of death, and that is now, unchangeably, how it is. In the present, the time which is the place of the voice, there can be nothing else to say.

'Eternally I': The Mobile Text

Quotation need not be the end; it depends what one chooses to quote. Beckett's later prose texts still draw some of their energy from quotations from the cultural heritage, despite his declared intention after the vision of summer 1945, echoed in *Krapp's Last Tape*, to abandon that heritage and turn inwards for his subjects.[39] That inward turn was not a question of searching for deep psychological insights, or undertaking elaborate investigations of feeling. The feeling is there, not least the anguish that comes with the recognition of mortality, but what interests Beckett most are the variations he can bring to the structures in which feeling takes shape. Most of his quotation is now of his own writing, echoing familiar figures, patterns, and concepts, inscribing himself into being through unending self-repetition. As David Watson points out, the concern of Beckett's later texts is not the production of the fixed subject, which is what readers see if they only pay attention to the narrative voice. Instead, here is the open subject, lodged in the writing process, whose being is identical with the play of the text:

> These texts (and others) constantly reopen their site of representation, disrupting its totality by the forms of intertextual repetition which I outlined earlier. [...] Beckett's texts constantly recross the same space, rewriting themselves in the same site of representation, but in ever-different contexts, repeating the movement of desire from a state of quiescence into a world of infinite difference.
>
> So to talk of the texts as merely representing something is to ignore the ritualistic processes of textual repetition, the process of performativity, the linguistic performance of the body in relation to desire and language, its dialectical relationship to the subject positions it adopts and refuses. To talk about narrative voice is to privilege the half of the text which installs fixed subjectivity and identification; it suppresses the play of the text [. . .].[40]

For David Houston Jones, it is the process of constructing images in narrative which is a central focus of attention in the later short prose texts (achieved, to the narrator's satisfaction, in *L'Image,* a small section of *Comment c'est*, which was published separately in 1959).[41] In those texts, play with repetition and play with images go together.

All Strange Away, begun and then dropped in early 1965, and first published in English in 1976,[42] is, as the title suggests, an exercise in self-estrangement, where writer and reader escape from the tyranny of language through the disruption of semantics and syntax. Words become as fluid as paint. The text operates in a single enclosed space, morphing between a cube of decreasing size and a rotunda. The space marks the limits of a perceiving body, origin of 'the glaring eyes' and 'flashes of vision' which generate the intense, mobile energy of this particular version of the creative process.[43] Imagination flicks on and off, through fixed patterns of repetition, and through images, all of them reflections of the perceiver, which are suddenly illuminated on the walls of the space. Movement is by extreme contraries (bone-white/ black, light/dark, ebb/flow, full/empty, female/ male, Emma/ Emmo, frustration/ satisfaction), with 'syntaxes upended in opposite corners'.[44] Vocabulary is an omnium gatherum of registers, ranging from algebraic notation (a, b, c) to crudely physical sexual terms, nouns and verbs (cunt, breasts, motte, 'sucking, fucking and buggering').[45] By the end of this intensive, increasingly frenzied accumulation of words, all meaning has been exhausted, leaving 'no more feeling apparently in hammock than in Jesus Christ Almighty', and in place of meaning, there is the image of nothing: 'nothing ever in that hand lightly closed on nothing'.[46]

Imagination Dead Imagine was written in French in early 1965, and published in French and English in the same year.[47] This text performs a similar exercise with fewer words, and in a simpler space: always a rotunda, inhabited this time by two still white bodies with piercing blue eyes, mirroring one another. The structure of thought is also simpler: the text moves by opposition of extremes of white and heat, and black and cold, and switches between the two in 'countless rhythms' of rise and fall.[48] The two bodies are the mirror-projections of the subject, joined in the creative process, and observed by the author-scribe. *Enough*, in more elaborate narrative form, represents that creative process from the perspective of the created object, housing the inspirations of ten years, who is taken for a walk to the sound of the pen of the author, as it starts and stops. Lurking behind this extended comic image, perhaps, is Paul Klee's conceit of painting as taking a line for a walk; and also lurking here is another answer to the question Beckett asked himself in the sixth of his *Texts for Nothing*: what happens to me when I am not consciously creating? 'When the pen stops I go on. Sometimes it refuses. When it refuses I go on.'[49] The body carries the continuation of being, even if the conscious mind does not.

Not all creations speak so clearly, and Beckett's interest in Bram Van Velde and Jack B. Yeats as painters who record honestly the impossibility of creating a 'true' image comes increasingly to the fore. *Ping* presents initially a highly visual image, of a bare white body surface, motionless, set against white walls, floor and ceiling; the only touches of colour are the eyes, light blue, almost white, and occasional glimpses of rose.[50] As the text proceeds, the created object is progressively stitched up by its creator into silence, the 'true' image only to be perceived as it vanishes from sight. 'All known', the text begins, but with such visibility, 'almost never all known', and as the end comes closer, 'known not'.[51] There are brief murmurs, but in the end, there is only silence. There is memory, but by the end it too is abolished. The blue eyes vanish, whited over. What is left is a black-and-white eye, half closed, 'imploring' – this is perhaps the 'elsewhere' of the observing self, whose presence is marked as an absence in relation to the body, said to be not quite alone, or through the repeated notes of 'ping' scattered through the text, like electronic soundings. The murmuring rhythms of repetition hold up strings of nouns and adjectives, with few verbs to stitch them together ('Head haught nose ears white holes mouth white seam like sewn invisible over').[52] This is perhaps as near as Beckett can come to writing the absence of exchange between creator and object – an absence which is his image of death. Notably, death, and especially the death of memory, is the motif illustrated in 'Bing Beckett Blin Bordeaux 2012', a short film with Beckett's text as voice-over, spoken by Roger Blin, made for France-Culture, in 1965. The camera roams over slabs in the three Jewish cemeteries of Bordeaux, lit by dazzling light.[53]

The Lost Ones (*Le Dépeupleur*), begun in October 1965, took five years to finish.[54] This is a very different version of how it is. Operating within a near-hermetically closed cylindrical space, the text is a representation, expressed as scientific and objective observation, of the external world and the multitude of its inhabitants. In these conditions, the human, for all its intellectual pretensions, is reduced to the animal, or even mechanical. Cruel, hopeless, and faceless, the crowd is condemned to an eternal, harshly-regulated circling inside the given space, each lost body 'searching for its lost one'[55] and also for a rumoured, and non-existent, way out. In this modern production of a Dantean Limbo, Beckett's earliest avatar, Belacqua, or rather, the form of his foetal crouch, again finds a place, mirrored by those sitting against the cylinder wall, who have given up searching.[56] This is the world, as the grim closing sentence discloses, that came into being when the first man bowed his head to invented authority – religion, reason, or science – and this is how the world will end as long as heads stay bowed.

Reiterated references to the harmony of the cylinder's construction recall the Leibnizian world view satirised most powerfully in Voltaire's *Candide*, the short story set in a world where all the characters are subjugated to the mathematician's philosophy of Optimism, and the belief that their world, with all its horrors, is the best of all possible worlds. There is much in this text to recall *Candide*, especially as the narrative progresses towards more violence and obscenity, focusing on the female who is the 'north' of the cylinder, the most fixed point within it, to whose unchanging body all its inhabitants turn. The figure is reminiscent of Candide's Cunégonde, who for her suitor is always the unchanging object of desire, even when the cruel world robs her of an eye and a buttock.[57] The light that turns from yellow to red, while vibrations fill the air, recalls the Lisbon earthquake that, for

Voltaire, swallowed up all the pretensions of Leibnizian Optimism, but which, as here, left the rest of humanity engaged in the same deep ruts. The beings who inhabit this world are, like Voltaire's, more cartoon figures than humans; but where Voltaire's characters were still in touch with their humanity, their loves and suffering, arousing laughter and sympathy, these are desiccated creatures, all surface and dry skin. There is no love, only occasional, hardly-registered, brief sexual congress. With people reduced to the simplest of shapes, circling round in a strictly limited set of options, Beckett's satirical image of the human treadmill is unique and unfunny.

The landscape of this world – the space-time of rationalism – is determined by numbers which constitute the most 'harmonious' of proportions: another grim joke at Leibniz's expense. All surface, the cylinder gives no access to any deeper significance, but the inhabitants strive repeatedly, in all directions, to find it. Like Beckett's Watt, caught in Mr Knott's house of Reason, they are doing their best to live within the limits they have fixed on themselves, physical and philosophical. There are ladders, which they queue to use, which lead more often than not to one of the few niches hollowed into the surface of the roof. Sometimes these niches are dead ends, in which the climber can however find temporary repose, and sometimes they are linked to another niche by a tunnel, thereby extending the deadness of the end. Either way, unlike Watt, the climbers do not have the freedom to go out and look for a more open space. There is a time limit enforcing their return to the floor. Time limits apply to all their movement; the direction of movements is limited and regulated; and different parts of the floor are allocated to beings at different stages of exhaustion. There are no options to change the rituals, and resistance to the rules is met with raging opposition from the rest of the community. Even the author of the text is caught in the endless circles, trapped in the reproduction of closure by his echoing of Dante and Voltaire. The narrative satirising obeisance to the past wryly undercuts its own critique with its reinstatement of old cultural forms, and spreads the infection to its readers, who must pick up the allusions.

Fizzles, first published in English in 1976, includes texts written in French as early as 1954, as well as more recent work.[58] These eight short prose poems explore the conundrum of being and consciousness. In Fizzle 3 ('Afar a bird'), the interplay of pronouns reproduces that contradiction of intellect and sense-experience that Beckett had seen painted in Giorgione's self-portrait. 'I', the intellectualising, creative, speaking self – speaking from within the object-self which is his material body – watches the body making its way through the landscape of human being, scattered with ruins. It is the speaking subject who creates all the parameters of the body's space: its time (night), its limits (the hedges and ditches), the cautious speed at which it travels, and the distance it covers. The speaker invents his material self, making of his body an unchanging image, leaning on his stick, wearing the 'same old coat', a fragmented, bony heap of a creature (hands, head, trunk, elbows, eyes, face). All 'he' ever uttered of his own was his birth cry, at his first sight of the light. At the moment of dying, the subject imagines, this body-object will grasp his life again. The syntax pauses, holds for a beat, and then breaks into a flurry of equal, strictly-rhythmed phrases, to capture, in the image of the bird, the elusiveness of free-flying being, the clarity of a life perceived in the fleeting moment of defying the limits and crossing into death: 'day dawns, he has only to raise his eyes, open his eyes, raise his eyes, he merges in the hedge, afar a bird, a moment past he grasps and is fled, it was he had a life'.[59]

But this, like everything else, is only imagining, and that imagining is corrupted by its origins. The hierarchy of the pronouns goes into reverse. The third person becomes the source of the first-person voice, now said to have been invented, in all its inadequacy, by the body, to suit its needs. The material body is the only source of knowing, and the mind is caught in its limits. The mind can know itself truthfully in the objects it creates, but it cannot know itself as a subject. The best it can aspire to is to formulate the debased and distanced first-person object. The rhythms and tone become bitter and vengeful, as the 'I' who can only know himself as me invents an alternative death for him, or better still, no death: the poem leaves this third person, the body who can never be more than an image, stumbling in panic through his field of being, his mind crowded with a confusion of memories, names, places, people loved and lost. Vision is gone, and the bird has flown.

The novella *Company* (1980), another confrontation with the presumptions of pronouns, expresses the truth of how, what, and who 'it' is, and 'I' am, in an extended image of the incessant creative activity of the living mind. Self-knowledge is only obtainable indirectly, through the objects of the mind's creation, and in the process of inventing: the subject knows itself in the devising of company.

The text begins from inside the subject, a nameless 'one', hearing himself addressed by a voice. The body of the subject provides reliable information about the place of the process: the nameless one knows that he is lying in darkness, on his back, from the pressure on his buttocks and the way the dark changes as he opens and shuts his eyes. But what the voice says is not reliable, as it speaks of past and future, and remembering and projecting are fictional processes. The best that can be done in the name of truth is to keep the pronouns straight. The one in the dark is the object of the voice, who uses the second person to address him. The third person is used of the body in the dark by the 'cankerous other', that is, the narrator and transcriber of the process. The first person is unthinkable and unnamable.[60] These are the conditions in which the one in the dark – the subject who is also an object – obeys the opening injunction of the voice to 'Imagine', and begins to devise other forms to keep him company. 'Devise' is the right word for the truth of his condition: 'Deviser of the voice and of its hearer and of himself. Deviser of himself for company. Leave it at that.'[61]

The company imagined in this fiction is of various kinds. Flashes of 'recollection' addressed to the second person by the voice evoke childhood scenarios, the boy walking hand in hand with his mother, and the day of his birth, when his father fled the house during the labour, and then himself as an old man, tramping the country road, listening to his own footfalls, and joined by his father's shade. All echo stories Beckett has told in earlier work. The voice has distinctive features; it varies place and tone, and it is repetitious. Repetitiousness is a trick of the voice, aimed at persuading him to believe in the past life and lives it conjures up, and at making him invent his own voice, to say: 'Yes I remember.'[62] The text underlines that this 'I' would be another fiction, and a welcome one: 'What an addition to company that would be! A voice in the first person singular.'[63]

There are games to play with sound, mimicking through rhymes and rhythms the shadow play which is living being: 'Some soft thing softly stirring soon to stir no more.'[64] The sibilants and the nasals combine to evoke the movements, both pleasing and repellent, in which the animal body reaches out for form, to be plunged immediately, by the determined syntax and the hard dental ('t'), into the stillness of death. The voice creates variations on light. It operates in many modes – statement, denial, question, exclamation – and all in the same flat tone, that of the scientist experimenting in his laboratory. There are reinventions of the originary scenario, centred on the one in the dark, which play with different versions of the voice, the hearer, and the material and dimensions of place, systematically exhausting the variants, and asking ironically 'What kind of imagination is this so reason-ridden? A kind of its own.'[65] The familiar stories return, this time told at greater length: the walk through the snow, and then the meeting with father, then lover, in the summerhouse. These tales too slow down and break down, into repetitiousness, or into the 'reason-ridden' exhaustion of counting and measuring that is all that can force words from a flagging imagination.

The one in the dark crawls on to the end of his text, crawling and falling, lying disheartened, and always bedevilled by his craving for company. Huddled in the dark, waiting to be purged, like Dante's Belacqua, he is caught inescapably in endlessly repeated reversals of stillness and movement, forever hearing words drawing closer to an end, but never hearing the end. This is how life is, the painful effort of being, the frustration of being without knowing, and without knowing an end, and being without articulate speech: 'Pangs of faint light and stirrings still. Unformulable gropings of the mind. Unstillable.'[66]

But at least, by the end of the novella, the trap of 'their' grammar has been seen and sprung: 'You do not murmur in so many words, I know this doomed to fail and yet persist. No. For the first personal and a fortiori plural pronoun had never any place in your vocabulary.'[67] In place of that closed and limited 'I', locked down into pasts foisted upon it, Beckett's text offers the mobile subject, intellect and imagination flickering into constantly changing forms, experiencing its own landscape through its own material body. The end is still a terrifying solitude, but the journey, the language, and the stories, are your own work:

> The fable of one with you in the dark. The fable of one fabling of one with you in the dark. And how better in the end labour lost and silence. And you as you always were.
>
> Alone.[68]

In the 1980s, the project of self-exploration, and the repeated disclosure of the different aspects of subject identity, perceiver and perceived, mind and body, had in Beckett's prose work become increasingly the exploration of the ageing self, mind and body dissolving and decaying. *Mal vu mal dit* (1981), published in English in the *New Yorker* in October 1981 as *Ill Seen Ill Said*, was performed on radio by Patrick Magee in September of the following year.[69] The broadcast text was praised by Anne Karpf as challenging all the conventions of the radio play.[70] There were no characters in the usual sense, no dialogues, and no indication of the status of the narrator's words, but still, Karpf said, the listener was mesmerised by the flow of sound and Beckett's dizzying puns.

The narrative voice is a poetic one, concerned to make clear from the start its status as inventor of its fiction, as it speaks ('On' 'Careful'), choosing its images out of the many in its store ('such as') and authorising its own choice of tenses ('All this in the present').[71] To move its inventions on, it asks and answers its own questions. It identifies and justifies the spaces of its fiction, beginning with the bed where the dying old woman he describes begins her journey ('From where she lies she sees Venus rise' – the rhymes spark multiple ironies), and then marking the situation – or non-situation – of her cabin ('At the inexistent centre of a formless place').[72] The voice goes on to give form to the formless place, flat and stony, meagre pastureland, with twelve figures on the horizon. In time, which is the true space of the text, the twelve figures emerge as standing stones, tombstones, surrounding the cabin, which is a hovel. (In *Cascando*, twenty years before, it was a shed, the house of stored images from which Woburn emerged to make his triumphant crossing to the island.)[73] The description is built up like an impressionist painting, stroke by careful stroke, and then spins into motion as the voice describes the woman's crossings, to and fro, of the stony space. From time to time, inspiration breaks down, and the voice must wait for vision and words to return. Here is the stumbling process of the making of the image, always difficult, and at the end of life, increasingly so, but for the artist there is no giving up:

> she can be gone at any time. [...] suddenly no longer there. [...] Then as suddenly there again. Long after. So on. Any other would renounce. Avow, No one. No one more. Any other than this other. In wait for her to reappear. In order to resume. Resume the – what is the word? What the wrong word?[74]

Beckett writes himself into the text as his object's other. They share the eye of washed-out blue that looks out onto their world, and blurs with tears, or too much light, or too much darkness. Only in the light of the moon, or Venus, can they journey together over the stones, to the tomb, and back to the cabin. They are both in 'the madhouse of the skull and nowhere else'.[75] Neither has any interlocutor but the tomb; both exist in stony silence, in the heart of the scream. Theirs is no longer the contented, remembering face of *That Time.* Instead:

> The long white hair stares in a fan. Above and about the impassive face. Stares as if shocked still by some ancient horror. Or by its continuance. Or by another. That leaves the face stone-cold. Silence at the eye of the scream. Which say? Ill say. Both. All three. Question answered.[76]

The whiteness that is the marker of death builds up as the words move on, and invades the blue eye, which becomes half-white, sclerotic, before it collapses, and then returns to life. In these dying moments, time is not linear, but leaps backwards and forwards, in anticipation of an ending that cannot come as long as the mind is still struggling to find the right word.

The figure of the mirror-woman is the bulwark of a mind no longer able to confront the terror of the void: 'Not possible any longer except as figment. Not endurable.'[77] Imagination puts flesh onto these fictional bones, detailing every facet of the 'scandal' that is the body,[78] and lingering over the invented detail of the wrinkled, swollen hands, the head, the face, and the spaces of the body's making and moving, obsessively revisiting and revising every trace, until the figure is finally dissolved.

The artist consumes his own woes as he devours the company he creates. With that recognition of the violence art does to the material of the real, a conclusion is finally possible. Words are no longer wrong, but fall precisely and smoothly together, to evoke the passage into a version of the void that is liveable and breathable, the space of the bird of artistic inspiration. This is not the freewheeling bird of *The Unnamable*, delightedly shitting on them all, but the terrifying vulture that first flew over the landscapes of *Echo's Bones,* taking into its maw everything below and above, and celebrating its power to devour death and turn it into life:

> Farewell to farewell. Then in that perfect dark foreknell darling sound pip for end begun. First last moment. Grant only enough remain to devour all. Moment by glutton moment. Sky earth the whole kit and

> boodle. Not another crumb of carrion left. Lick chops and basta. No. One moment more. One last. Grace to breathe that void. Know happiness.[79]

Beckett's earlier work focused on the struggle to understand life in the light, bounded by the dark of unknown, beyond the beginning and the end, birth and grave. The last prose works reverse that scenario, to address head-on the dark in itself – contemplation and consumption of the void.

The title of *Worstward Ho*, begun in 1981, is a rueful joke.[80] Embedded in it are layers of cultural archaeology, echoing Charles Kingsley's popular novel of 1855, *Westward Ho*, and the early Jacobean play by John Webster and Thomas Dekker, a parody in its turn of *Eastward Ho*, the Jacobean satire by George Chapman, Ben Jonson, and John Marston. It also points to a real place, which is the ultimate no-place, the village of Kingsley's novel. When Kingsley wrote his book, this was only the site of a farm and a few houses on the edge of a cliff, miles from anywhere, with no name of its own; it acquired its name later, from Kingsley's fiction. None of the historical or geographical references has any significance for Beckett's text, which is a performance, in 'voice' and writing, of the unspeakable and unsayable nature of what there is when all references are gone.

The reviewer in the *Listener* was disappointed by what he saw as the element of predictability in the text, read on the radio by Norman Rodway, detailing Beckett's customary struggles to begin, to continue, and to end.[81] The text is self-confessedly more of the same, one more failed attempt to say something that cannot be said, and the voice, comically, is sick of it, to the point of throwing up. But the pleasure is in the poetry, plangent but without self-pity, which, in terms of 'Meremost minimum', draws the reader into the understanding of how it is, and feels, to be on the edge of departure, moving, as the initial statement of purpose puts it, 'Somehow on' towards the point where movement ends in 'nohow on' – rewriting end of moving as a new form of beginning.

The beginning records the bleak knowledge that everything is signifier, words and images, signifying nothing. All saying is missaying. All images are shades in the void. On that understanding, the voice of the text (which is never an 'I') builds a sequence of images that marks out this particular perception of how the void is bounded. First comes an image of the point from which perception is generated. Then three images of what is perceived.

By the end, the text has established the cold geometry of the space of being that surrounds the void: 'Three pins. One pinhole. In dimmost dim. Vasts apart. At bounds of boundless void. Whence no farther.'[82]

Between beginning and end comes the representation of all that constitutes life, at least in this version: movement and feeling. The syntax, short abrupt sentences of assertion and negation, mimics the movements of the ageing body: in and out, moving and still, standing and lying down, old bones filled with pain. The old head, with its staring eyes, Beckett's familiar image, which is the source of it all, is now sunk on 'crippled' hands. Head and hands dissolve, and all that is left is the skull and its stare: 'Scene and seer of all.' With the pun on 'scene' is also evoked the divided nature of the self, both perceiver and perceived. As the body decays, the mind decays with it, and words, out of control, threaten to 'ooze'[83] – a simpler, but equally terrifying version of the panic evoked in *From an Abandoned Work*.[84]

The three pins seen through this pinhole are an old man and a child, first moving hand-in-hand then separated, and an old woman with a bent back, ultimately seen bending over gravestones. At one point, the bent back of the old man and the old woman ooze into one another, but by the end, the precision of gender difference is restored, and the manifold potential of human relationships emerges: connections between old and young, male and female, hands joined in love, hands separated in loss. At the end there is the pain of loss and mourning, but mourning is the memory of love.

The perspective of *Worstward Ho* is double, or rather oscillating. Writing the fearful void is certainly the declared aim. But there is no way of writing the void except by writing its outlines, which in Beckett's text is always his own vision of human life, at the moment of writing. Against the dark mystery marked out by the human points, with all its richness of feeling, the darkness of the void is shown up as a nonsense jingle of empty, invented words: 'Thenceless there. Thitherless there. Thenceless thitherless there.'[85] At the end is a triumphant rejection of the old bogeyman: 'A pox on void. Unmoreable unlessable unworseable evermost almost void.'[86]

NOTES

1 Letter from Beckett to Yvonne Lefèvre, 27 April 1950, *Letters* II, p.181n; letter from Beckett to Georges Duthuit [before 1 March 1950], *Letters* II, pp.185–7; letter from Beckett to Georges Duthuit [30 March or 6 April] 1950, *Letters* II, pp.192–7.

2 Letter from Beckett to George Reavey, 11 December 1950, *Letters* II, pp.206–7.

3 Letter from Beckett to Pierre Bordas, 22 January 1951, *Letters* II, pp.227–9. After the success of *Waiting for Godot*, Barney Rosset of the Grove Press, New York, was happy to publish the novels, as well as the play, and Beckett began discussions with him on the translations (Letter from Beckett to Barney Rosset, 25 June 1953, *Letters* II, pp.384–6). Patrick Bowles translated *Molloy* into English with Beckett for the Grove Press edition, and Beckett himself took on the other two.

4 Letter from Beckett to Barney Rosset, 11 February 1954, *Letters* II, pp.456–7.

5 Ibid.

6 Mark Nixon, Preface to Mark Nixon (ed.), *Samuel Beckett. Texts for Nothing and Other Shorter Prose, 1950–1976* (London: Faber and Faber, 2010), p.vii.

7 *Texts for Nothing*, I; *TN* 2010, p.5. First English publication of the *Texts for Nothing* was in 1967.

8 *Texts for Nothing*, VIII; *TN* 2010, p.33.

9 Letter from Beckett to Barney Rosset, 11 February 1954, *Letters* II, p.457.

10 Letter from Beckett to Mania Péron [16 April 1951], *Letters* II, pp.240–41.

11 Beckett, *Texts for Nothing*, I; *TN* 2010, p.3.

12 Beckett, *Texts for Nothing*, II; *TN* 2010, p.7.

13 Beckett, *Texts for Nothing*, VIII; *TN* 2010, p.33.

14 Beckett, *Texts for Nothing*, III; *TN* 2010, p.11.

15 Ibid.

16 Beckett, *Texts for Nothing*, IV; *TN* 2010, p.17.

17 Beckett, *Texts for Nothing*, IV; *TN* 2010, p.18.

18 Beckett, *Texts for Nothing*, XIII; *TN* 2010, p.53.

19 Beckett, *Texts for Nothing*, VI; *TN* 2010, p.28.

20 Letter from Beckett to Barney Rosset, 11 February 1954, *Letters* II, p.457.

21 Letter from Beckett to Pamela Mitchell, 26 September 1953, *Letters* II, p.406.

22 Letter from Beckett to George Reavey, 11 December 1950, *Letters* II, p.207, n.3.

23 Knowlson, *Damned to Fame*, pp.400–2.

24 Knowlson, *Damned to Fame*, pp.463–4.

25 See Preface to Samuel Beckett, *How It Is*, ed. Edouard Magessa O'Reilly (London: Faber and Faber, 2009).

26 Beckett, cit. Knowlson, *Damned to Fame*, p.461.

27 Knowlson, *Damned to Fame*, pp.461–2, gives the extract from McWhinnie's letter.

28 Beckett, *How It Is* (1964), in O'Reilly (ed.) *How It Is*, p.3.

29 Ibid.

30 Beckett, *How It Is*, in O'Reilly (ed.) *How It Is*, p.4.

31 Beckett, *How It Is*, in O'Reilly (ed.) *How It Is*, pp.7–8.

32 Beckett, *How It Is*, in O'Reilly (ed.) *How It Is*, p.5.

33 Beckett, *How It Is*, in O'Reilly (ed.) *How It Is*, p.18.

34 Beckett, *How It Is*, in O'Reilly (ed.) *How It Is*, p.62.
35 Beckett, *How It Is*, in O'Reilly (ed.) *How It Is*, p.61.
36 Beckett, *How It Is*, in O'Reilly (ed.) *How It Is*, p.100.
37 Beckett, *How It Is*, in O'Reilly (ed.) *How It Is*, p.128.
38 Beckett, *How It Is*, in O'Reilly (ed.) *How It Is*, p.129.
39 See above, Chapter 1, p.36.
40 David Watson, *Paradox and Desire in Samuel Beckett's Fiction* (Houndmills, Basingstoke: Macmillan, 1991), p.115.
41 David Houston Jones, *Samuel Beckett and Testimony*, p.78.
42 Nixon, Preface to *TN* 2010, p.xiii.
43 Samuel Beckett, *All Strange Away* (1976); *TN* 2010, p.76.
44 Beckett, *All Strange Away*; *TN* 2010, p.74.
45 Beckett, *All Strange Away*; *TN* 2010, p.75
46 Beckett, *All Strange Away*; *TN* 2010, p.84.
47 See Nixon, Preface to *TN* 2010, p.xiv.
48 Samuel Beckett, *Imagination Dead Imagine* (1965); *TN* 2010, p.88.
49 Samuel Beckett, *Enough; TN* 2010, p.93. The text was written in French (*Assez*) at the end of 1965, and published in 1966; English translation published in 1967 (see Nixon [ed.], *Texts for Nothing*, p.xv).
50 Published in French in 1966 (*Bing*); Beckett's English translation (*Ping*) was first published in 1967 (see Nixon [ed.], *Texts for Nothing*, p.179).
51 Samuel Beckett, *Ping* (1967); *TN* 2010, pp.123–5.
52 Beckett, *Ping*; *TN* 2010, p.124.
53 'Bing Beckett Blin Bordeaux 2012.' Essai filmique. Texte de Samuel Beckett (1966, Editions de Minuit), voix de Roger Blin sur France-Culture 1965, images des trois cimetières juifs de Bordeaux (1724 à nos jours). Published on 29 October 2012. (http://www.youtube.com/watch?v=x3Zyt4XLHs0. Consulted 9 July 2013.)
54 James Knowlson, *Damned to Fame*, p.535.
55 Samuel Beckett, *The Lost Ones* (1972); *TN* 2010, p.101. Original written in French 1965–66, and published as *Le Dépeupleur* in 1970 (see Nixon [ed.], *Texts for Nothing*, p.xv).
56 Beckett, *The Lost Ones*; *TN* 2010, p.103.
57 Mary Bryden discusses the importance of this female figure for Beckett's representation of gender roles, and she points to Avigdor Arikha's three illustrations for the 1972 edition of the episode, published separately, in which she appears as central (Samuel Beckett, *The North*, limited edn [London: Enitharmon Press, 1972]). See Bryden, *Women in Samuel Beckett's Prose and Drama*, pp.144–5.
58 Nixon, Preface to *TN* 2010, pp.xvii–xix.
59 Samuel Beckett, *Fizzles* (1976); *TN* 2010, p.143.
60 Samuel Beckett, *Company* (London: John Calder, 1980), p.32.

61 Beckett, *Company*, p.34.
62 Beckett, *Company*, p.21.
63 Beckett, *Company*, pp.20–1.
64 Beckett, *Company*, p.24.
65 Beckett, *Company*, p.45.
66 Beckett, *Company*, p.30.
67 Beckett, *Company*, pp.86–7.
68 Beckett, *Company*, pp.88–9.
69 Dirk Van Hulle (ed.), *Samuel Beckett, Company, Ill Seen Ill Said, Worstward Ho, Stirrings Still* (London: Faber and Faber, 2009), Preface, p.x.
70 Anne Karpf, 'Radio', *The Listener*, 2785 (4 November 1982), p.29.
71 Samuel Beckett, *Ill Seen Ill Said* (1981); *Van Hulle* 2009, p.45.
72 Beckett, *Ill Seen Ill Said*; *Van Hulle* 2009, pp.45–6.
73 See below Chapter 7, p.181.
74 Beckett, *Ill Seen Ill Said*; *Van Hulle* 2009, p.51.
75 Beckett, *Ill Seen Ill Said*; *Van Hulle* 2009, p.53.
76 Beckett, *Ill Seen Ill Said*; *Van Hulle* 2009, p.58.
77 Beckett, *Ill Seen Ill Said*; *Van Hulle* 2009, p.59.
78 Beckett, *Ill Seen Ill Said*; *Van Hulle* 2009, p.60.
79 Beckett, *Ill Seen Ill Said*; *Van Hulle* 2009, p.78.
80 Written in English, the text was first published by John Calder in 1983, and collected with *Company* and *Ill Seen Ill Said* in *Nohow On* (London: John Calder, 1989); see Van Hulle (ed.), Preface to *Samuel Beckett,* p.vii, p.xiii, p.xxvii.
81 Nigel Andrew, 'Meremost Minimum', *The Listener*, 2821 (11 August 1983), p.26.
82 Samuel Beckett, *Worstward Ho* (1983); *Van Hulle* 2009, p.103.
83 Beckett, *Worstward Ho*; *Van Hulle* 2009, p.96.
84 See below Chapter 7, p.173.
85 Beckett, *Worstward Ho*; *Van Hulle* 2009, p.83.
86 Beckett, *Worstward Ho*; *Van Hulle* 2009, p.101.

CHAPTER 5

Drama from *Eleutheria* to *Happy Days*

A Material Stage

By the beginning of the 1950s, the originality of Beckett's prose fiction, his lively and shocking humour, and his unrelenting attack on all things conventional, from subject to story, were winning a following of friends and admirers. But it was his work on the stage during that decade which first brought him to the attention of the public at large. *Waiting for Godot* made him first notorious, and then famous; and it is by his work for the stage that he is perhaps still best known.

As an undergraduate at Trinity College Dublin, he had experienced drama from the audience's side of the footlights, especially at the Abbey Theatre, where he enjoyed the work of Seán O'Casey, W.B. Yeats, and John Millington Synge, whose influence marked him most: 'He was drawn to Synge's unusual blend of humour and pathos, his stark but resilient tragicomic vision, his imaginative power and clear-sighted pessimism. And he was impressed by the rich texture and vitality of Synge's theatrical language and the striking, bold simplicity of his verbal and visual imagery.'[1] He was less enthusiastic about Yeats's work, writing to MacGreevy in August 1934 of a visit to the Abbey to see his latest plays (*Resurrection* and *The King of the Ould Clock Tower*), and commenting scornfully on Yeats's attempts at daring blasphemy, and on his poor sense of theatre: 'Balbus building his wall would be more dramatic.'[2]

He also enjoyed more popular forms, such as music hall, variety and comedy, and the silent films that were increasingly standard fare in the capital.[3] In Paris, before the war, he visited the Bobino, in Montparnasse, converted from theatre to music hall in 1926, and through Lucia Joyce he became familiar with dance theatre.

In those inter-war years, French drama took on a new lease of life, and afterwards, during the Occupation, radical directors continued to flourish, such as Jean Vilar, director of the Théâtre National Populaire, and the actor-director Jean-Louis Barrault, both of whom brought the actor's body, mime, and gesture to the centre of the stage. The wartime and post-war scarcity of resources worked to the benefit of avant-garde directors such as Roger Blin, committed to the subversion of the ideas and expectations of conventional boulevard theatre which still dominated the scene in both Paris and London.

On his return to Paris after the war, Beckett had renewed his avant-garde contacts. In 1953, when his friend Con Leventhal, husband of Ethna MacCarthy, was preparing a lecture on modern French theatre, he strongly recommended to him the work of Adamov and Ionesco, and offered to have Ionesco send Leventhal a copy of the newly-published first volume of his theatre.[4] Staged at the Royal Court theatre in London, Beckett's work was associated from the start with the exponents of new French ideas and forms. French drama – Ionesco, Sartre, Duras – ran alongside the Royal Court's standard fare of drama of ideas and politics, represented chiefly by John Osborne, and George Devine considered it at least as important.[5]

Except at the very beginning, in *Eleutheria*, which has echoes of Ionesco and Pirandello, Beckett's dramatic writing made few gestures towards other models. There are within it processes of defamiliarisation that might invite comparison with Brecht. Beckett saw the Berliner Ensemble in Paris for the first time in the 1956–57 season; pressed to go by the painter Avigdor Arikha, he liked Brecht's staging, but it was too rich for his taste.[6] Richard Eyre and Nicholas Wright, comparing the two dramatists, could rightly indicate the substantial difference: 'Beckett took the one-place, time-unbroken drama of Sophocles or Racine and distilled it to the point where its off-stage life is reduced to nothing.'[7]

More interesting than what Beckett doesn't show is what he does put on stage, for which 'distillation' is a good term. His drama aims to create an image of presence, and present-ness, a compound of emotion, intensity, and immediacy, which absorbs and engages the spectator. To speak, as many do, of his creating a stage 'icon' might be helpful, except that an icon is a static form, and in Beckett's stage images it is the movements of bodies, and rhythms of speech, which are key for the transformative effect his plays work on their audiences. Jonathan Kalb, challenging Charles Lyons's approach to Beckett's drama, argues that the spectator's expectation should be of an affective experience, not an intellectual one:

> [Charles Lyons's model] neglects the music of the plays and other aspects of their intense affect in the present, and assumes that the most sophisticated viewer is the one who pays closest attention to the words, which is too intellectual a process to account satisfactorily for the characters' or most spectators' responses. [...S]pectators do not just wonder about plot information; they are also enveloped by a prominent sound pattern and a startling *live* stage picture. [...] The intellectual is only one of several faculties called into play by Beckett performances, and usually not the first one.[8]

Billie Whitelaw, describing her first acting experience with Beckett (in *Play*), made the same point. Her fellow-actors, Rosemary Harris and Robert Stephens, wanted more information about their characters, but she felt that psychology, like story, was not the point of Beckett's plays. Rather, their interest lay in the music of the text, and the representation the music created of a particular aspect of the human situation, or a structure of human feeling.[9]

The transformative effect, operating through emotional affect, is there in the prose, working between the printed words on the white page, and engaging the imagination of the individual reader, to generate a uniquely personal induction into new modes of perception. The careful reader of the prose cooperates in her/his own destabilisation, to emerge into different rhythms of being. But the same process, in the drama, can call on instruments and techniques that create not merely an individual but a collective experience, and one that, by the nature of the form, is intensely physical and material.

In Beckett's drama, the actor's body is central. More often than not, the body is a whole unit, journeying, stumbling, or fixed within its defining landscape. From *Waiting for Godot* to *Quad*, his stage is often occupied by pairs of bodies, interconnecting and intersecting with other pairs, coming and going, in a visual performance of the patterns of relationships that constitute the body collective. Other plays are dominated by fetishised parts of the body: head, face, eyes and mouth. The voice that appears at one remove in the written texts, the subject making itself through words on a page, is on stage a primary and audible presence.

The stage space encodes Beckett's insights into the material nature of existence, and, crucially, the role of perception in relation to 'reality'. The audience is a necessary part of the performance – watcher or listener, the mirror in which the action on stage is caught and reflected. Setting was not of central interest for Beckett, who while Roger Blin was hunting for funding for *Waiting for Godot* complained of what he called the Wagnerist fashion for collaboration in the arts, and expressed his preference for drama stripped down to words and action: 'Je veux un théâtre réduit à ses propres moyens, parole et jeu, sans peinture et sans musique, sans agréments. [...] Il faut que le décor sorte du texte, sans y ajouter.'[10]

But there is a role for a minimal amount of scenery to represent the physical landscape which conditions the characters' situation: the growing pile of sand in *Happy Days*, or the tree in *Waiting for Godot* around which Vladimir and Estragon try to organise their lives into some form of order. The boundaries of the stage space have their own significance, dividing the light of performance and action onstage and the darkness of the unknown where action ends.

Stage time operates on different levels. There is the playing time of each drama, a limited period of chronological time during which the audience sits in its paid-for seat. Against this unbroken time, time onstage is constantly broken and reconstituted. Onstage is the continuous present of existence, reworked into rhythms and rituals of repetition and variation, productions of memory and imagination, which abolish the familiar conventions of past, present and future.

Most of all, the words that fill Beckett's stage have material force. For one critic, Beckett's turn to drama gave him new freedom to investigate the blanks between words, and to show onstage the unreliability of language.[11] But by the time he started writing his plays, Beckett was already less concerned with indicting language as not fit for use, and much more preoccupied with exploring its malleability and its application to new purposes: the way words might be made to resonate, and to combine with other carriers of meaning, such as gesture, rhythm, and visual images, to find new ways of representing the process of being human, and the shape of the chaos the human inhabits. Words on his stage are no longer script – as early as *Eleutheria*, the prompter threw in the script. They are sound, and the syntactical rhythms of Beckettian utterance are given body by the actor's voice. Anne Atik, Beckett's friend and translator, noted how he urged his actors to stop acting, to keep colour out of their voices, and to concentrate instead on getting across the shape of sentences, and the rhythms created by pace and pauses – the tension between words spoken and words withheld.[12]

Eleutheria: Subverting the Spectator

Beckett's first play, written in January and February of 1947, marks the beginning of a very sharp learning curve. After *Eleutheria*, he had a much better idea of what could and could not be made to work on the modern stage; in a sense, for all its faults, this first play sets the pattern for the great plays to come.

The opening scenes operate in the mode of Feydeau's farces, with stock family characters, much rushing in and out of rooms, self-conscious wittiness, and smart one-liners, but the action soon takes on a surreal edge. Knockabout becomes overt violence, and slapstick pushes towards obscenity, with references to sex and pissing intruding into the respectable exchanges of this middle-class world. It was considered for staging at one point by the Grenier-Hussenot company, who specialised in light popular productions;[13] as the characters keep saying, it is an entertainment.

As in many of Beckett's later plays, farce, repeated, turns to tragedy. In the end, Beckett thought it failed on both counts, telling Georges Duthuit in August 1948 not to try to have it staged; he would write something funnier and more significant ('nous rigolerons mieux autrement, nous puiserons ailleurs, loin de là, un meilleur sérieux)'.[14] It did the rounds of directors in the 1950s, but despite offers of production and publication, Beckett decided it needed rewriting; it was, he told Maurice Nadeau, enclosing the typescript, even worse than he remembered.[15] And after the success of *Waiting for Godot* he must have decided he had better things to do.

The 'Freedom' of the title is what Victor, only son of the Krap family, wants: to be left alone, not to be required to provide explanations, and not to be caught in the words, rites and conventions of the familial and social trap. His is an impossible ambition, and Beckett's satire shows no mercy. The play could equally well, he said, be called *Eleuthéromane*.[16] He wrote to Georges Duthuit of his impatience with those who took seriously Victor's pretentious desire for freedom, which was certainly not Beckett's own. Victor, he added, was no kind of exemplar; for all his bluster, he would fawn on the authorities and say whatever they wanted, to shut them up ('ce qu'il doit dire, pour avoir le droit de se taire, c'est les vieilles blagues au fond, il a peur, il dit Monsieur l'Inspecteur, il a l'air de les engueuler, en réalité il leur lèche les bottes, leur parler c'est leur sucer le cul').[17]

An inventive stage set makes visible the constraints set on the would-be individual living in society, who can never be other than a form of collective property. A split set divides the stage between the Krap family salon and their son's rented room. Each space has its own doors and its own interior lighting, but they have similar windows, looking onto the same daylight, and there is no dividing wall between them. The stage directions distinguish them as the spaces of marginal and main action, and the balance between the two changes over the three acts. In Act I, the family salon is the main set. In Act II, Victor's room slips increasingly into the family space, following what Beckett implies is the normal trajectory, and taking on its respectability and public character. By Act III, the salon has slipped into the orchestra pit, leaving Victor's space apparently triumphant. But in the last scene, Victor pushes his bed into a new relationship with the space of others, up against the fourth wall of the stage. He makes a final gesture of curling up in bed, and turning his back on humanity – but only once he has stared into every area of the theatre, and made himself subject to the gaze of the audience, who, it has emerged, share the role of guards and monitors played by his family.

The unfolding of the play discloses the absurdity of Victor's desire to be a free subject. From the start of the two-year voluntary isolation that is his family's obsessive concern, he has been subsidised by his mother, and looked after by his landlady. His sleep is occupied by a recurrent nightmare of the trap man hands on to man, in which his father, sitting in a pool full of stones, summons him to join him. There is no lock on his rented room, and anyone can and does walk in. Victor sometimes walks out, to rummage through dustbins for food, without registering that living on others' rubbish is still living on others. There is no rejecting the imperatives of life on earth: the demands of the body, the demands of gender, the landscape given to the body to inhabit, and the interfaces between body and landscape – windows, words, and senses – are irrefutable.

The human condition is one of limits and confinement. It is also one of theatricality. The Krap family, and their relations and friends, all marked down for disease and death, know that their role in life is to distract one another, with talk more or less witty and more or less small, playing up to their cues, and accepting their assigned parts. The theme of theatricality is embedded in the language. Mr Krap asks Dr Piouk what he will be contributing to 'this comedy', while Piouk responds in kind ('If you make a little effort, you might manage to keep the punters amused') and Madame Meck upstages everyone.[18] Life, as the dying Mr Krap spells out, is an absurd performance. People start and finish, but it's all only bluff. 'Why can't we be satisfied with a life that is only bluff? It must be because of its divine origin.' Life is, he adds, 'merely the fear of doing nothing'.[19] He would have liked to content himself simply with having been born and not yet being dead, but since this is impossible, his solution is to 'pretend' that he, and other people, are living. He concedes that Victor is right to resist incorporation, but he still lets the comedy roll on around him, right up to his onstage death. Like so many of Beckett's father-figures, he is the primary betrayer, responsible for his son's internalising and perpetuating his own surrender to the tyranny of the normal.

The logic of the spectacle dictates the logic of existence. Act II opens with Victor's self-destructive but necessary commitment to his situation: he looks at the audience, and feels impelled to declare that he must start. Unable to find words to start with, he resorts to gesture, throws a shoe, breaks his window pane, and lets in the Glazier and his son. As he later comments, not to start would have been simplest. But not starting is not an option, and once the machinery is engaged, he has no chance of escaping the Glazier, whose mission is to maintain a transparent connection between Victor and the rest of the world now that Victor has entered the public domain. Everyone in the public domain, according to the Glazier, is there to entertain the others, and help provide them with some *raison d'être*. Victor, he says, has to explain himself, 'so that the whole thing can look as if it makes some sort of sense'.[20]

In the final act, Victor is still resisting the increasing pressure to explain himself, or as the Glazier puts it, take shape. What finishes him is the audience. *Eleutheria* is the only play in which Beckett provides an extended (and unflattering) analysis of his audiences, and the part they play in shaping a drama. The Spectator climbs down from his box onto the stage. He knows himself, he thinks, with all his faults and virtues: he has common sense, he is like blotting paper, absorbing and retaining everything he sees, and he represents 'a thousand spectators, all slightly different from each other'.[21] The Glazier's view of 'the thousand-arsed character' is less flattering: 'Bezique, billiards, good substantial meals, pain in the caecum, love on Saturday after the show, partiality for clarity, moderation in all things.'[22] This monstrous representative of bourgeois culture is also a familiar of the stage and its performances, and he asks many questions of the dramatist, which are neither original nor interesting.

The Prompter throws in the script and leaves. The Spectator finally finds a good question, which is why the audience doesn't walk out. There is, he suggests, a peculiar tension created by a play that demonstrates total incapacity. This play always seems to be on the edge of providing entertainment, 'but it never gets there, it's awful. (*pause*) Actually, who wrote this rubbish? (*programme*) Beckett (*he says 'Béké'*), Samuel, Béké, Béké, he must be a cross between a Jew from Greenland and a peasant from the Auvergne.'[23]

With the play collapsing, and the script thrown away, the Spectator brings on his own Chinese torturer, to extract a serious answer, and the terrified Victor finally explains the life he leads: 'It's the life of someone who doesn't want to lead your kind of life [...] always the same old grind.'[24] He claims, in the language of a Molloy, to have been trying to abandon himself to negation: 'By being the least possible. By not moving, not thinking, not dreaming, not speaking, not listening, not perceiving, not knowing, not wishing, not being able, and so on.'[25] But no one believes that, and he acknowledges, as Beckett said to Georges Duthuit, that it was all a story, to get people to leave him in peace.

The best he can do, something a little less dreadful than their same old grind, is find a way of feeling that he is 'becoming free. (*pause*) I'll tell you how I'm going to spend the rest of my life: I shall rub my chains one against the other. From morning to night and from night to morning. That useless little sound will be my life. [...] My limbo.'[26] Victor clears the room, pushes his bed towards the footlights, stares round at the audience, and lies down on his bed with his back to the eyes he knows are watching. The fall of the curtain marks an end without closure.

Loose and baggy, its themes blatantly spelled out, and the switch between farce and tragedy crudely done, *Eleutheria* was a play Beckett was happy to abandon. He may also have felt it was too reminiscent of Pirandello and Ionesco, in its foregrounding of the theatricality of living, and its satire of the disintegrating bourgeois family, and have preferred to strike out in a direction more clearly his own – rattling his own chains. But as a key starting point for his dramatic experiments, it identifies a thematics of four basic elements that would reappear in Beckett's next plays. Human living is 'nothing doing'; it would be best not to start living, but there's no way of avoiding it; bluff (playing the part, and telling stories) is the only way to go on; and there is a responsibility on everyone to keep the punters amused.

One last lesson learned from *Eleutheria* is the importance of keeping the audience in their proper place. In *Waiting for Godot* they are briefly evoked as the fourth wall, both terrifying and depressing, and acknowledged as the ultimate drivers of the action on stage, the watchers who watch Vladimir watching the sleeping Estragon. But in *Godot* and later plays, their powers are muted, and for the most part, the characters on stage are left with the illusion that they are living their own lives. No Chinese torturer appears to force them to spell out their anxiety; instead, it is the interplay of relationships on stage that generates the boredom, anguish, frustration, and terror that characterise the waiting mode in which they exist. The entertainment wears thin, but life continues unchanging, clinging to the mode of bluff.

Waiting for Godot: Doing Time

Beckett's most celebrated play was written in French between 9 October 1948 and 29 January 1949, and he described it as a relaxation from writing the novel trilogy.[27] Some of his sense of release may have come from the knowledge that the final responsibility for this particular creation would be shared, with actors, directors, and set designers. As productions succeeded one another there was certainly an element of surprise, pleasant as well as not, in the variations supplied by different companies.

The first performance at the little Théâtre de Babylone, on the Parisian Left Bank, in January 1953, was directed by Roger Blin, and supported by a subsidy from a French government programme to encourage first plays. It was also helped by publicity from French national radio (the ORTF), which broadcast an abridged version in February 1952.[28] The theatre audience was small, but it was sympathetic, and relatively familiar with post-Artaudian efforts to find new ways of creating significance out of the stage space. The radical left-wing director had already staged Strindberg and Büchner, and was about to stage the first plays of his close friend Adamov. Beckett told Georges Duthuit that he thought Blin neither a good actor nor a good director, but he had a great love of the theatre.[29] Tristan Tzara, the grand old man of Dada, had recommended the play to Blin, having read the manuscript, and Blin said later that what he liked in *Godot* was its humour and its subversive nature.[30] The highly successful production was welcomed by critics, including three major playwrights – Anouilh, Audiberti and Robbe-Grillet. Beckett wrote to his French publisher, thanking him for a copy of *Critique*, with Robbe-Grillet's article, and describing it as 'excellent'.[31]

The English version, directed by Peter Hall, opened in August 1955 at the Arts Theatre, London, a private club, which enabled the producers to circumvent censorship by the Lord Chamberlain. Censorship in Paris had not been a problem. London audiences were not used to minimalism, and a bare stage, and the set, for a start, struck the wrong note, picturesque rather than desolate, and featuring an inappropriately solid tree.[32] Among critics, only Harold Hobson and Kenneth Tynan understood what the playwright was trying to do, but even so, the play was a success, and together with Osborne's *Look Back in Anger*, staged the following year, it became known as the dividing line of old and new theatre in England.

The first Irish production was at the Pike Theatre in Dublin, October 1955, directed by Alan Simpson, which subsequently transferred to the Gate Theatre. The Dublin voices, and the down-to-earth delivery, helped found a successful run, but critics and audiences still complained that the play was hard to follow, and too intellectual.[33] A translation into Irish, Beckett reported, was in process in 1956.[34]

Nothing doing, or, as Estragon puts it, 'Nothing to be done', is the leading concept from the start.[35] The famous formulation by Vivian Mercier, that in this play, nothing happens, twice, is accurate, but open to misunderstanding. The effort of doing nothing is what Beckett stages, and the fullness of that nothing, which is the whole of the human situation. Towards the end, Vladimir's meditation over the sleeping Estragon is a lyrical and compassionate expression of the pain and anxiety of the struggle, which encapsulates and intensifies, in a few telling phrases, all the futile activity deployed in the drama of Everyman: 'The air is full of our cries. (*He listens.*) But habit is a great deadener.'[36] To the director of the first West German production, eager to bring out symbols and emblems, Beckett wrote to emphasise that his characters must be treated as real-life beings, caught in a material situation of daily routine: 'et c'est cette quotidienneté et cette matérialité qu'à mon avis il importe de faire ressortir.'[37]

The audience empathises with the couple's valiant survival through their attempts at doing, and their comic recognition of the unremitting darkness of their situation. Their stoical persistence in making do on scanty and diminishing resources is admirable. To eat, they have carrots, turnips, decaying radishes, and the occasional snatched bone; they have boots to help them move, though the boots are too tight, and they make their feet stink and hurt; and they have words, increasingly hard to utter and string together. They have another couple, passing through their landscape, Pozzo and Lucky, and a boy, or perhaps his brother, who at first brighten their situation, and then bring more confusion and devastation. They have an apparently open landscape, on a country road, and they have time, which moves, over two different days, bringing change – not always a blessing – as well as more of the same. Dailiness ('quotidienneté') is a focus in this play, an aspect of time which, intensely focused on doing nothing, creates an atmosphere of terrifying claustrophobia entirely absent from *Eleutheria.*

The unavoidable start opens both acts, as the couple are thrown together, fleeing the gathering dark. In Act II, the eternal necessity of starting is enshrined in Vladimir's round song about the dog's coming into the kitchen in search of a bone, in an unending circle finally inscribed on the dead dog's headstone.

'Bluff', playing roles to keep going, is the nature of all that the couple do as they wait for Godot, from playing at conversation to playing at hanging, rehearsing their daily routines, with small variations. In Act I, they are in slapstick mode, though the mood is black – this is all, they agree, worse than the pantomime, the music-hall, the circus. If this is circus, they are not playing the part of clowns, but trained animals: 'People are bloody ignorant apes.'[38] In Act II, the mode is dialogue. They must converse, they say, they can't keep silent. Dialoguing is hard work, with its own technical machinery. It needs a kick-start, and there are standard modes of procedure, echoes, questions, and repetitions. It can develop in short, breathless sentences and phrases, or be carefully balanced and rhythmed. In any event, it soon ends in silence. First time round, Pozzo and Lucky give Vladimir and Estragon the chance to play audience, listening to stories and a monologue, and watching Lucky dance. Second time round, Vladimir and Estragon play an active role, acting the Good Samaritan to the crippled pair. The Boy who appears with a message from Mr Godot formulates his answers in the language of their questions, simply responding to cues – another form of bluff.

Providing entertainment for audiences onstage and off is a central preoccupation of the play. For the characters onstage, entertainment represents a serious engagement with time. After the first set with Pozzo and

Lucky, filled with dialogue, stories, Lucky's dance and Lucky's monologue, Vladimir has a sense of satisfaction: 'That passed the time.'[39] Estragon notes that it would have passed in any case, but it wouldn't, Vladimir replies, have passed so quickly. But dragging or flying, time slips out of human hands. When he first appears in the stage twilight, Pozzo has a watch, that symbol of the rich man's power to control the time of others, and a schedule of his own to observe, and he can evoke with confidence the passing of the day and the setting of the sun, cheerfully contradicting the gloomy Vladimir, who says that time has stopped. By the time Pozzo leaves the stage, the watch has gone, and he has forgotten he had it with him. The second time he appears, struck blind, he must ask the others what time it is, and he falls into frustrated rage at their attempts to find out how long Lucky has been dumb, railing at the curse of human time, that meaningless space between birth and death.[40] As Act II opens, at the end of another day, what passed yesterday, when and where, defies Vladimir's best efforts at recovery; and as the Act closes, the prospect of a tomorrow also slips away from them. Time, as Vladimir muses over the sleeping Estragon, means only one thing: 'We have time to grow old.'[41]

The tears of the world, like its laughter, are a constant quantity, according to Pozzo. Beckett was concerned for productions to communicate the interpenetration in the play of laughter and tears: 'Le côté farce me semble indispensable aussi bien du point de vue technique (moyen de détente) que par rapport à l'esprit de la pièce. Donc ni à escamoter ni à exagérer. Ici le malheur est le comble du grotesque et tout acte est clownerie.'[42] This is probably of all Beckett's plays the most satisfying for an audience in search of comic entertainment, and great comic actors have been happy to accept the challenge of its roles, though with varying success. Jean Martin played the first Lucky, setting the tone for Luckys to come; Dermot Kelly and Max Wall have been highly praised in the part of Vladimir. The unfortunate Bert Lahr, at first hailed as a catch for the first New York production, directed by Alan Schneider, contributed to its failure by overplaying Estragon for laughs, throwing off the balance, and leaving Schneider with the problem of dealing in future productions of *Godot* with the public memory of the Bert Lahr fiasco.[43] Playing for easy laughs, and losing the thrill of the dark side of the farce, remains a temptation. Sean Mathias's highly popular production of 2009, revived in 2010, was described by at least two critics as 'Godot Lite'. Charles Spencer complained in 2009 that the jokes were there, but none of the dark side.[44] It was, said Lyn Gardner, in 2010, made to be easily swallowed, sparing the audience from having to engage with its meaning and its anguish.[45]

From Roger Blin's first production, the balance between comedy and tears has not been achieved by relying on star performers but by exploring the underlying rhythms of contradiction driving the performance as a whole, in order to stylise and intensify its energies. Blin asked his actors to develop their characters by working from the outside inwards, looking for each one's particular form of movement, which was determined by their distinctive physical maladies. Vladimir has prostate problems, so it hurts when he laughs; Estragon has bad feet, Pozzo a bad heart, and Lucky demonstrates the symptoms of Parkinson's disease.[46] But Herbert Blau's 1957 production at the Actors Workshop of San Francisco was the first to grasp fully the musical quality of the play, and to understand the importance of its rhythms for the construction of its meaning, and the need to subordinate the visual impact of particular stage images to the dance of the whole.[47] (Sean Mathias's production of 2010 was to demonstrate the danger of prioritising the image, showing the famous tree forcing its way up through the planks of the stage, in a very obvious attempt to communicate the idea of theatre within theatre.) The next watershed in the rhythmic development of the play was Beckett's own production in the Schiller-Theater, Berlin, in March 1975, assisted by Walter Asmus, whose later productions at the Gate Theatre, Dublin 1991–99, carried on the traditions established by Beckett in Berlin. The author revised his text, and worked painstakingly with the actors, to make visible the patterns of repetition and variation which structure the waiting game, introducing a strong element of mirroring into all the stage moves, and using sudden frozen moments to emphasise the theme of bodies caught in time.[48]

The play also communicates with its audiences through the immense variety of its comic tones. Against the background of gentle knockabout and crosstalk provided by Vladimir and Estragon, Pozzo and Lucky burst on stage to create a loud, jarring discord, an enormous comic shock that unfolds into a sustained sequence of violent black humour. The gross, wealthy, well-dressed Pozzo, hauled on stage by the thin, weary Lucky, on the end of a long rope, makes one of the best-known entries in the business. Pozzo flourishes all the things that signify the man of property: a watch, bag, stool, picnic basket, greatcoat, and a whip. Lucky has nothing to signify, only his hands and his brain, which are dwindling assets. On the way to market, in the hope of selling Lucky, Pozzo takes time out to kick his jester into entertaining the audience. Lucky's is a gabbled and rushed monologue, but still highly coherent, structured to underline fragmented phrases that, like Vladimir's monologue over the sleeping Estragon, encapsulate the situation of the human in time: 'shrink and dwindle'; 'I resume'; 'the great cold'; 'the skull'; 'labours unfinished'; 'labours lost'.[49] Comic entertainment turns to terror; and in Act II, when the pair return, with Pozzo blind and Lucky dumb, falling over and unable to get up again, knockabout is overwhelmed by cruelty and vengeful violence.

Entertainment in the form of movement and spectacle is paired with verbal entertainment. Speech, story and song are not only a way to pass the time, but to define the form time takes. Living through the chaos is not enough; as with all the dead leaves, in the most lyrical of the play's dialogues, it's not enough for men to have lived, they must talk about it. Lucky's tirade holds up for his horrified onstage auditors, as well as the thousand-arsed Spectator, the mirror of man at the end of his tether, driven to destruction by a centuries-long inheritance of exploitation by religious and rationalist fantasies. Lucky's version of the dead-end of life can be silenced by force, and Vladimir can simply refuse to listen to Estragon's accounts of his personal nightmares. But the story that cannot be silenced, and whose phrases have become embedded in everyday speech, is the Christian narrative, the rope to which Vladimir, Estragon, and their audience, are all tied. Here is the reason why people nurtured in the Western cultural tradition put up with their suffering, encouraged by the prospect of salvation and a last Providential home. Estragon has, he says, throughout his life, compared himself to Christ.[50] There are, the two friends note, variant New Testament accounts of the fate of the thieves crucified with Christ, but one of the two was saved, and that seems acceptable odds. Estragon is more sceptical than Vladimir, but they still depend on the Christian template for the idea of Godot, whom they invent, with a plethora of realistic detail about the time they met him, in one of the first dialogues of the play. Their Godot is all bluff, a pure effect of discourse.

The most entertaining and satisfying form of story is song, which will figure increasingly in Beckett's drama. The song puts meaning into its most intense form, with words and music combining in well-rhythmed harmony to create the sense of a satisfactory ending. Two songs point up the lyrical thrust of this quiet tragedy: the round song which opens Act II, the eternal cycle of the dog who died still searching for his bone, and Vladimir's lullaby for Estragon, the long dying fall into sleep.

Death, like Godot, exists only in the form of story – or offstage, where, figured as night, it is the space of separation, terror, and beatings. On stage, there is only life. The skull in Lucky's tirade may be in Connemara, but Connemara is not here. The threshold of death lies in the past (it's too late, they agree, to jump off the Eiffel Tower, and when Estragon was near-drowning in the Macon country, Vladimir saved him), or in a future that never comes. They might hang themselves tomorrow, but not today. In any case, they can't hang themselves, because the branch or the rope will break. Like the Unnamable, Vladimir and Estragon can only go on; unlike the Unnamable, their ending is not in the moving form of a new rhythm, but in immobility and stalemate. They should go, says Estragon; but no one moves.

Endgame: Playing to Lose

Beckett's next play was written, and rewritten, in French, between December 1955 and September 1956. The first draft, in two acts, was begun shortly after the death of Beckett's brother Frank. He finished it in February 1956, but told Barney Rosset, his American publisher and agent, that he was not happy with it.[51] He wrote to Rosset again three months later, to comment that '*Godot* is rollicking beside this awful thing'; he was compressing it into one act for the Marseille Festival in August, but was still very unhappy with it.[52] Compression did not secure acceptance for the Festival, but was good for the play, ensuring a tighter presentation of the rhythms and tensions of the interminable routines of everyday life. This time, there would be none of the compassion and dignity that distinguishes the lives of Vladimir and Estragon, only spite, recrimination, and bitter black humour. Here, unlike *Godot*, there is at least one death on stage.

Beckett told Pamela Mitchell at the end of September that the play was as near final as was possible before rehearsal, reduced to one act, and with the addition of a supporting couple, legless and living in rubbish bins; Roger Blin would be directing, but there was still no theatre booked.[53]

Endgame was first performed, in French, directed by Roger Blin, and starring Jean Martin as Clov and Blin as Hamm, at London's Royal Court Theatre, on 3 April 1957, because French theatres, despite the success of *Godot*, were reluctant to take it.[54] The reviews were poor.

The drama opens in a single claustrophobic interior set, minimal in its content, and offering the characters who inhabit it no way to find any other space. Hamm, the master, confined to a wheelchair, and Clov, his servant, bicker and snarl away their time in a bare room with a high window. There is nothing outside but greyness, and inside there are only the two bins with the legless bodies of Hamm's parents, Nagg and Nell. Clov has his kitchen, into which he retreats, but the kitchen is only a subset of Hamm's domain, and Hamm has the key to the food cupboard. Hamm's room is a domestic version of the nightmare cylinder that Beckett would evoke over a decade later, in *The Lost Ones*. Here is the space of modern humanity, inhabited by self-conscious and self-centred individuals, joined by necessity in the anxieties of survival, moving in the same endless circular routines. Competitive, callous, cruel, these earlier figures are also highly intelligent, creative performers, dreamers, and storytellers. From the 1970s, various directors have tried to set the play in more particular spaces: an old people's home in Cologne in 1973, a padded room resembling a mental ward, a skull, a womb, a fallout shelter, a wire cage.[55] The American director JoAnne Akalaitis set her 1984 production in a subway, in order to make it real in terms she thought her audience in the United States would recognise, and she costumed her characters to bring out what she thought of as a thrilling, urban kind of energy, appropriate to people of her own time, not merely European actors from the 1950s.[56] Too much specificity loses the point. Beckett's original interior presents the universal situation of the twentieth century, through characters stripped down to their simplest form, locked into the sadistic power games of possessive individualism: parents and children and masters and servants, Baudelairean tormentors and victims, exploiting and suffering the reversals of power and weakness. This is, as Beckett was about to show in prose form, how it is: things are grasped and abandoned, and the identity of one is scratched bloodily onto the back of the other.

Time in Hamm's room is reduced and restricted, an accumulation of sterile, repetitious moments. In *Godot,* the characters fantasised a future to wait for, there were leaves growing on a tree, and a track crossing their space, suggesting, however untruthfully, other spaces where comings and goings might still generate new games. In *Endgame*, nature supplies no changes except the death of the mother, the one female, and the pieces left in the game move round in a closed field, towards a stalemate both willed and imposed by circumstances. Offstage, the light is dying, the surrounding waters are rising, and there is, says Clov, looking through his end of the telescope, nothing, zero, greyness. In the distance, there may be a small boy, but he comes no nearer, and he will be killed if he does. The flea in Clov's trousers and the rat in his kitchen are promised the same end.

Movement is restricted. Blind Hamm, the king piece in this game, scripts and directs the action from his armchair on castors, pushed sullenly by the stiff-legged Clov. Nagg and Nell crouch in their dustbins. Paradoxically, within these tight constraints, the urgency of bodily performance is more frenetic than in *Godot*, and more so for its centring on the stiff-legged Clov, who staggers in and out of the kitchen, climbing ladders, checking on the bins, pushing Hamm's chair round the room to mark the parameters of their action. The body struggles to assert its presence, though nearing its end and vanishing into fantasies: Nagg and Nell's recollections of the sensual bliss of rowing their boat on Lake Como, Hamm's erotic and sadistic fantasies of murder, and his near-final fantasy of committing suicide, throwing himself out of his wheelchair to end it all, and clawing his way over the floor. The last refuge of the decaying body is the voice that still gives form to fantasies and memories. The grand narrative of God, or even Godot, is swiftly dismissed. Hamm orders a collective prayer, but receives no reply. These characters know they have no recourse.

Structured on the same fourfold thematics as the first two plays, *Endgame* twists the strands together more tightly. The inevitable start and the declaration of nothing doing are simultaneous. The start of the action is a matter of deadly, and deadening, habit. Clov climbs up to the windows, draws back the curtains, takes the sheet off the bins and lifts their lids, and takes the sheet off the sleeping Hamm. Immediately, Clov negates the beginning he has made ('Finished, it's finished, nearly finished'), and as he leaves, Hamm makes another start: 'Me (he yawns) to play.'[57] As Hamm makes his final moves at the end of the action, he echoes Clov's opening: 'The end is in the beginning and yet you go on.'[58] Going on involves the re-enactment of a worn-out dialogue of animosity, where there is never anything new to say, only the same old questions and answers.[59] Hamm and Clov, Beckett said, were Suzanne and himself;[60] and certainly, the killingly recognisable language of the bickering old couple, together too long to part but unable to find peace together, is, for all its stylisation, acutely observed.

Living is nothing but bluff, a playacting which is also a kind of mutual entertainment; though the entertainment is wearing thin, and life's ironic edge pokes through. Clov asks: 'Why this farce, day after day?' and Hamm replies: 'Routine. One never knows.'[61] Laughter and tears are not in balance here. The comedy is turning sour, as Nell acknowledges: '[I]t's like the funny story we have heard too often, we still find it funny, but we don't laugh any more.'[62] Nagg's well-worn joke about the tailor is killing; Nell fails to smile, and dies. The audience laughs at the characters, not with them, and there is no compassion, only cruelty, in the comic routines of the servant running backwards and forwards at his master's commands, to bring catheter, painkiller, tonic, or a three-legged stuffed dog, for consolation.

The stories Hamm tells constitute the real fabric of the world inside this room, a 'prolonged creative effort'[63] which becomes more violent, sadistic, and then masochistic, as his energy runs out. This is 'my chronicle', to which the others are expected to play audience. It was once packed with characters, the many people he fantasises he might have helped, and joyfully turned away: Mother Pegg, to whom he refused a light, the mad painter, and the starving man, who begged for food for his children. Like the voice of the Unnamable (Beckett was translating the novel into English as he wrote his play), Hamm lives by inventing and consuming characters, and finding them, he confesses, is increasingly hard. A flagging narrative finds new resources in metanarrative. Hamm muses on ending his present story, and beginning another. In the next story he makes himself his own character, and his own victim, as he fantasises throwing himself suicidally onto the floor; and then, his audience on stage having disappeared, he becomes his own audience, like the lonely child who invents more like himself, for company, to babble and whisper together and fend off the dark.[64] This is the ultimate endgame, where the creative mind collapses in on itself and vanishes into its own labyrinthine inner spaces.

The complex word-music of later texts written for reading, such as *Company*, can dwell at length on Beckett's terrifying fantasies of the threshold of dying, where imagination still echoes inside a decaying skull. *Endgame* pulls back into the conventional terms of dramatic entertainment, and restores equilibrium with a burst of comic relief. Clov, having left the stage in pursuit of his rat, returns to report ruefully that the rat got away. Hamm inaugurates a final fantasy, telling Clov that away from Hamm, and outside Hamm's space, is death. Clov, as ever, plays along, in a final sequence in which the two entertain one another by playing out a ritual of parting, as an emblem of dying. Hamm invents a final speech for Clov, and Clov mirrors it with a speech of his own, mourning the absence in their world of all the friendship, beauty, and order that life, he says (ironically), promised him. He leaves the stage, in a model declarative performance ('This is what we call making an exit'), and Hamm in his turn makes a final speech, returning to his opening words of the play: 'Me to play. [*Pause. Wearily.*] Old endgame, lost of old, play and lose and have done with losing.'[65] Clov returns, dressed as if ready to depart, and watches silently, an unseen audience, as Hamm throws away all his things, and places his handkerchief over his face. The curtain falls on a devastating performance of a way of living where the end of doing is losing, and even dying is a form of bluff.

Krapp's Last Tape: 'Drowned in Dreams and Burning to be Gone'[66]

Beckett began writing his next play in English, in February 1958, two months after learning that Ethna MacCarthy had been diagnosed with terminal cancer. For the next eighteen months, up to her death, he wrote her long letters, and the time he devoted to writing the play, James Knowlson surmises, would have been filled not only with the sense of present sorrow and imminent loss but also happy memories of earlier times in the Ireland of their youth – a mood far removed from the angry bitterness of *Endgame*.[67]

Krapp's activity with his tape recordings was adumbrated by Hamm's brief self-splitting into two or three children, whispering in the dark, but it goes much further, with an exploration of how imagination, combined with memory, can create a more substantial and aesthetically more satisfying version of the self. Here, doing and playing leads, as always, to the recognition of the dead end of all endeavour, but this time the process of making and editing also results in a pleasurable image in which the maker can briefly contemplate himself.

Krapp's one-act monologue is, like Hamm's, a dialogue with himself as both speaker and listener, but it strikes a new note as he doubles and multiplies his voices not in fantasy but through recordings of past selves, or rather, recordings of the different ways his younger selves perceived themselves. The newly-developing technology of the tape recorder, which Beckett discovered when he came to work at the BBC, offered him a means of inscribing the perception of self, which is the only kind of truth about itself that the subject can reach; and the piling up of recordings, continually processed through an auditor, is a way of acknowledging and incorporating the discontinuities of self-consciousness in a form that can contain the disorder. Beckett and Patrick Magee worked together to make clear the differences between the two voices of older and younger Krapp, and to establish the distinctive rhythms of his past recordings, as well as the illusory present of the onstage voice that brings everything together.[68] These insights into the operations of perception and memory are not new, and the student of French must have been influenced not only by Proust but by Jean-Jacques Rousseau's autobiographies, the *Confessions*, and especially the *Rêveries d'un promeneur solitaire*.[69] The technology however makes all the difference, bringing the multiple presents, and presences, of voiced selves together on the living stage.

Krapp's carefully-filed collection of tapes, numbered and entered in a ledger, each one recorded by him on his birthday, captures the passing years in the form in which he each time perceived their passing. Each new start of a new year of his life is embedded in the years past; here again are the turning cycles of Vico's history. As he sits listening to selected tapes, and sections of tapes, Krapp comments on how he now perceives what he hears, and records his comments. Layers of perception pile up and interconnect, as time slips past, filling the stage with a new version of nothing doing. *Waiting for Godot* stages what it is like to live in the illusion of a linear future. *Endgame* attempts to lock down the present by walling it up inside the projections of a single imagination, from a fixed point. *Krapp's Last Tape* addresses time passing, through a character who repeatedly operates a distinctive and changing self-positioning in relation to a past that has its own substance and consistency, and this drama produces onstage a figure of present as process. Beckett challenges traditional assumptions of theatre's unique ability to communicate presence, through the 'reality' of actors' bodies on stage, and the 'immediacy' of actors' voices.

Steven Connor has analysed the new dimensions that Beckett's use of recordings has brought to the way speech operates on his stage, reducing the sense of immediacy, originality, and continuity, which for a Western audience it traditionally connotes.[70] More accurately, perhaps, *Krapp's Last Tape* rewrites dramatically the ways that the immediacy, originality, and continuity of speech can be thought. The body of Krapp seen on stage is lacking in presence and impact – grubby, carelessly dressed, impoverished, a gorilla chewing on bananas, slipping on their skins. Krapp's speech is something else, filling the stage with an intense and complex version of what it is to be human, which involves multiple modes of being and speaking, self recorded, self listening, and self re-recording, self-assessing self, and self-addressing self.

The Krapp presented in his onstage body enjoys his repeated new starts, and his creative mind is not engaged in 'bluff' but is painstakingly collecting, assessing and editing aspects of his objectified selves, that is, the versions of his past that his present mind intends will survive the passing of his present body.[71] For the 'me' onstage, not everything is worth hearing again, but in place of the anxiety and terror elsewhere associated with loss, there is sadness and lyricism. Imposing order on speech and memory with his tape recorder, as he controls the demands of the body with his rituals of eating and drinking, Krapp recognises the changes in himself over time, and in the end finds what, for the time being, he decides is the best of what he feels he has been.

Krapp, unlike his predecessors in Beckett's drama, is not concerned with holding off the dark, and has no fear or need of watchers. Seated centre stage, in the spotlight which has its analogue in the bright light of his own self-awareness, he is as indifferent to the audience's gaze as a gorilla in its cage, peeling and eating bananas, slipping on the skins without bothering to acknowledge the comic cliché, or tossing them into the pit. He leaves the circle of light to pop open a bottle in the darkness, and returns refreshed. The darkness is the place of inspiration and knowledge, the source of the drives that have made the man who is now remaking himself.

On the day of this performance, the first spool he chooses – box three, spool five – was recorded on his 39th birthday when, the recording says, he had been listening to a tape from ten or twelve years earlier. This tape mentioned the warm eyes of Bianca, with whom he was living at that time, and was full of resolutions to drink less and lead a less active sexual life. These remarks, along with his hint at a great work to come, are greeted with derision by the two listeners, the middle-aged man recording spool five, and the old man sitting on stage, in the spotlight of the present. In the memories accumulated on this tape's narrative, another erotic encounter follows. Sitting in the park, watching his dying mother's window (her death less interesting to the old man than the legal term his pretentious younger self uses for her widowhood, 'viduity', which he now has to look up in a dictionary), young Krapp was distracted by a dark-haired nursemaid, with eyes, he says, like chrysolite. He remembers in vivid sensuous detail the feel of the little old black rubber ball he was about to throw for a little white dog when the blind went down at the window to signal the moment of his mother's passing.

After a short pause, indicative perhaps of grief (or perhaps not), he recounts his unforgettable vision at the end of the jetty in March, recording, he says, lest he forget it in old age, the storm-tossed moment that set his work alight, and his discovery that 'the dark I have always struggled to keep under is in reality my most –'.[72]

Onstage Krapp, infuriated in his old age by the rehearsal of these youthful aspirations to greatness, switches off and runs the tape forward, finding instead, by chance, an episode in a punt, where the speaker sat with an unnamed she, drifting in the hot sun. He told her they must end it, and she agreed, with closed eyes. At his request, she opened her eyes, and his words re-enact precisely how they opened, and let him into her gaze. The syntax recreates the driving of the boat into the bank, and then the rocking of the boat, mimicking a sexual union that never took place, a performance of completeness, out of human time and space, in which the self that knows and the self that is known, subject and object, tormentor and victim, sadist and masochist, are distinct and united, moving in perfect equilibrium.[73] This is the best that Krapp can make of the feeling called 'love': a mirroring of oneself in the depths of the accepting eyes of another, infused by intense sensuous and erotic awareness, and made more intense by its enclosure in loss.

Krapp switches off. His new birthday recording is a rejection, and then an acceptance, of that younger self, and then a bitter account of his own year just gone, with no fame and no love, only drink, and the memories caught in the spooling tape. He switches off the new tape and throws it away, to return to spool five and the sequence in the punt, in all its rhythmic completeness. But no memory, even recorded, can be the same. This time round he finds the closing comments of the young man full of confidence in his own future, assured of his creative powers, who has no regret for lost happiness, and thinks he will never want that time back.

The mirror-eyes of love, mirrored by the eyes of ambition, are in their turn mirrored by the eyes of the old man left with neither ambition nor love. The play ends in that profoundly ironic evocation of absolute desire and absolute loss, and the curtain falls on Krapp, his own inventor and his own auditor, his eyes fixed on emptiness as the tape runs silently on.

Here is the perfect realisation of nothing doing, in a dramatic performance where man, the maker, embraces the instruments with which he makes himself (his memories and words, and his recording machine), and the spooling and switching, on and off, which are the rhythms of making. The emphasis is on the materiality of the process. In the collected performances which constitute Krapp, there is continuity in his material body, eating and drinking the same foods, in the same rituals, performed in the same preferred costumes and spaces,[74] at a well-lit table covered with the records of past experience and the instruments to inscribe new ones, and surrounded on all sides by the darkness that comes before and after all experience. What the records show is that the body, sensuous and sensual, strikes the primary note of being, across the years, as the source of the voice in which, eventually, it speaks itself. Most of all, what distinguishes Krapp, binding together body and senses, voice and inscriptions of voice, is the fire of desire by which he has always been consumed: his vision of his creative power ('the fire that set it alight'), the heat of his sexual drive ('Sun blazing down'), and at the end, the old man's intense longing for death: 'drowned in dreams and burning to be gone.'

At the end of the 1950s, Beckett wrote two short scenarios in French, *Rough for Theatre I* and *Rough for Theatre II.* Neither was staged, and both are, as the titles suggest, just practice pieces. The first, which takes itself seriously, is reminiscent of *Endgame* in its structure (a blind beggar and a man in a wheelchair are engaged in competition and mutual exploitation), but is no more than self-pastiche. *Rough for Theatre II* shows Beckett practising his comic skills. It stages two men employed by a third to go through his papers, while the third stands at the window with his back to them and the audience, apparently ready to jump. The pair read extracts from testimonies by his family and friends, and his own account of his problems, which are all caricatures of the Beckett persona promulgated in the popular press, as received by uncomprehending audiences and critics. There are some good one-liners and many perceptive self-putdowns, as when one of the examiners struggles with their subject's long, rambling account of his morbid sensitivity to the opinions of others, rummaging desperately through the sentence to find the verb.[75] In the end, they leave him to jump.

Happy Days: The Dance of Love

Two years later, in October 1960, Beckett began writing, in English, the drama of Winnie, finishing the second draft in February 1961.[76] *Happy Days* is a feminine counterpart to *Krapp's Last Tape,* presenting the other side of Krapp's experience of 'love': in her role as mirror to the man, the woman is trapped and destroyed. The play is Beckett's most painful and also most heroic representation of the human condition, and the pain of losing and ending. Winnie, up to her waist in sand in Act I, and then up to her neck in Act II, is the archetypal feminine of modern culture, defined in terms of her body, and objectified by the gaze of others to a degree that her husband has not known. The sun that blazes down on Winnie never affects Willie, who can move at any time into the shade of his wife. The universal truth intuited by Vladimir that someone is always looking at 'me' signifies for Winnie a very different experience.

When the play begins, Winnie is already aware of the difference that gender makes to the experience of time: 'natural laws, I suppose it's like everything else, it all depends on the creature you happen to be.'[77] She knows that her material situation, the bodily space she has always inhabited, and the accumulation around that body of the weight of time, leaves her powerless. By the second act, she is becoming even more painfully aware that materially and physically she has changed, though her awareness of some form of self, what she calls her 'mind', slight as it is, remains the same: 'what difficulties here, for the mind. [*Pause.*] To have been always what I am – and so changed from what I was. [...] And no truth in it anywhere.'[78] The men in Beckett's dramas had had some measure of control in their lives, however little, or memories of moments when they felt they did, and awareness of a potential for imagination and creativity that is a form of control. Winnie has none of these. Only in these end days does she finally objectify herself, in a memory that surfaces of a couple watching and criticising her condition, and in the first story she invents for herself, of her dolly, Mildred; and then she begins at last to grasp her condition as the sexualised object of the gaze of the male.

Winnie is the first female character to appear on Beckett's stage since Hamm's mother Nell, who died quiet and uncomplaining in her dustbin, her death, like her life, hardly noticed.[79] With Winnie, Beckett wanted to create an extreme image of the human situation, and a corresponding image of humanity's heroic ability to survive its condition. He told the actress Brenda Bruce, who played Winnie in the first British performance at the Royal Court in November 1962, how the inspiration came to him. He imagined, she reported, a collocation of awful situations, starting with the most terrible: being prevented from sleeping, sinking down into the ground, under an endless sun, with nothing but '"a little parcel of things to see you through life." [. . .] Then he said: "And I thought who would cope with that and go down singing, only a woman."'[80]

The stage directions for Winnie's appearance describe her as a plump, 50-year-old blonde, with a low-cut bodice, big breasts, and a pearl necklace. The stage set emphasises the illusion of happiness inside which she lives: a *trompe l'oeil* backcloth representing a receding plain and sky, horizons way out of her reach. A dazzling sunlight shines on her all through the play. Beckett's favourite actress, Bille Whitelaw, probably the best-known Winnie, directed by Beckett himself at the Royal Court in 1979, commented on its ferocity. Jack Raby, the lighting technician, focused all the lights he had on her face, stopping only when she finally complained that her eyes were burning.[81]

The sun that shines on the living is more pitiless with each passing day, but Winnie survives. She has no option. The earth that holds her thwarts her desire to be sucked up into the blue. Killing herself is impossible. She once took a revolver away from Willie, at his request, and she now lays aside her own revolver, taken from her well-supplied bag, onto the ground. By the time she thinks she might use it, the earth has buried her arms. She adapts to everything, including the dominant masculinity of language: 'That is what I find so wonderful. [*Pause.*] The way man adapts himself. [*Pause.*] To changing conditions.'[82] As she speaks, the parasol that has been tiring her arm bursts into flame. The black comedy intensifies, bringing a new frenzy to the balance of laughter and tears. As the end draws nearer, Winnie finds herself, in the language of the (male) poet, 'laughing wild amid severest woe'.[83]

She survives on an unceasing fountain of speech. Her language is coherent, but it consists, to begin with, of trivia, delivered to strict speech rhythms and marked by ritual gestures, between bells that mark each day's start and end. Habit, the great deadener, is her mainstay. Beckett set up a metronome for Brenda Bruce's speech and pauses, and instructed her in regular ritual movements. A *Guardian* interview with Billie Whitelaw on the occasion of the forthcoming production of *Happy Days* at the Royal Court, directed by Beckett (opening 7 June 1979), reported that:

> Beckett, she says, is very precise, and right to be; he does not direct, he conducts, as though it were music. 'It's painful for him to hear me miss a comma, physically painful. But we've made a pact that that is his problem, not mine.'

She will ask him whether Winnie's gesture should be at eye level or throat level (it can make all the difference to Beckett). But he never says what the play means, and she doesn't ask.[84]

Winnie's rhythms include hesitation over words, and pauses. Her particular experience, Beckett says, is of a basic 'discontinuity of time ... Her time experience is an incomprehensible transport from one inextricable present to the next, those past unremembered, those to come inconceivable'.[85] Occasional fragmentary, baffling memories surface, triggered apparently gratuitously, which are forms created by the emotions and pressures of a situation she cannot consciously articulate. She may not remember the name of the couple called Shower, or Cooker, who watched her and wondered aloud why Willie didn't dig her out of her mound, but her feeling of humiliation and sadness is intense. Hers is the contrary of Krapp's experience. He has control of the instruments that record and play back his feelings, and he can create his own continuities. Winnie's anxious wriggling on the hook of her present, the victim of all stories, is in dramatic tension with the inexorable continuity of earth time, piling up around her.

She has her own resources. There will always, she says, be her shopping bag, with its rich collection of things: toothbrush, handkerchief, spectacles, medicine, looking glass, lipstick, and hat. She can read the packets, unpack, and pack again. Like the 'man' in *How It Is*, at the start of his journey to himself, she identifies the things she has collected in her bag as markers and makers of her survival. But all that the painkillers and beauty aids can do is create anxiety, through the fear of their loss. In Act II, with the bag out of reach, it turns out that things are not the best resource after all, and that words will outlive them.

At the start of Act II, up to her neck in sand, her hat on her head, Winnie can only move her eyes. She opens them at once when the bell rings that starts all her days; the bell hurts, but the pain confirms she is still there. The light that burns and blinds her is another reassurance; someone is still looking at her. Her own body is also still there; she has no arms, and, she mourns, no breasts, but she can see bits of her face and touch them with her tongue. And words, it seems, have not failed. As a last resource, she begins to tell herself 'my story [...]. A life'.[86] The story of Mildred and her doll provokes the further recollection of the trauma that was the commentary of Shower or Cooker, and its significance emerges in the images of a doll with nothing on underneath her dress, terrified by the mouse that runs up her legs. The deeply repressed terrors of sexual experience surface, in the complex language of sadomasochism, but this talking cure comes too late to rescue anything past. There is still time, though, for a dramatic reversal in her relationship to Willie.

Her chief resource, or so the audience and Winnie herself believe, to begin with, is Willie, the other half of the heterosexual couple into which the two of them are locked. She needs Willie, she constantly tells him, even if he does not answer, to save her from the unbearable feeling that she is talking to herself. If he died or left her, she thinks, she would be left with nothing to do but stare silently into space.[87] As time will tell, Willie, like the bag, is less necessary than either of them thought. In Act I, she is delighted when, in answer to her repeated calls, he finally crawls out from behind her mound, and too grateful for the crumbs of recognition he throws her to let herself think about what they imply about how he, and the world at large, views women. He reads bits from his newspaper: 'Opening for smart youth', 'Wanted bright boy'.[88] He hands her a pornographic postcard. He draws her attention to a passing ant, and makes a joke about fornication. Willie is turning his own repressions and failures into sadistic taunts, and Winnie, in the growing insecurity of her own body, laughs and plays along. In Act II, as circumstances force her to recognise the humiliation and terror in which she has lived her life, and the loss of everything on which she pinned her identity, Willie's deafness to her calls for help changes the balance of their relationship. He finally emerges on all fours, costumed like the first day he came to woo her, in top hat and tails, the comically recognisable signal of class and gender power, stroking his long white Battle of Britain moustache. The clumsy attempt at a renewed seduction is too little, too late, and serves only to remind her of how time has passed, and how much of it has been wasted. She mocks him, abuses him, and gibes at his impotence.

The closing sequence is full of vicious ironies. Like Beckett's male couples, neither has anywhere else to go. They return to their habitual patterns. Winnie welcomes another happy day, and, as Beckett planned, ends singing. The song is sung not to celebrate her heroic optimism, but to rejoice in her reversal of power, moving from victim to tormentor. The popular music-box tune, celebrating the dance of love, is heavily ironic. 'Love', like everything else that was promised in 'their' world – friendship, justice, and order, said Clov – is an empty term, just one more bluff, a means to amuse the punters; or worse, as here, a gloss thrown over the cruelty, violence, hatred, and loathed dependency which join two animal bodies together. The final image of the play, the end of Winnie's song, is another ritual performance: the two smile, the closing bell rings, they look into each other's eyes, and switch off the smiles. The curtain falls on the long, unsmiling gaze which is their counterpart to Krapp and his tape-recorder. Whatever paths are chosen, the end is the same: nothing doing.

NOTES

1 Knowlson, *Damned to Fame*, p.57.

2 Letter from Beckett to Thomas MacGreevy [7 August 1934], *Letters* I, p.217.

3 Bair, *Samuel Beckett*, pp.47–8.

4 Letter from Beckett to A.J. Leventhal, 17 November 1953, *Letters* II, p.417.

5 See for example Peter Lichtenfels, 'Afterword. British Intersections with Paris,' in Bradby and Delgado, *The Paris Jigsaw*, pp.283–4.

6 Anne Atik, *How It Was. A Memoir of Samuel Beckett* (London: Faber and Faber, 2001), p.16.

7 Richard Eyre and Nicholas Wright, *Changing Stages. A View of British Theatre in the Twentieth Century* (London: Bloomsbury Publishing Plc, 2000), p.214.

8 Jonathan Kalb, *Beckett in Performance* (Cambridge: Cambridge University Press, 1989), pp.21–2.

9 Billie Whitelaw, *Billie Whitelaw ... Who He? An Autobiography* (London: Hodder and Stoughton, 1995; Sceptre Paperback, 1996), p.76.

10 Letter from Beckett to Georges Duthuit [3 January 1951], *Letters* II, p.216.

11 Michael Robinson, *The Long Sonata of the Dead: A Study of Samuel Beckett* (New York: Grove Press, 1969), p.230, cit. David Bradby, *Beckett, 'Waiting for Godot'* (Cambridge: Cambridge University Press, 2001), pp.15–16.

12 Atik, *How It Was*, p.40.

13 Letter from Beckett to George Reavey, 15 August 1947, *Letters* II, p.60, and p.61n5.

14 Letter from Beckett to Georges Duthuit, 11 August 1948, *Letters* II, p.95.

15 Letter from Beckett to Maurice Nadeau, 25 June 1956, *Letters* II, pp.628–9; see also letter from Beckett to Christian Ludvigsen, 23 April 1956, *Letters* II, p.616.

16 Letter from Beckett to George Reavey, 14 May 1947, *Letters* II, p.55.

17 Letter from Beckett to Georges Duthuit, 11 August 1948, *Letters* II, p.95.

18 Samuel Beckett, *Eleutheria*, trans. Barbara Wright (London: Faber and Faber, 1996), p.24, pp.32–3.

19 Beckett, *Eleutheria*, p.51.

20 Beckett, *Eleutheria*, p.82.

21 Beckett, *Eleutheria*, p.128.

22 Beckett, *Eleutheria*, p.155.

23 Beckett, *Eleutheria*, p.136.

24 Beckett, *Eleutheria*, p.146.

25 Beckett, *Eleutheria*, p.149.

26 Beckett, *Eleutheria*, p.164.
27 Bradby, *Beckett: Waiting for Godot*, p.15.
28 Bradby, *Beckett*, p.51.
29 Letter from Beckett to Georges Duthuit, 27 [February 1950], *Letters* II, p.182.
30 Bradby, *Beckett*, p.46.
31 Letter from Beckett to Jérôme Lindon, 17 February 1953, *Letters* II, p.366. The article by Alain Robbe-Grillet, 'Samuel Beckett, Auteur Dramatique', appeared in *Critique* 9 (February 1953), pp.108–114.
32 Bradby, *Beckett*, p.75.
33 Bradby, *Beckett*, p.85.
34 Letter from Beckett to Thomas MacGreevy, 4 June 1956, *Letters* II, p.624; see also *Letters* II, p.625n. A translation by Liam Ó Briain and Seán Ó Carra (*Ag Fanacht Le Godot*) was staged on 28 November 1971, with T.P. McKenna as Estragon, directed by Alan Simpson, at An Taibhdhearc, Galway (Playography Ireland, Irish Theatre Institute. [www.irishplayography.com/play.aspx?playid=3376. Consulted 18 September 2013]).
35 Samuel Beckett, *Waiting for Godot*; *CDW* 1986, p.10.
36 Beckett, *Godot*; *CDW* 1986, p.83.
37 Letter from Beckett to Carlheinz Caspari, 25 July 1953, *Letters* II, p.389.
38 Beckett, *Godot*; *CDW* 1986, p.14.
39 Beckett, *Godot*; *CDW* 1986, p.45.
40 Beckett, *Godot*; *CDW* 1986, p.82.
41 Beckett, *Godot*; *CDW* 1986, p.83.
42 Letter from Beckett to Carlheinz Caspari, 25 July 1953, *Letters* II, p.390.
43 Letters from Alan Schneider to Beckett, in Harmon (ed.), *No Author Better Served*, 22 January 1962, p.120, and 27 January 1970, p.232.
44 Charles Spencer, '*Waiting for Godot*, Haymarket Theatre Royal', *The Telegraph* (8 May 2009).
45 Lyn Gardner, '*Waiting for Godot*, Haymarket, London', *The Guardian*, 26 January 2010.
46 Bradby, *Beckett*, pp.59–61.
47 Bradby, *Beckett*, p.100. Blau's production is famous for its impact on the audience in the San Quentin prison, November 1957, where the theme of anguished waiting, with nowhere else to go, spoke directly to convicts' experience of prison life. One result was the contact made with Beckett by one prisoner, Rick McCluchy, on his release. With Beckett's support, McCluchy went on to found the San Quentin Theatre Company.
48 Bradby, *Beckett*, p.116.
49 Beckett, *Godot*; *CDW* 1986, pp.40–2.
50 Beckett, *Godot*; *CDW* 1986, p.49.

51 Letter from Beckett to Barney Rosset, 22 February 1956, *Letters* II, p.602.

52 Letter from Beckett to Barney Rosset [15 May 1956], *Letters* II, p.619.

53 Letter from Beckett to Pamela Mitchell, 28 September 1956, *Letters* II, p.657.

54 Requests to see the MS of *Fin de partie* came from Jacques Hébertot, of the Hébertot Theatre, Montmartre, the American producer, Michael Myerberg, and the Schiller Theater in Berlin (Letter from Beckett to Barney Rosset, 30 August [1956], *Letters* II, p.647). By November, the play was in rehearsal, along with *Acte sans paroles*, for a projected January start at the Théâtre de l'Oeuvre (Letter from Beckett to Nancy Cunard, 7 November 1956, *Letters* II, p.670).

55 See Jonathan Kalb, *Beckett in Performance*, pp.77–88.

56 Jonathan Kalb, interview with JoAnne Akalaitis (7 March 1986), *Beckett in Performance*, p.171. For more interviews with Beckett's directors on their approaches to his theatre, see Lois Oppenheim (ed.), *Directing Beckett* (Ann Arbor: University of Michigan Press, new edn 1997).

57 Samuel Beckett, *Endgame* (1958); *CDW* 1986, p.93.

58 Beckett, *Endgame*; *CDW* 1986, p.126.

59 Beckett, *Endgame*; *CDW* 1986, p.94.

60 Bair, *Samuel Beckett*, p.483.

61 Beckett, *Endgame*; *CDW* 1986, p.107.

62 Beckett, *Endgame*; *CDW* 1986, p.101.

63 Beckett, *Endgame*; *CDW* 1986, p.122.

64 Beckett, *Endgame*; *CDW* 1986, p.126.

65 Beckett, *Endgame*; *CDW* 1986, p.132.

66 Samuel Beckett, *Krapp's Last Tape* (1958); *CDW* 1986, p.222.

67 Knowlson, *Damned to Fame*, pp.442–3. Written in English, with Patrick Magee in mind, the play was first performed at the Royal Court, October 1958.

68 Knowlson, *Damned to Fame*, p.455.

69 He had certainly read the *Rêveries* (Letter from Beckett to Thomas MacGreevy, 5 December [1932], *Letters* I, p.145).

70 Steven Connor, *Samuel Beckett: Repetition, Theory and Text* (Oxford: Basil Blackwell, 1988), Chapter 6, 'Voice and Mechanical Reproduction: *Krapp's Last Tape*, *Ohio Impromptu*, *Rockaby*, *That Time*'.

71 Beckett, *Krapp's Last Tape*; *CDW* 1986, p.217.

72 Beckett, *Krapp's Last Tape*; *CDW* 1986, p.220. The stormy vision is frequently, and erroneously, attributed to Beckett himself, but although he decided on a change of direction during his trip to Ireland in summer 1945, the setting was different, and the decision much less melodramatic (Knowlson, *Damned to Fame*, p.352 and p.772n. 55. See above, Chapter 1, p.36.)

73 Beckett, *Krapp's Last Tape*; *CDW* 1986, p.221. This is Krapp's/ Beckett's version of Rousseau's famous experience of absolute self-awareness, evoked in the *Rêveries*,

in his Swiss exile, in the rhythmic rocking of the boat on the lake surrounding the Île de Saint-Pierre. While Rousseau's was a solitary experience, an arch-Romantic narcissism, Krapp's narcissism is situated in a heterosexual mirroring. Beckett mentions the Île de Saint-Pierre in a letter to Thomas MacGreevy [16 September 1934], *Letters* I, p.228.

74 Beckett, *Krapp's Last Tape*; *CDW* 1986, p.217.

75 Samuel Beckett, *Rough for Theatre II* (1976), *CDW* 1986, p.243.

76 Knowlson, *Damned to Fame*, pp.475–7. The play was first performed in New York in September 1961. It was produced in London in November 1962, with Brenda Bruce as Winnie, and in Paris, in autumn 1963, with Madeleine Renaud in the role. Jean-Louis Barrault asked to play Willie, and an important friendship began between Beckett and France's most famous theatrical couple. John Beary produced the play in Dublin in September 1963, with Marie Kean as Winnie.

77 Samuel Beckett, *Happy Days* (1961); rpt. James Knowlson (ed.), *Happy Days/ Oh Les Beaux Jours* (London & Boston: Faber and Faber, 1978), p.46.

78 Beckett, *Happy Days*, p.66.

79 See below, Chapter 7, pp.167-171, for Beckett's presentation of Mrs Rooney, in the radio play *All That Fall*, broadcast in 1957.

80 Brenda Bruce, interviewed by James Knowlson, 7 April 1994, cit. Knowlson, *Damned to Fame*, p.501.

81 Whitelaw, *Billie Whitelaw*, p.153.

82 Beckett, *Happy Days*, p.48.

83 Beckett, *Happy Days*, p.42. The quotation is from Thomas Gray, 'On a Distant Prospect of Eton College.' Beckett sent Alan Schneider a list of all Winnie's thirteen references, which are mostly from Shakespeare and Milton (Letter from Beckett to Alan Schneider, 25 August 1961, in Harmon (ed.), *No Author Better Served*, pp.96–8).

84 Anon., 'Billie up to her neck in Beckett', *Arts Guardian* (30 May 1979), p.12.

85 Samuel Beckett, Schiller Theater Notebook, cit. Knowlson, 'Afterword', *Happy Days*, p.118.

86 Beckett, *Happy Days*, p.70.

87 Beckett, *Happy Days*, p.38.

88 Beckett, *Happy Days*, p.26.

CHAPTER 6

The Shorter Plays – Diminishing Returns

From the early 1960s onwards, working through the processes of dramatic production, as with his prose, Beckett had seen the principal elements of his conceptualisation of the human condition – who, what, and where 'one' is – taking shape. To begin with, he had negotiated, through and out of the story form, with the conventions of realism, time, space and language; but he soon went beyond them to establish aesthetic forms which made very different demands of the senses and imagination of directors, actors, and the thousand-arsed Spectator. Beckett's next task was to condense, intensify, and deepen his perceptions, and to explore the visual and auditory resources of the stage to produce images that would draw audiences more closely into the shapes and feelings of his world. In the language of *Rockaby*, he was looking out for eyes as famished as his own, mirroring his search for another living soul. The shaping of the first plays involved a long build-up of action that poured multiple significances into a final scenic image. The next experiment was to present a single image from the start, and expand its meaning as the audience watches, condensing the time and the impact of understanding into a single space – an urn, a mouth, a strip of carpet, a rocking chair, each one the limits shaping and containing a particular life.

The chronological framework of the previous chapter was convenient to show the process of patient working and reworking through which – to use the language of *How It Is* – Beckett learned to realise the tones and rhythms of the voice of his making. The stage plays of this second period will be approached in two thematic groupings, to bring out some key aspects of the concepts and feelings that were taking shape from his particular perspective in among the chaos. Not all this work was developed solely within the enclosed walls of the theatre; from *Krapp's Last Tape* onwards, Beckett's stage work runs parallel with his exploration of the new technologies of radio, film and television, which will be reviewed in the next chapter.

The Gender Gap

From the middle of the 1950s, with his first radio play, *All that Fall* (written in 1956), and then in 1960, with *Happy Days*, Beckett had recognised the different perspectives gendered acculturation brings to the human condition. In the next two decades, four shorter plays set up his vision of the relations between men and women, and the particular situation of women.[1]

Play, a 20-minute piece, including the reprise, written in English, is generally acknowledged as marking a major change in Beckett's writing for the stage, which became more static and more lyrical, committed to balancing visual and poetic images.[2]

Play was first conceived in April 1962, and the world premiere in Germany, in a translation by Erika and Elmar Tophoven (*Spiel*), which Beckett reviewed, took place in June 1963.[3] Three identical urns stand front centre stage, each a metre high, and sticking out from them are the heads of one man, and two women. Theirs are ageless faces, washed out, almost identical to each other and to the urns, of which they seem part. In the first English production, the make-up devised for the actors matched the green and brown of the urns.[4] The faces are expressionless, and the voices mostly toneless. A glaring spotlight projected onto one face at a time forces them to pour out stored memories and feelings. They don't speak to each other; absence of communication and understanding is the condition of gendered relationships. The single mobile spot, the eye of the dramatist interrogating his subjects, is their only interlocutor. Whitelaw described the play as not a trio but a quartet, in which the light, she thought, played the most important role.[5] There is no mutual questioning, or self-questioning, to challenge their fixity. They simply utter their (determinedly partial) perceptions of themselves and each other, recounting events as they remember living them, and the operatic structure of the play collects, repeats and condenses the elements of each one's separate song into the harmony of the performance. The play offers an image of relationships created and torn apart by desire and fear. Individual minds crack open under the pressure, and plunge into chaos;[6] the mess is put into new order in the forms selected by the dramatist. Ordering their affairs, as the man in the jar says, is what men do[7] – though in his case, the cliché is an evasion, not a means to understanding.

The spotlight in *Happy Days* glared down on Winnie, leaving Willie, relatively speaking, silent and in the shade. *Play* gives voices to both sexes, not in the form of the couple, but the triad created by male power and female insecurity, which Beckett presents as the shaping dynamic of heterosexual relationships. Here is another dance of 'love', in all its negative aspects: competition, jealousy, hatred, violence, sadism, indifference, abandonment, humiliation, and loss. The drama, carried entirely in the intersecting rhythms of the words, is in the irreducible tension between the passionate clashes of feeling, and the longing for dark, silence, and peace. These are all emotions Beckett must himself have experienced, or inflicted, in the course of his many extra-marital affairs. There is apparently no evidence that Suzanne ever complained of situations that everyone knew about (though her hostility to him in the last years of her life may well have had its source in long-standing grievances), but not all his lovers were equally complaisant – Barbara Bray, for example.[8] But there is no sense of any intrusive autobiographical dimension in the well-observed psychology, and the carefully selected clichés, of the appropriately named eternal triangle. Aesthetic distancing universalises the view.

Structured like a piece of music, *Play* requires a balance to be maintained between the drive to a totalising communication, and the separate notes, the melodies of each character, which must all remain audible, with their own value. To communicate the sense of the whole, speed is of the essence. Billie Whitelaw, who reduced the running time to fourteen minutes, understood the imperative to go as fast as possible, at the risk of compromising the audience's understanding.[9] To capture the precise tone of each individual, well-timed speech rhythms are essential, to throw points into relief. For Whitelaw, this was a musical exercise, and she marked on her script where the stress should fall on syllables, so that she could dwell on them to bring out the rhythms.[10] The role was exceptionally demanding, especially as the play ran in the repertory for some months, and the actress had to undertake regular exercises for her face muscles.[11]

There is an introductory movement of five seconds, after which the voices speak together, in faint light, in disjointed phrases, each with their own leitmotiv. The first woman and the man, in their different ways, want the situation to be over; she desires to return to the dark, he wants peace. The second woman, the mistress, is anxiously preoccupied with her unimportance, and then, as now, feels herself to be no more than a shade. After another five seconds of darkness, a strong light shines on all three faces, and each speaks out the first phrase of their own story.

The main dramatic movement, an outpouring of frenzy, begins with another five seconds of darkness, and then the spotlight switches from face to face, and the conflict between the three is narrated from each separate perspective, each reporting their own version of the others' actions and speech. The scaffolding of the affair is a sequence of confrontations. The wife accuses her husband of cheating, and then bursts in on his mistress and denounces her; the husband confesses and promises to leave the mistress; the wife bursts in again on the mistress, and gloats over her success. The husband tries to keep up with both, then gives up the struggle and leaves them both. Each woman thinks he has left her for the other.

In the closing movement, introduced by five seconds of darkness, there is half light on all three faces, voices are at half volume, and calm is apparently restored. The man marks the end, with relief, hoping for a descent into darkness and peace.[12] The mistress records an ending that underlines yet again her dependent subjectivity: he goes out, and so then does she. But there are still explosions, of energies not entirely repressed. The man, the survivor, finds his own ways out, in bluff, deciding that everything that happened was 'just … play',[13] and fantasising that they might all three have come together, in the same boat, with him driving it. The women, with no capacity for bluff, are left 'weary', and 'unhinged'.[14]

After five seconds of darkness, there is a reprise of the first movement of the play. This was originally meant to be identical, but in rehearsals for his French version (*Comédie*), Beckett decided with Jean-Marie Serreau that a variation with reduced and slower lighting and voice would be more effective.[15] As Beckett became ever more closely involved in directing and producing his own work, as well as translating his texts, variant versions proliferated. As Gontarski points out, it becomes difficult to establish which text, or performance, should be viewed as definitive; more important is to register the shift in Beckett's thinking to a more formalist, minimalist aesthetics, which can be traced through the notebooks on staging that he began to keep methodically.[16]

Distancing is achieved not only by speed of delivery, but by the blackly comic tone that is Beckett's hallmark. The frenzied central movement is crammed with grotesque comic effects. There is the shock of surprised laughter at the contrast between the wife's crude outbursts ('He stinks of bitch'),[17] the husband's obsequious platitudes, and the mistress's carefully controlled, complacent speech, in the early stages of the affair when she thinks the wife is going to be abandoned. The hypocrisy and evasions of the husband, and his familiar excuses, provoke a knowing smile. The clichés of women's willingness to be deceived, or pretend to be deceived, are a source of patronising laughter, and the husband's smug self-satisfaction also requires a smile of superiority. The audience is drawn into the music of its own derelictions. The comedy persists through the evocations of the raw violence of feeling, including implied threats of physical violence, suicide, murder, and castration. There is a razor in the wife's vanity-bag, and the sound of an old lawnmower in the background of the lovers' exchanges; in the French version, though not in the English, the mistress reports having cut off her lover's excuses. But no comedy can disguise the notes of jealousy and humiliation, and the pervasive fear of abandonment, experienced not only by the women but, in the end, by the man: 'Am I as much as ... being seen?'[18] The need to be seen and recognised pierces through as the mark of the human, beyond gender.

While the interwoven voices of *Play* have their own harmony and form of order, the flood of words that pours from the Mouth of *Not I* (1973) struggles to establish intelligible shape. No longer in physical contact, the triad of *Play*, fixed in their urns, still shape each other's present in the remembered dialogues of the past. Mouth, poised eight feet above stage level, has nothing to support herself and her words except the words themselves; no mirroring interlocutor is present to give depth to her utterance. The Auditor, of undeterminable sex – a tall figure standing downstage audience left, who punctuates Mouth's speech four times with a brief, sympathetic and impotent raising and dropping of arms – appeared only in the original version. Jocelyn Herbert, the theatre designer, reports having dinner with Beckett after watching a poor performance of Ionesco's *Le Roi se meurt*. '[A]ll the night through, the conversation had been as to whether it was possible to write a play with no action. Could you be only dramatic in words? And out of that came *Not I*.'[19] Dramatic monologues are nothing new, but the dramatic content of this one certainly is: the tragedy of a woman who, paralysed from the neck down, trying at the end of her life to tell a kind of story of her life, all fragments and repetitions, cannot figure herself as more than a third-person object ('she'), and cannot even cross the threshold to the illusory first person. No one has ever seen her, let alone watched her, but herself.

Winnie, in *Happy Days*, could make a bravura first-person production of her present, but she too could only speak of the traumatic core of her remembered life in the third person, through her story of Mildred and her dolly. Giving voice to her repressed fear of sexual invasion liberated the equally repressed knowledge that a sexual identity, as a reproductive female, is all she has, or, crucially, has lost. The whole of Mouth's life is staged in terms of story, as a continuing trauma where the only present is past. Now cut off from her body, her recollection of herself as a sexual body is minimal. Describing her birth, she first calls herself 'thing', corrects the word to 'girl' (using the term just that once), then describes herself as an 'old hag'. These moments of recognition of herself as feminine are the only times she reports having wept, once at birth and once on recognition of herself in ugly old age.

Anecdotally, the figure of Mouth was reportedly said by Beckett himself to have been inspired by the many bent old women who staggered along the country roads of Ireland; it was their voice, he said, that he heard and transposed for *Not I.*[20]

The landscapes and the events of Mouth's life may well have Ireland for their original inspiration. But out of that particular space, and beyond that particular gendered experience – or rather, that experience of the loss of gender identity in old age – Beckett has created an extreme image of the situation of many impoverished old women, in many places, unseen and ignored, and in the last analysis, an image of destitute humanity everywhere. In that sense, as Mouth says, hers is a 'typical affair'.[21]

Linda Ben-Zvi has seen in Mouth's situation the theme central to all Beckett's work, that of the unnamable subject who must speak unceasingly while recognising that words offer no knowledge of a 'real' self.[22] Feminist readings, she indicates, can present Mouth's outpourings as the suppressed of patriarchal discourse or its triumphant subversion in the form of hysteria. As in Hélène Cixous's *Portrait of Dora*, they are both; though unlike Dora, who silenced Freud and walked away from his talking cure, Mouth's ending has no hint of triumph, nowhere else to go, and no means of going. For ten seconds before the curtain rises and after it falls, her voice is heard in a continuous, unintelligible stream, signalling that the speaker is on earth, and there is no remedy.

Written in English in the spring of 1972, *Not I* was first performed in New York in September 1972 by Jessica Tandy. Directed by Beckett, the first performance in Britain was at the Royal Court on 16 January 1973 with Billie Whitelaw. Whitelaw, much later, told an interviewer that *Not I* was a play she would never do again. 'With *Not I* I did actually say "you've finally done it – you've written the unlearnable and you've written the unplayable"'; and she went on to say that doing the play was 'like falling down a long, dark narrow tunnel, with your arms and legs up and your bottom going first. Backwards into Hell. Emitting cries.'[23]

Whitelaw's description of a dizzying, intensely physical feeling of falling out of control, deep into the dark, with screams replacing speech, gets to the heart of the experience explored here, which is a darker version of the journey figured in *How It Is.* The man in that tale was crawling forward through the darkness of origins, working his way through and into a voice whose powers of creative imagination give shape and direction to the processes of his becoming. Mouth too is slowly emerging from the inchoate state of a beginning-human, working towards the will to know and say. Her voice rushes and stumbles towards the same key questions of what, who, and how it was. She too has a story to tell, formed by the experiences of her 'own' life up to her present age of seventy, marked by submission and passivity, which come as sudden, short flashes of memory. These meld with a very different kind of experience, shaped by an imperative to 'imagine' and 'understand' – directives from a mind at last becoming critical, and groping for speech. 'She did not know' moves to 'she suddenly realized'.[24] The starting point of her story takes the shape of a moment in an early April morning when she suddenly found herself in the dark. From the sudden blackout, never explained, she begins again, literally finding herself, hearing undifferentiated sound (a buzzing), seeing a faint light come and go, and establishing her position (lying down). Whereas the man in *How It Is* moves on to discover and actively explore the body of Pim, down to the genitals, Mouth is confined to her own physical form, and to the head alone; below the neck, nothing registers. There is no active exploration; she waits passively for illumination to come. Her sense-functions slowly establish themselves in this limited form. The buzzing is in her ears, or rather, she decides, her skull, and as she focuses the sound becomes a distant bell. The faint light, felt through the eyelids and then the eyes, resolves itself into the specific time of an April morning; and then come words, and her own voice, and her lips moving, cheeks, jaws, and tongue. She is holding up to herself as if for the first time the mirror of herself, naming the parts that show who, what and where she is. But she still cannot say herself as subject, only as object. Apart from her head, her body is numb.[25] Without the body, the road to the illusory 'I' is impassable.

Billie Whitelaw called Mouth's monologue unlearnable and unplayable. Syntactically fragmented, it is however not without shape. As well as the rhythms to which the actress is required to yield her voice, there are semantic structures to be grasped in Mouth's flood of phrases. There is an unfolding, sequential drama in her discovery of her thinking self. The increasingly fast- and furiously-moving operations of a brain suddenly appear in the text of a life until then 'unquestioned', 'unexamined', and are figured in a stream of unfamiliar words: 'questioning', 'realized', 'reasoned', 'awful thought', 'imagine!', 'trying to make sense'. These new conceptualisations are matched by the emergence of increasingly precise sense-responses: 'feeling so dulled', 'hearing', 'listening', 'fixing with her eye', 'words coming', 'lips moving', 'feeling coming back'. As both linguistic strands develop, the story Mouth repeatedly tells fills out, and by dint of repeated sound-strokes, builds into a powerful Impressionist sound-picture of what she is, why she has become so, and where she is now. The woman never really born, never possessed of her own body, her own experience, and her own speech, never spoken to, discovers the knowledge of body and speech in the moment of being divided from them. Like Clov as he prepares to part from Hamm, she enters the knowledge that there was something she was promised but never had, and now never will have. In her case, it was a story she could have told, but now never can.[26]

There are very few markers to her bleak story, and she passes swiftly over its trajectory. Born prematurely, abandoned by parents she never knew, she was brought up in a loveless orphanage. Nothing of importance happened to her until, as an old woman, she collapsed in the field. In the orphanage, a place she dwells on, belief in a merciful God was driven deep into her being, along with the presumption that she was destined for punishment and suffering – an idea that she now almost, but not quite, dismisses as vain and foolish. As her voice returns, it brings with it the awareness that all her life she has been denied speech, crystallised in the detailed rehearsal of three scenarios. In the shopping centre, she would stand silently in the crowd, mouth half-open, waiting for the assistant to return her old black shopping bag, so she could pay and go away. In court, in the dock, object of some unspecified charge, she had nothing to say and simply waited to be led away. Occasionally, driven by the need to speak, she would stop people in the street, pour out an unintelligible stream of words, and shrink back in shame at their stares. Unloved, unlovely, accused, guilty, despised, and ashamed; the curtain falls on an image of human waste, knowing only the imperative to go away, grabbing vainly for words to fill the endless devastation before her ending. Her last intelligible utterance links together the promises, disappointments, and appeals that have shaped the shell of an empty life: 'God is love ... tender mercies ... new every morning ... back in the field ... April morning ... face in the grass ... nothing but the larks ... pick it up –'.[27] The appeal to God is as hopeless as Winnie's invocation of the dance of love. The unintelligible muttering after the curtain falls is Mouth's final marker: the broken machine stutters on, but it can never be picked up and mended.

In *Footfalls*, written for Billie Whitelaw, which opened at the Royal Court in May 1976,[28] Beckett created a very different image of the woman who is hardly there. The play presents the hostile, mutually destructive relations of a mother aged ninety and a daughter aged forty, from the well-to-do middle class. Class status is established in swift comic detail. May's tread wears out the deep pile of the carpet; and she was, her mother says, self-confined to the house when other girls of her age were playing lacrosse. The humour is short-lived. Woman's body is again the heart of the matter, not, this time, figured onstage as an absence, but as a presence which creates another variant on the broken machine. May is a moving figure, pacing out the rhythms and patterns of her progressive abolition in the crippling confinement of the domestic space, marked out by the authority of her mother's voice.

Talking about the play to Billie Whitelaw, Beckett said he was striking out in a new direction, and he told her husband, Robert, that he was no longer sure whether the theatre was the right place for him.[29] His emphasis now was on the visual image created by the moving body. He was less concerned with his character's words than her movements, the essential point being that as the play moved forward, May's body posture should change, to communicate her progressive withdrawal into herself.[30] May's unending pacing of a strictly limited strip of floor was the image he was most concerned to get into correct shape: a regular sequence of nine paces followed by a wheel and return. The emphatic rhythm of her pacing is underlined by the scratching of her feet on the floor. In the Royal Court production, Jocelyn Herbert put emery board on the soles of May's shoes and lined her costume with taffeta to highlight the swish of her turn.[31]

The play is divided into three sections, or stanzas. The latter is Whitelaw's word, and it effectively conveys the new nature of the play, which is a lyric written in words and movement. The short playing time is important; the shorter the play, and the more condensed, the more powerful is the impact of the rhythm, the syntax, and the tone of the particular mode of being it presents. The rhythms, as always, required special attention. Whitelaw describes how with each stanza May's movements become slower, until the lights go up on the final section and the woman has evaporated, like smoke, completing the moving image of the body's inward spiral into the void.[32] The actress felt as though she was being sculpted, choreographed, painted with light, or sometimes her movements erased, all in the interest of creating an image of something not quite there, shreds of grey, fading to nothing.[33] She told James Knowlson in an interview:

> We spent hours on the walking up and down, and hours getting the relationship of the arm and the hand and the bringing down of the hand from the throat and how far this should go to the elbow. [...] I felt like a moving, musical Edvard Munch painting [...] I almost felt that he did have the paintbrush out and was painting, and, of course, what he always has in the other pocket is the rubber, because as fast as he draws a line in, he gets out that enormous india-rubber and rubs it out until it is only faintly there.[34]

As May disappears, so does her tyrannical mother. The mother's voice is in dialogue with May in the first section; it is heard in monologue in the second, repeating a dialogue between herself and May as a child; in the third, it is completely gone, a mere echo in the story May tells of the dialogue between Mrs Winter and her daughter Amy. The mother and May enact their mutual destruction, exchanging the roles of executioner and victim, the mother out of selfishness and May as revenge.

The ritual exchanges of the first stanza display May's resentment of the dutiful services she performs for her mother, and the mother's iron grasp on her authority. The language of feigned compassion (from the daughter, 'your poor lips', and from the mother, 'your poor mind') barely veils the hostility and contempt that bind them together.[35] In the second stanza, the mother's voice dominates, telling her own version of what she has done to her daughter, in language riddled with unconscious irony and double takes. Watching and monitoring her daughter, the mother speaks as the voice fully aware that she has inscribed herself in her child. This is the process adopted by the 'man' in the dark of *How It Is*, carving a name of his own invention on the body he has found, to take possession of it. Infantilising the adult woman, she drags her back into the past, describing May's confinement since she was a girl, in the space of domesticity. In an anecdote of an incident when May was still little more than a child, she interprets May's complaint about being forced to march to order ('this is not enough') as an expression of compliance.[36] She allows May no autonomous, unmonitored speech, describing contemptuously how her daughter only tries to speak for herself at night, when she imagines no one can hear her.[37]

In stanza three, May unexpectedly utters her version of her story. The first half of her monologue, starting in the third person, at first implies that the mother–daughter identities are still merged, but the listening audience slowly separates the two. The one who is forgotten emerges as the mother, now dead, and the one who is the daughter walks out of the house at nightfall, slips somehow into the locked church, and there resumes her incessant pacing. This figure is only a semblance, faint, pale grey, an object rather than a person, who commands listeners to watch the transparent shade passing by.[38] There is a brief reference to 'his poor arm' 'that poor arm'.[39] Arms reach out tenderly, hold, help up, or sometimes they attack. May has no more to say about what happened with that masculine arm, but in the language she learned from her mother, in which she is still confined, mock sympathy was the victim's instrument of attack. There may have been an attempt to create a heterosexual relationship, thwarted by May's inability to act in any mode but the tormentor–victim binary learned from her mother. There is no way of knowing, as, like all May's experience, what happened has been repressed.

The second half of May's monologue switches abruptly into what sounds like a reading from a book. This is May's attempt to vary the language she has learned, using a different learned language, to force a way out of the pit. The reader she addresses, like the listeners and watchers she invokes in the church, are invented interlocutors: the sounding-boards that create the semblance of communication. She ventriloquises a dialogue over supper between old Mrs Winter and her daughter, Amy. The mother insists, in an increasingly hectoring tone, that her daughter was in church that evening, and she heard her say Amen, while Amy insists she was not there. She does not concede, but her silence allows the mother's words to win by default.

May returns to her pacing, and then picks up again the voices of Mother and Amy, this time reprising her own dialogue with her mother in the first stanza, where Mother enjoined May to have done turning it all over in her mind. The light fades out and up again, faintly, and fades out on the strip of stage, with no trace of May left. The confining domestic space and the mother's overpowering voice, even after her death, have internalised their rhythms in the daughter, diminishing and dissolving her. May's minimal attempts to resist, producing only minimal changes in names and places, could only identify her as a string of negatives: 'I saw nothing, heard nothing, of any kind. I was not there.'[40]

Against these not-women, who end in desolation, *Rockaby*, written in 1980 and first performed in Buffalo, New York, in 1981, with Billie Whitelaw in the rocking chair, develops a very different image of a daughter, which ends in rhythms of fullness and consolation. The woman who dies in the rocking chair where her mother died rocks to her end at the moment she chooses, effortlessly, and to the pre-recorded sound of her own voice, in a rhythm far removed from May's strict, tense pacing. The stage directions show her dressed to impress, as for a party, in a black high-necked evening gown, studded with jet sequins, that, like her headdress, glitters as she rocks in the subdued spotlight that sits constantly on her face. She speaks only to command that the recording play more, a little more softly each time. Her eyes, in section 1 alternately open unblinking and closed, are increasingly closed in sections 2 and 3, and closed for good in section 4, where the recorded voice itself softens. In this play, Billie Whitelaw said, the eye movements, and keeping the eyes open, were the acting challenge; her own eyes were completely wrecked by the fierce light of particular plays.[41]

What she listens to is the long, lulling poem, a litany of short, repeated phrases, of a long, full life, lived to the beat of her own choices ('time she stopped', she says seven times from her chair, along with her recording). She spent her life looking, like everyone else, for 'another like herself', 'another living soul'.[42] She was locked, like everyone else, into the gradually slowing rhythms of life's stages, inhabiting worlds outside and then worlds within. Her imagery is shaped by domestic spaces and places, windows, stairs and chairs; but hers is not the home satirised in *Footfalls*, the limited strip of carpet, watched over by a controlling mother. She has lived in an outside, public world, busy with movement, seeing and being seen by others, before going back in to look out from her window at other windows, all with lowered blinds, then descending the steep stair to the rocking chair her mother died in, lowering her own blind, and sinking gratefully into the arms of the chair, and the mother, to become 'her own other / own other living soul'.[43]

There is a strand of keening sadness weaving through her poem, in the failure of her lifelong search for some other like herself, hungry to be seen, and in her recognition that the unrequited longing to know one's own desire mirrored in others is a universal source of grief. On the threshold of death, as her eyes close, the long-desired rhythms of recognition and merging intensify.[44] But at the end she can choose to embrace the sadness of having done with the search. Like Winnie, she goes down singing, but, unlike Winnie, there is no irony in the rhythms of her song. She is not disappointed by the gaze that mirrors her own, for she never deluded herself that she had found one. Control is relinquished to the arms of her mother, and she herself, the mother's arms, and the rocking machine, dissolve into a single injunction to 'stop her eyes/fuck life/stop her eyes/rock her off'.[45] The languages of love and death fuse together in the vanishing rhythms of a gentle ending, both accepted and inevitable, which is the culmination of a life that has enjoyed its full complement of desire, loss, and failure, lived with eyes always wide open.

The mother this daughter follows into silence was said by others to be mad, but unlike Beckett's other mothers, she is the figure of a nurturing inheritance. This mother is the analogue of the father of the old man whose eye presides over the unrolling of *That Time*, and whose green greatcoat, the analogue of the old woman's rocking chair, holds the son in its embrace. *That Time* is another version of *Rockaby*'s evocation of time stopped, a life-narrative commanded to unroll under the unblinking gaze of its author, in the form of his and her own preferred words. The shape of the chaos of being – how it is – is a matter of vision and sound, eyes and rhythms.

Watch this Space

Beckett's anxiety that the theatre might no longer be the right place for him had little justification in the changing conditions of the stage in the second half of the twentieth century, which he himself had done so much to bring about. Peter Brook's autobiography, *The Empty Space* (1968), points to the openness of the terms by which drama now operated. Any empty space could be termed a stage; and for an act of theatre, all that was required was for someone to walk across that space, watched by someone else.[46]

Beckett's plays work on the new definitions of stage, actor and audience that Brook's simple statement implies. Most important is their emphasis on the role of the audience, who must be made aware of their responsibilities as watchers, eyes that participate in the creation of meaning in the empty space of the stage. The search for living souls is conducted from both sides of the footlights. As Beckett's actors are trained to adapt their bodies to the rhythms of his words and movements, and to respond to the spotlights and fades his careful stage directions stipulate, so the thousand-arsed Spectator is required to look at productions from inside Beckett's perspective, and to see not what s/he is used to seeing, but what Beckett wants to be seen: a new form of performance. Jonathan Kalb has described 'a performance sensibility specific to late Beckett', which needs acting styles very different from those of the earlier plays, and also raises different issues of audience perception and aesthetic form.[47] In some plays, he notes, confronting an often motionless tableau, the audience is required to meditate on its metaphoric significance while 'a flow of words emanates from the stage, guiding meditation'.[48] Other plays reduce words to a minimum, a litany of repeated phrases, or pre-verbal sound, or silence, or they play words off against music, and run the gamut of motion from a minimum of gesture to choreographed patterning by players who criss-cross the stage in various combinations. In every variant, what remains constant is the requirement laid on the audience to think about the image created on stage: not necessarily, perhaps, pondering its metaphoric significance, but pondering the performative nature of what they are seeing, and the fact that performance and process is basically how it is.

Later Beckett began quite early on. *Act Without Words I*, a mime for one player written in 1956 with music by Beckett's nephew, John Beckett, was first performed at the Royal Court in April 1957. In a parody of comic knockabout, the mime plays through the hopes and disappointments that constitute the human journey. Thrown abruptly backwards onto an empty stage, flooded with dazzling light, the player responds to a sequence of whistles from right and then left, following them offstage, only to be flung back again. More whistles attract his attention to a sequence of things that appear on stage, lowered out of nowhere, seeming to promise distraction or relief: a tree, a pair of scissors, a carafe of water, three cubes of different sizes, and a rope. All of them, despite his ingenuity in devising ways of reaching them, are raised out of his grasp. The clowning is exploited for maximum entertainment value. He climbs and falls, moving with careful, exaggerated attention to details of his actions and gestures, and at each repeated attempt and failure, in the tradition of clowns, his crestfallen disappointment produces more laughter. Finally, having exhausted his options, he turns to the scissors with the clear intention of killing himself. At this point in the drama, all the things are whisked away. On his side, motionless, facing the auditorium, he ignores each thing as they descend in turn, one more time, and in a final gesture, looks away to his empty hands. Knockabout plays out into the tragedy of failure, and the audience's laughter trails away into embarrassment, with the realisation that they have misread the signals, and that their discomfiture is as much a part of this performance as the downfall of the player on stage. The watchers must now watch themselves, and each other.

This is the process described by Wolfgang Iser. The 'toppling' of audience expectations, created by the complex contradictions within the comic experience, is for Iser one of the fundamental dynamics of comic effect: the spectator, taken by surprise, loses all sense of his distance from the action, and, caught inside its tensions, thrown into confusion, takes refuge finally in laughter.[49] This laughter is the body's response to the recognition that it is in a situation beyond its control, which it can no longer understand, and the collective laughter of conventional comic theatre provides the audience with mutual reassurance. Beckett's on-stage characters and his audiences mirror one another in their persistent expectation of conventional interpretations and resolutions, but they don't get them. In Beckett's theatre, collective laughter gives way to the hesitant, repressed laughter of scattered individuals, no longer sure of themselves. The distinctive feature of Beckett's comedy, Iser argues, is that it repeatedly plays with, destabilises, and reassures its audience, only finally to plunge them into a gulf of anxiety that offers no way out. Laughter, conventionally, enables the audience to claim to itself that the situation is not serious. As soon as that happens, Beckett twists back into seriousness; laughter is no longer an option, and the audience must recognise the anguish it creates for itself by its refusal to think outside the walls of the box.

Act Without Words II, written at the same time and produced at the ICA (Institute of Contemporary Arts) in London, in January 1960, is a mime for two players. It plays out on a brightly-lit narrow platform across the back of the dark stage, which creates the effect of a frieze. At the beginning, two sacks, each with a player inside, and a heap of clothes, are lined up at the right of the stage. At the end, the three bundles are lined up on the left. In turn, players A and B are prodded out of their sacks by a goad, reminiscent of the compère's stick in the music-hall tradition. Each in turn mimes his way through his daily routine, dresses in the piled-up clothes, undresses down to his shirt, and returns to his sack. Player A is slow and clumsy. He broods, swallows pills, and prays his way through his allotted time, and he has comic difficulty with his dressing and undressing. Player B is smart, vigorous, clean and tidy, and keen: he has a watch and a map to keep him up to scratch. He gets through more comic business than A, but each has the same time to fill. The mime ends as A is goaded out of his sack once more to start his routine, and once again, laughter sours as the audience recognises that they have misread the performance. They are not watching a one-off clown show, just for laughs, but a serious representation of the repeated trivialities in which men spend the time between birth and death. The watchers must reassess the content and the form of what they have seen on stage, which can now be read as the running frieze of human history. In the process, their own lives are called into question. Audience response here is not intellectual but affective, and Beckett's approach is very much in line with Antonin Artaud's design for a new kind of theatre, which aims: 'To reforge the links, the chain of a rhythm when audiences saw their own real lives in a show. We must allow audiences to identify with the show breath by breath and beat by beat.'[50]

Breath and beat are the primary elements of the stage image offered for meditation in *Breath* (1969). For five seconds, the audience observes a stage scattered with rubbish, all lying on the same level, and lit by a faint light. A recording plays of the faint, brief cry of a new-born infant, and an indrawn breath, lasting ten seconds, while the light increases slowly to maximum. After another five seconds of silence, there is an exhalation of breath (another recording), as the light slowly decreases, over ten seconds, to its original faintness. An identical cry is heard, and the faint light is held in silence for five seconds. The stage directions stipulate that the sounds are recorded, the cries identical, and the switching on and off of the light, and the breathing, are strictly synchronised. The light makes visible the basic rhythm of life, the breathing in and out whose counterpart in *The Unnamable* was the thudding syntax echoing the systole/diastole of the heartbeat. Life and death cries are clearly human, and the rubbish is equally clearly the waste of human living, where there is nothing doing and nothing to be done. Things are there, unconnected, at the start, and still there, unchanged, at the end, marks in a landscape unchanged by human passage.

The essence of being is evoked in the sole movement of sound and light, in a cool aesthetic form which invites meditation not, perhaps, on the metaphorical but the material nature of the image. Famously, Beckett conceived this work for Kenneth Tynan, who had been pressing him for a piece. He gave it to Tynan with strict instructions not to vary from the stage directions. The director and critic, who in earlier days had shown sympathetic understanding of the intentions of Beckett's theatre, used the piece in his New York revue, *Oh Calcutta!*, and added to the rubbish on the stage a scattering of naked bodies – turning a scientifically objective observation into a machine for creating a cheap thrill, and ensuring, for this particular performance, the comfortable return of the thousand-arsed Spectator.[51]

Ohio Impromptu, written in 1981 and first performed at Ohio State University in the same year, is an induction for the audience into a new experience of listening, which opens doors for each one to create their own dream. It stages an identical Listener and Reader, in long black coats and with long white hair, sitting on opposite sides of a table, each leaning his head on his right hand, with a black hat between them which could belong to either, or both. The Reader reads a story about a lonely man in a long black coat, whose love has gone, who is visited time after time by another man in a long black coat, who reads to him through the night, a sad tale, a rhythmic litany of regret and loss. The Listener, his face hidden throughout, knocks on the table from time to time to require the repetition of a phrase, enhancing the swing of the narrative. The story of the repeated visits ends with the visitor, having closed the book, saying he will not return again; the two characters sit motionless, staring at each other.[52] The story of the two on stage also ends; the Reader closes the book, and they sit staring at each other until the light fades out. The final image on stage is as close a representation as can be made of the unspeakable mystery of death. In the story read by the Reader: 'With never a word exchanged they grew to be as one.'[53] The self knows itself as living, alongside its invented company, as long as the words go on. Without dialogue, the split aspects of the knowing self collapse into the unknowing point of origin. Here is almost the end, but not quite, for the mirror-personae are still reading one another, through their mutual gaze.

The piece begins 'Little is left to tell', and ends 'Nothing is left to tell'.[54] In between is the performance of the brief span of human life, situated from the beginning in its ending. The short space has infinite depths, created by the infinite duplication of the tale-telling that resonates between the frame of the two black coats. The mirroring-effect of the onstage action has its counterpart in the relationship created between the performance and the audience, drawing them too into the music of time passing, loss, losing, ageing, and ending. Beckett the tale-teller finds a different kind of company, something more than a mirror, in the listening and watching audience, who recognise something of themselves in the story of love and loss. Caught in the mutual fascination figured on stage, they are drawn into a deep place of some deeper, inexpressible mood and feeling of their own, beyond intellectual understanding and beyond sense-perception: 'Buried in who knows what profounds of mind. Of mindlessness. Whither no light can reach. No sound.'[55]

Catastrophe, written in French for the Avignon Festival of 1982, and dedicated to the Czech playwright, poet and dissident Václav Havel (at the time in prison in Czechoslovakia), stages the process of creating the stage image. The plot follows the interactions of the director, his female assistant, the actor, and the (invisible) lighting man, through to the final performance. This is a crueller and more violent version of the relation of audience to performance than that offered in *Ohio Impromptu*, and the self-knowing it inspires is harsh and ugly. In *Catastrophe*, the tormentor–victim binary is the basic mode of being, and meaning is created through the subjection of others.

The Director appears in a fur coat and his female assistant in a white overall, with a pencil behind her ear. The stage directions say the rest of their appearance is unimportant, as is that of the solitary actor, who shivers in pyjamas and a dressing-gown. The players are all functions of the performance, and their costumes make explicit the power relations at work. Having first demonstrated his power over his assistant by systematically substituting his version of how the victim should look for hers, the Director moves offstage to pre-empt the space of the audience, and in their name demand more nudity and whiter flesh from his increasingly humiliated actor. By the end, the victim has been reduced to a lowered head. The artwork completed to the Director's satisfaction, he commands a final run-through, declaring that the actor will have the spectators standing to applaud. The offstage audience dutifully produces loud applause – which dies as the actor raises his head, and fixes the real-time audience with his gaze. Catastrophe, the denouement of the play, no longer merely an image, crosses the footlights, and the eyes of the victim reverse the balance of power.

The doubling of the audience in this play underlines the role and responsibility of those who think they only watch. There is the on-stage audience, invoked by the Director, which applauds and then freezes into terror; and there is the audience in the real theatre. They too have acquiesced in the process of exploitation and humiliation, the whole performance of costuming, make-up and lighting, and the director's pre-emption of their response. At the end they are left shifting uncomfortably in their seats, abandoned to deal by themselves with the challenge of their collusion in atrocity.[56]

What Where, Beckett's last play for the theatre, produced in New York in June 1983, has four near-identical players, in grey gowns and with grey hair, Bam, Bem, Bim and Bom, and Bam is doubled as his Voice, speaking over the exchanges of the four. They are, Voice says, the last five. Voice, off to one side, in shadow, speaks at start and finish, to state what and where the performance is to show; to determine its mode (first 'without words', and then 'with words'); to switch on and off the light that prompts the onstage action to begin; and to comment on the progress of the action ('good', or 'not good').[57] This is the voice of the author, who chooses and experiments with the shape and development of his artwork, and who alone can finally deem it a satisfactory presentation of what and where he is. As in *How It Is*, to have achieved the capacity to voice himself as his own author, the individual subject must already have made the journey into awareness of split selfhood, as his own subject and object, which he now rehearses for an audience of watchers and listeners; these are the third party of this creation, without whom the totality of being is not reached. The process of becoming self loops round, and being, like a play in a theatre, only exists in replay.

The opening chant, a schematic, still-life presentation of what and where, expressed in the language of time, evokes beginning ('In the present as were we still./ It is spring./ Time passes.').[58] It unfolds into a series of variations without words, presenting the originator of this time in the figure of Bam, the prime actor in his own production, and the sequence of his creations. There is a false start in which Bam stands with an interlocutor, but Voice rejects this and starts again: the vision of self as a singular element must be grasped intuitively, before the self can be totally known as a working process, coming into being through the conscious creation of other aspects of itself. Bam now speaks in his own right, and engages in dialogue with his secondary creations, three variations on himself. Two acts might have made a series in *Waiting for Godot*, but here three movements have been chosen. In *Waiting for Godot*, time also passed, and the leaves appeared on the tree, but for the figures in that play, locked in delusion, the only knowledge of their own being in time came in the form of frustration, fear, and anxiety. In *What Where*, as time passes, says the Voice, from spring to winter, there is a journey into truth. It is a minimal truth ('Is that all?' is repeated several times, by Bem), but Voice finds it satisfying enough.

Truth emerges as the audience listens to the dialogue exchanges. Bam instructs each of his delegates in turn, in the form and language of a gangster film, to 'give the works' to an unseen victim. Violence and the threat of death are the conditions in which Bam/ Beckett makes sense of himself; as Voice says at the end, 'Make sense who may.'[59] The form that mediates this search for sense is also a distraction, and the audience must discover for themselves that hearing only the obvious, thrilling words (the object of violence screams, weeps, begs for mercy and passes out) deafens them to the small, important variations in the delegates' reports. Over time, Bam repeats his demands on his delegates, threatens to give them too the works if they don't do better, and challenges them if they say that they can't keep alive the subject given them, or find the answer he wants. In time, small variations emerge in small words, and the sense Bam is looking for comes closer. What 'he' says is first reported as 'anything', then 'it', and finally 'what'. In another sequence, 'it' is replaced by 'where'. Bam finally calls stop, at a point that seems no different from any other, and leaves the stage. Voice approves, announces that it is winter, and announces at last his own appearance: 'In the end I appear.'[60] Bam reappears, to stand silently on stage. Voice repeats his opening chant, but now the first-person plural has become first-person singular, and there is a new attribute to Voice's position: 'Without journey'; so that Voice can conclude, 'That is all'.[61] Self has been represented as being alone, figured more fully than at the start, in the retrospect of the stillness after all the false starts and searches for what and where are over. Voice switches off the light on Bam, and then the light goes off on Voice. At the end, it is the audience that remains, enjoined to make its own sense of that final play of light. The variations of performance are not exhausted; they go on resonating in the theatrical space beyond the footlights, where the audience, engaging in the process of performance, has its own chance to become 'who'. 'Who', 'what', and 'where' are not questions with definitive answers, but states to be explored and experienced.

NOTES

1 A selection of stage and radio drama on a range of themes, including gender, was made in 'Beckett Shorts', part of the French Theatre Season, 30 September–20 December 1997, performed at the RSC, Stratford-upon-Avon, and directed by Katie Mitchell, with a cast including Juliet Stevenson. The brochure announced that 'For the first time, *Footfalls*, *Rockaby*, *Not I*, *Embers*, *A Piece of Monologue* and *That Time* have been thematically selected to provide a fascinating programme which explores time, memory, death and gender' (p.10).

2 S.E. Gontarski (ed.), Introduction to *The Theatrical Notebooks of Samuel Beckett, Vol. IV, The Shorter Plays* (London: Faber and Faber Ltd, and New York: Grove Press, 1999), p.xv.

3 The English-language premiere was in New York, in January 1964, directed by Alan Schneider, and the play opened in London, at the Old Vic, in April 1964, directed by George Devine, and in Paris, directed by Jean-Marie Serreau (*Comédie*), in June 1964. Beckett was heavily involved with all four productions. Gontarski's Introduction to *The Theatrical Notebooks … IV*, pp.xv–xxix, discusses the different productions, and the authorial revisions to the text which were generated in the production process.

4 Whitelaw, *Billie Whitelaw*, p.80.

5 Ibid.

6 See Whitelaw, *Billie Whitelaw*, p.76.

7 Samuel Beckett, *Play* (1964); *CDW* 1986, p.311.

8 On Beckett's relationship with Barbara Bray, see Chapter 7, p.166, pp.177–8, p.196.

9 Whitelaw, *Billie Whitelaw*, p.77. The most recent performance of *Not I*, by Lisa Dwan, who was advised on technique by Whitelaw, reduced the running speed to nine minutes (see the article by Lisa Dwan, 'Beckett's *Not I*: how I became the

ultimate motormouth', *The Guardian* [8 May 2013], at http://www.theguardian.com/culture/2013/may/08/beckett-not-i-lisa-dwan. Consulted 28 October 2014.) Dwan's performance was televised on Sky Arts 2 on Wednesday 31 July 2013 as part of an hour-long documentary, *Samuel Beckett: Not I* (see Rupert Hawksley, 'Samuel Beckett's *Not I* to be performed on television', *The Telegraph* [27 June 2013], http://www.telegraph.co.uk/culture/tvandradio/10146406/Samuel-Becketts-Not-I-to-be-performed-on-television.html. Consulted 29 October 2014.) See also Adam Mars-Jones, '"Not I"', *London Review of Books*, 36, 5 (6 March 2014), p.22.

10 Whitelaw, *Billie Whitelaw*, p.78.

11 Whitelaw, *Billie Whitelaw*, p.81.

12 Beckett, *Play*; *CDW* 1986, p.312.

13 Beckett, *Play*; *CDW* 1986, p.313.

14 Beckett, *Play*; *CDW* 1986, pp.316–17.

15 Gontarski, Introduction to *The Theatrical Notebooks ... IV*, p.xxii.

16 Gontarski, Introduction to *The Theatrical Notebooks ... IV*, pp.xxiii–iv.

17 Beckett, *Play*; *CDW* 1986, p.308

18 Beckett, *Play*; *CDW* 1986, p.317.

19 Jocelyn Herbert, in Knowlson and Knowlson, *Beckett Remembering*, p.167.

20 Deirdre Bair quotes Beckett himself telling her this (Bair, *Samuel Beckett*, p.623).

21 Samuel Beckett, *Not I* (1973); *CDW*, 1986, p.376.

22 Linda Ben-Zvi, '*Not I*: Through a Tube Starkly', in Linda Ben-Zvi, *Women in Beckett: Performance and Critical Perspectives* (Urbana and Chicago: University of Illinois, Illini Books Edition, 1992), pp.243–8.

23 Deborah Philips, 'Interview: Billie Whitelaw', *Women's Review*, Issue 4 (February 1986), p.8.

24 Beckett, *Not I*; *CDW*, 1986, p.377.

25 Beckett, *Not I*; *CDW*, 1986, p.381.

26 Beckett, *Not I*; *CDW*, 1986, pp.381–2.

27 Beckett, *Not I*; *CDW*, 1986, p.383.

28 Programmed by the Royal Court for Beckett's seventieth birthday celebrations, the play was staged together with *That Time*, centred on Patrick Magee, the two described by Billie Whitelaw as complementary pieces (Whitelaw, *Billie Whitelaw*, p.144).

29 Whitelaw, *Billie Whitelaw*, p.145.

30 Whitelaw, *Billie Whitelaw*, p.141.

31 Whitelaw, *Billie Whitelaw*, p.144. Hildegard Schmahl, playing May in the German premiere, argued at length for Beckett to supply some psychological motivation for her character, and was not satisfied with his advice to emphasise her footsteps, and his explanation that his play had been built up round the picture of pacing: her

character was living a particular form of the human condition, so what mattered in this performance was the bodily image she created (Jonathan Kalb, *Beckett in Performance*, pp.64–5).

32 Whitelaw, *Billie Whitelaw*, p.142.

33 Whitelaw, *Billie Whitelaw*, p.147.

34 Billie Whitelaw, in Knowlson and Knowlson, *Beckett Remembering*, p.170 (extract from interview by James Knowlson in *Journal of Beckett Studies*, 3 [Summer 1978], pp.85–90).

35 Samuel Beckett, *Footfalls* (1976); *CDW* 1986, p.400.

36 Beckett, *Footfalls*; *CDW* 1986, p.401.

37 Ibid.

38 Beckett, *Footfalls*; *CDW* 1986, p.402.

39 Ibid.

40 Beckett, *Footfalls*; *CDW* 1986, p.403.

41 Deborah Philips, 'Interview: Billie Whitelaw', p.7.

42 Samuel Beckett, *Rockaby* (1982); *CDW* 1986, p.437.

43 Beckett, *Rockaby*; *CDW* 1986, p.441.

44 Beckett, *Rockaby*; *CDW* 1986, p.441.

45 Beckett, *Rockaby*; *CDW* 1986, p.442.

46 Peter Brook, *The Empty Space* (1968); rpt. Harmondsworth: Penguin Books 1990, p.11.

47 Kalb's analysis of *Ohio Impromptu*, for instance, shows how different actors, like different directors, can bring out different levels of meaning or create more or less ambiguous experiences. The actor Alvin Epstein ignored the ambiguities, and looked for realistic motives to shape his presentation, while David Warrilow, not interested in psychological reality, aware that there are questions, but believing it not his job to find and suggest answers, thought that the way forward was to establish the right musical tone (Kalb, *Beckett in Performance*, pp.59–60).

48 Kalb, *Beckett in Performance*, p.49.

49 Wolfgang Iser, 'The Art of Failure: The Stifled Laugh in Beckett's Theater', Chapter 8, *Prospecting: From Reader Response to Literary Anthropology* (Baltimore, MD and London: Johns Hopkins University Press, 1989); see especially pp.152–74.

50 Antonin Artaud, *Le théâtre et son double* ([1938] Paris : Gallimard, 1964, p.95), cit. Susan Bennett, *Theatre Audiences. A Theory of Production and Reception*, 2nd edn (London and New York: Routledge, 1997), p.38.

51 See Peter Lennon, 'Evenings with Sam', p.23. Tynan's revue was staged at the Eden Theater, New York, 16 June 1969.

52 Samuel Beckett, *Ohio Impromptu* (1981); *CDW* 1986, p.448.

53 Beckett, *Ohio Impromptu*; *CDW* 1986, p.447.

54 Beckett, *Ohio Impromptu*; *CDW* 1986, p.445, p.448.

55 Beckett, *Ohio Impromptu*; *CDW* 1986, p.448.

56 See Susan Bennett, '*Theatre Audiences*', p.11, for a discussion of audience doubling.

57 Samuel Beckett, *What Where* (1984); *CDW* 1986, pp.470–2.

58 Beckett, *What Where*; *CDW* 1986, p.471.

59 Beckett, *What Where*; *CDW* 1986, p.476.

60 Ibid.

61 Ibid.

CHAPTER 7

Broadcasting Beckett

One of the many paradoxes Beckett presents is the contrast between the shy speaker, who opens up only to his closest friends, and the exuberant writer, with his driving need to communicate as clearly and truthfully as possible, to the widest audience possible. The fast-developing wireless and electronic technologies of the post-war world offered him a whole new range of ways of saying, and of enabling the thousand-arsed Spectator to construct new responses to what was being said. Between the two worlds of live and mediated performance, Beckett's work built its distinctive bridges. In the 1980s, Ronald Hayman, writing in *The Listener*, suggested that it was the Third Programme that had laid the foundations for the success of *Waiting for Godot* in the 1950s; the BBC, he thought, had taught its audiences how to listen.[1]

Beckett on Radio

The restricted space of the little theatre – with the spectators pressed up close against the action, pulled over the fourth wall when required, to become part of the performance – was one kind of ideal workshop for Beckett's creative projects. Radio, with its potentially huge, faceless audiences listening to equally faceless voices, which nevertheless creates a sense of real presence in unbounded space, held a very different kind of attraction. Beckett seems to have been fascinated from an early stage by this medium of pure sound, where voices exist in a net of resonance, and the essence of the artwork was defined by its emergence from darkness.[2] He welcomed the opportunities as well as the challenges emerging in the new technology. 'He was very, very technical,' according to Martin Esslin, who took over as Assistant Head of the Radio Drama Department of the BBC in 1961, 'his interest in the purely craftsmanship side of things was absolutely fascinating. [...] He was asking people how does one cut the thing and what's the best way of doing it and so on.'[3]

Roger Blin organised the first radio broadcast of Beckett's work, the shortened version of *En attendant Godot*, which preceded the stage production.[4] A broadcast of the English translation was mooted by the BBC Drama Department in the spring of 1953, but the plan fell through. The first English-language broadcast of *Waiting for Godot* took place late on 27 April 1960 with Patrick Magee, by then one of Beckett's favourite actors. Magee was paid thirty guineas, plus eight guineas for the extra rehearsal the play was felt to need.[5]

From the start, there were keen admirers of Beckett's work in the drama department of the new BBC Third Programme. John Morris and Donald McWhinnie became close friends as well as collaborators. Barbara Bray, Beckett's future lover, who had begun with the BBC in 1953 as a script editor, was one of the few women of senior standing in the department, and also an important and respected translator. She first met Beckett in 1956, during the production of his radio play *All That Fall*. There was serious commitment to the introduction of avant-garde drama to British radio audiences, and Bray, like Morris and McWhinnie, regularly travelled to Europe to seek out and commission work by Marguerite Duras, Robert Pinget, Ugo Betti and Luigi Pirandello.[6] The Third Programme struggled hard to get Beckett's work before audiences, to explain it, and as Barbara Bray put it, to educate the public's ear.[7] Listening figures were slowly pushed up over time, and the proportion of listeners who liked what they heard gradually increased, though the majority remained resistant. The Audience Research Report on the half-hour *New Comment* programme on Beckett that was transmitted on the Third Programme, at 8.00 p.m. on Wednesday 11 October 1961, reported on a sample of 61 people, the 8 per cent of the Third Programme Listening Panel who had heard all or most of the broadcast, and calculated an Appreciation Index of 56 per cent (the average for the *New Comment* series was 61 per cent). The negative comments were very strong. A farmer noted that 'Not being a passionate adorer of Samuel Beckett, these rhapsodies make me sick.' A retired art mistress wrote that 'Beckett's plays mean absolutely nothing to me and are a further proof of decadence in literature.' A teacher joined her in condemnation, declaring that '[Beckett] is on a par with some modern painters and composers – meaningless to normal people'. However, it was also generally agreed that the short discussion that had taken place between Martin Esslin, Patrick Magee, and Karl Miller had been interesting and useful in clearing some of the fog around Beckett's work.[8]

The Head of Drama, Val Gielgud, was not a fan of Beckett's work, but he saw it as his duty to keep his listeners up to date with new developments, and he invited Beckett to write a play for radio. Beckett found the invitation very attractive, and he wrote to Nancy Cunard to tell her that inspiration for the work was already coming through to him in the form of sound effects: 'Never thought about Radio play technique but in the dead of t'other night got a gruesome idea full of cartwheels and dragging feet and puffing and panting which may or may not lead to something.'[9] He wrote to another friend, the writer Aidan Higgins, to report that he was tempted by the offer: 'feet dragging and breath short and cart wheels and imprecations from the Brighton Road to Foxrock Station and back, insentient old mares in foal being welted by the cottagers and the devil tattered in the ditch – boyhood memories.'[10] The rhythms of the play, *All That Fall*, were already taking shape.

All That Fall was broadcast on the Third Programme on 13 January 1957.[11] Patrick Magee was paid ten guineas, plus eight guineas for extra rehearsals.[12] It was welcomed by Roy Walker, writing in *The Listener*, as an important example of pure radio drama, and a number of congratulatory letters from ordinary listeners appeared in the same issue.[13]

Beckett was preoccupied then, and later, by the quality of the sound effects. He wrote to his producer, Donald McWhinnie, that he wanted sounds coming from real animals not human imitations; he agreed that they should have the unreal quality of the other sounds in the production, but he thought that their absurdly appropriate occurrence should manage that. He suggested there might be some distortion of the real originals by technical means, and in the event, real sounds were enhanced electronically.[14] Later, Beckett was to express dislike of the electronic drone heard under the waves in *Embers*, and the sound of the chamber door closing at the beginning of *Rough for Radio II*; he made a point of asking Everett C. Frost, who organised a set of new recordings for the American market, not to copy them.[15]

Frost notes correctly that the aim of *All That Fall* was not to render the story as an objective natural reality, but to represent Mrs Rooney's experience of her reality, in the form of its processing through her perceptions and responses – the experience that creates existence. Radio, in his opinion, was uniquely able to do this. The audience experiences her as she experiences herself, as an accumulation of sounds: the countryside around her, her own dragging footsteps, and the music of 'Death and the Maiden', coming from an old house on her road. The first words she utters are produced out of the sounds of her everyday life, prompted into form by the rhythms of art.[16] It is of course not just the assemblage of sounds but the rhythms into which they are shaped, cut and timed by Beckett, that create Mrs Rooney's existence for the audience as an effect of calculated form.

This play saw Beckett's first placing on centre stage of the relationship of the heterosexual couple. Between the radio play and the stage drama, *Happy Days*, the differences are not only the formal ones that arise from different media, sound and vision, but also thematic. The ugly viciousness of gendered dependency is more to the forefront throughout the Rooneys' situation and relationship, and the listeners' participation in Mrs Rooney's despair is more intimate and more intense. There is none of the distraction provided by the 'things' that populate Winnie's happy days, and the final confrontation of female powerlessness with the knowledge of murderous masculine violence is uniquely stark and terrifying.

The body of 70-year-old Maddy Rooney, grossly fat, breathless, just out of hospital, and childless since the death of little Minnie, is the formal centre of the play. The weight of the body is amplified to bring out the stifling material experience of the human condition, trapped in the enclosure which is earthly form.[17] Mrs Rooney's panting is the sound correlate of Winnie's mound, and it also points to the narrow frontier that separates the human condition and the animal. The farmyard sounds on which the broadcast opened do indeed have a human edge to them, despite Beckett's requests, and they match the grunts of the woman as she drags herself along the lane. The motif continues in her grunts as she is pushed into Mr Slocum's car, and in her cackling laugh. What differentiates her noises from the animals is the brief phrase of the death march she hums as she goes, which disappears into the funereal drum beat that rhythms the Rooneys' final walk home from the railway station. Consciousness of waiting death is what makes her human, and the second of her songs is 'Lead Kindly Light', the dirge-like hymn that mourns the darkness of the night and the distance from home.

The private body and the social body are the source of her woes, succinctly spoken: 'destroyed with [...] gentility and churchgoing and fat and rheumatism and childlessness.'[18] She cannot endure, and yet heroically she drags herself along. No space is safe. On the road, she and the passing cyclist are almost knocked over by Connolly's van, but staying at home is no safer: simply, a more protracted form of ending.[19]

Murderous violence and unrequited desire for love, tears and wild laughter, the grunts of animals and the roar of the train that joins country home to city office, come together in a synthesis of the universal human road to nowhere. But there are also specific referents. The play was written in a moment of European-wide desolation, in the aftermath of the Suez Crisis, and Beckett was experiencing the hardships of daily life in Paris without fuel, as he wrote to Barney Rosset in December 1956, promising him a copy of *All That Fall*.[20] More particularly, the Ireland he had left behind him determines the setting, with the landscape and inhabitants borrowed from Foxrock, and the mood, coloured by the death two years earlier of his brother Frank.[21] David Warrilow, who acted in Frost's 1986 production, pointed in an interview to the distinctive Irishness of the play which, to Beckett's surprise, had been delivered in Irish accents; Warrilow had, he said, himself seen the Foxrock railway station which supplied one of the settings of the play.[22] Propped up by Miss Fitt against the wall of that station platform, Maddy Rooney surveys the setting in all its local detail – the station, the racecourse with rails and stands, surrounding hills, the respectable villagers, and the blue sky – painfully and tearfully aware of how different it is, seen through her eyes.[23]

There is indeed an Irish accent to the language, especially Mrs Rooney's, although again she is aware of her difference, and the way her simple words are distorted by the strangeness of her rhythms and inflections. Christopher Ricks has brilliantly analysed the comic effect of her speech.[24] But both language and situations go far beyond the Irishness in which they began, as does the comedy of character. The slapstick humour, like the comic stereotypes, is transnational. The fat woman stuck in a car, or half way up the station steps, is straight out of Bamforth's seaside postcards, while Miss Fitt, frequently rendered 'distray' by thinking of her Maker, to the point where she eats the doily instead of the bread and butter, is any middle-class spinster with pretensions.[25] Only Maddy Rooney escapes the stereotypes, declaring the gulf that divides her from her fellow-villagers and puts her firmly alongside her creator: 'I estrange them all.'[26] Demanding Miss Fitt's reluctant arm to help her climb the station steps, she brushes aside all norms and conventions, threatening to 'scream down the parish! [...] Pismires do it for one another. [*Pause.*] I have seen slugs do it.'[27]

The road Mrs Rooney travels stinks of decay, with its mixture of dung and scented laburnum. Dung, for some, might also connote fertiliser, but not for Mrs Rooney, who has, she says, no use for it at her time of life. Fertility and nurture abandoned her world with the death of little Minnie. Everything on her road is breaking down, falling into dissolution: Christy's cart (loaded with manure), Mr Tyler's bicycle, Mr Slocum's car. The train she is going to meet, as a birthday surprise for her husband, is mysteriously stopped.

The source of her sufferings is the blind Mr Rooney, cruel, sour, irritable, self-centred and a bully. He is verbally as violent as Mr Tully, whose wife's scream attracts their attention. Mr Rooney blames his wife for all his ills, and brushes aside her placatory gestures of affection. His account of the mysterious halt of the train begins with a lengthy meditation on the horrors of his home discomforts (the disruption caused him by her cooking and cleaning), and the greater horrors of being buried alive all day in his office. He describes graphically the anguish of realising the train was stopped: 'You know, the feeling of being confined. [...] I got up and paced to and fro between the seats, like a caged beast.'[28] Mrs Rooney does indeed know that feeling, she murmurs, and she recalls the lecture by a psychoanalyst she once attended, and the lecturer's comment on a little girl who died, for whom he could do nothing: 'The trouble with her was she had never really been born!'[29] Mr Rooney hears nothing of what she says.

The woman who feels she has never been born, and the man who feels buried alive, drag their way home together, weeping, through wind and rain. The melodramatic moment is punctured by sudden laughter, as they think of the theme proposed for this week's sermon: that God will raise up all that fall. God supplies the rhetoric of life in this village, but he has no remedy for the living death, or the final dying, into which all must fall. For Miss Fitt, he is a sticking-plaster for the desperate loneliness of spinsterhood, and the demands of an oppressive mother. For the Rooneys, like the characters in *Endgame*, he is a shared joke that briefly unites them in their misery. Such unity is short-lived. The play closes with the shocking revelation of the ineradicable difference between men and women. Mr Rooney, heedless of the memories he will conjure up of little Minnie, asks his wife if she had ever wished to kill a child. The train, the audience might conjecture, may well have stopped because Mr Rooney, the caged beast, pushed a child out of the carriage to be crushed under the wheels. The woman of the couple endures by turning inwards, into tears and self-repression, while the man fantasises violence, and, more likely than not, acts it out.

The play takes ordinary people, in a commonplace situation, and discloses the knife-edge of repressed pain, rage, and violence on which they live. Billie Whitelaw, preparing for Frost's recording project, explained to Frost how Beckett worked to build tension to a point of sustained climax:

> The work with Sam has been trying to get the right music, the right sound, the right color; these are words that he uses a lot: Color. He'll say, 'That's too much color.' I think he's terrified that actors will start acting, and so he always says 'no color, start with no color,' and gradually it starts to build and starts to roll and nine times out of ten one ends up with an absolute powerhouse of emotion. ... And of course this lady is getting more and more in a state of exhaustion and panic and distraughtness. Sam described her as – oh, he had a marvelous expression for it, what was it? – in a state of abortive explosiveness.[30]

The Third Programme scheduled an hour-long reading of an extract from *Molloy*, at Beckett's suggestion, in the early evening of 8 December 1957. The reader was Patrick Magee; his words were accompanied by the music of Beckett's nephew, John Beckett.[31] On 17 December, Donald McWhinnie forwarded to Magee a letter from Beckett praising Magee's performance, and the way the music and words had worked together, and saying he was looking forward to hearing Magee read *From an Abandoned Work* on the following weekend.[32] That twenty-minute reading took place on 14 December 1957 at 8.45 p.m. and earned Magee another twenty guineas on top of the thirty he had been paid for *Molloy*.

The work that is abandoned is the daily struggle for being, the losing battle of mind to hold together the always-deteriorating body. A croaking voice delivers the recollected narrative of a life expressed in the form of journeying, day-long walks going away from the family home, and then coming back again. Three days are selected for narration – none any different, the voice says, from any other. All the comings and goings are crossed by the same repeated impulses of fear and desire, both almost always experienced as violence, and the surrounding landscape and its creatures are felt as an overwhelming force, variously of pleasure or pain. Into his memories, inconsequential thoughts, interminable mutterings, and evocations of activity – often without a subject, simple gerunds or abstract nouns – the narrative voice weaves sudden, sharp comments on his past and present situations. Over the three days, the structure and the rhythm of performance draw the listener into the energies of human beginning, the accelerating shortness of days and confusion of perceptions, and finally the degeneration of articulate energy into the dreamtime of old age, stumbling towards the threshold of death. These are Joyce's three beats of narrative, noted in Beckett's essay of 1929, each 'embossed' with the knowledge of the others. As the time of the narrative voicing runs on, time within the days becomes a blur, events leach into each other, old things are perceived as new things, and all, never clear from the start (since all voice comes from the end) is increasingly confusion. The final going is there in the earliest coming. Already on the first day, the voice is meditating that soon, he will at last be happy, merging with the earth which has always been the space of his being. He envisages his own imminent total dissolution, separating out in the earth, consumed by the worms, and washing into the sea.

The first day starts in the early fresh morning of youth, waving goodbye to Mother, while Mother waves back in sad, helpless love, her frantic waving spoiling his peaceful view. There is rain all day, but there will be blue sky to be seen briefly at the end of this day, before night falls. Walking is its own end; he has never had a goal for his journeys.[33] Sometimes he walked slowly, and sometimes he ran in sudden bursts. He felt violent impulses against snails, slugs, and the birds that swoop to attack him; and for no reason, he felt sudden savage rage. As he walked on, there were no more creatures on the attack, only the vision of a distant white horse, the *Schimmelpferd*, the German icon of desire. Flashes of white throughout the narrative signify, like all the whitening in Beckett's writing, the levelling down into non-differentiation which is dying, and death. The violence in him persists, for no reason he can tell. He wonders if he has killed his father and mother (though earlier, it was only his father who was dead on this day). He sometimes beats his own head against things. Briefly, erotic desire enters this 'day' in the form of guilty self-reproach, for thinking too often of love in his youth. He regrets not having pursued that quest; he might have fathered a family and have done with his roaming.[34]

By the start of the second 'day', nothing is left but the watching mother and the angry rain pouring down on his own fury.[35] The violence within the narrator is now also outside, and from murderer, he becomes victim. He was pursued by a family of stoats, and was lucky to escape with his life. This day's start was a shaky one but the remarkable thing remains: that every day still always had its start, and its return home. There are fewer things to pick out: seeing some stars on the way home, the importance of his stick, and now, the memorable event, the first of numerous falls. But after his mother died, there seemed less and less need to chart differences. All he does now is wait for his own end.

The memorable event that began the third day was the look the roadman gave him, old Balfe, who terrified the speaker as a child; now Balfe is dead and the speaker looks like him. Time, marked on the body, has circled round, and in the mirror of Balfe the coming is merging into the going. This last beat, the space of waiting for death, follows through to the threshold of final separation and dissolution of mind and body. Body, out of control, thrashes round violently in the tall primitive ferns, in fear of the stoats. Here is heroic resistance; fighting back against the landscape, and the things of the earth, that are pulling him back into themselves to consume him. All the while, mind drifts off into unknowing, and even voice vanishes into a dream of senseless sound.[36] Here finally is an end to one form of movement, the conscious comings and goings, however aimless, and to the work that was mind's frenzied effort to keep hold of the dissolving body. Words are slipping away, and the pronouns shift from first to second person, and from subject to object case. In the closing line, the last thing that can be recorded is the distanced object: the body that is still mine but no longer mine, being abandoned by the conscious subject but continuing still, in its own way.[37] The rhythms, grammar and syntax of human being are never-ending; at the threshold from being alive to being dead, the forms change, but the story goes on, telling itself.

Embers, a funny, cynical, and bitter play, broadcast on the Third Programme on 24 June 1959, was the BBC's entry that year for the Italia Prize. In the introductory information he provided for the Prize submission, Beckett noted a key difference between *All That Fall* and his new play. The first, he felt, had theatre echoes, while *Embers* was related rather to the novels, especially *The Unnamable*; the text had been conceived for radio, and the production was more lyrical and personal.[38] He was writing a first draft in mid-December 1957, but had put it aside by mid-February 1958, in order to finish translating *The Unnamable* from the French. He submitted his script to the BBC Drama Department a year later, in February 1959.[39]

All That Fall had a clear setting, with multiple triggers for the audience's visual imagination; it had a strong plot line, and developed dramatic and complex relationships between characters. In *Embers*, plot is near-invisible, the creation of characters is subordinated to the drama of the creation of meaning, and the imaginations of author and audience come together purely on the basis of sound. Henry, the narrative voice, invokes and controls some specific and repeated sound effects (horses' hooves, the drip of water, the slamming of the door behind his departing father, the clash and thud of stones), and explains their significance. His voice splits to mimic the voices he invents in his embedded story of Bolton and Holloway, and the interlocutors he invents for his dialogues with his dead father, his daughter Addie, and his wife, Ada, both also dead, or as good as. He summons up Ada, who speaks with her own quiet, die-away voice; the frontiers blur between Henry's reality and his imagination. Voices rise, fall, merge and blend. Henry's own voice functions in a landscape that is not under his control. The surge of the sea comes and goes in its own time, sucking at the hard shingle beach at the water's edge, where he clings on to his control of life. Like his father before him, he looks across the sea at an inaccessible horizon, and invokes family and professional duties to justify his failure to take up its challenge. The monstrous sea, like the horses, represents the doubleness of living, the lure of infinite possibilities, promises of potency, a vehicle to somewhere new always coupled with the terror of engagement and risk: 'Lips and claws!'[40]

The foreword to the radio broadcast pointed listeners to the special capacity of radio to represent the operations of creativity:

> In all the work of Samuel Beckett the drama is the poetry and the poetry the drama; in all his work the subject is at one and the same time life and art. That is why his plays for radio – the medium where word, sound and silence are all – represent modern poetic drama in one of its purest forms, and why *Embers* in particular discloses a vivid image of the creative mind at work.
>
> For in *Embers* we are not simply concerned with the attempts at communication, self-knowledge and self-preservation of an old

> man alone on a deserted shore; but also with those of the artist, who struggles constantly by means of his creations to build up his (and our) defences against the irrational unknowable forces that threaten always to encroach on and destroy his existence as an artist and as a man.[41]

A platitudinous preoccupation with the threat of 'irrational unknowable forces' is to be attributed to the BBC itself, especially at this time of Cold War, rather than Beckett, whose play is a lucid analysis of the actual threats to the artist, and the modern Everyman he represents, against which there is no defence. The sea of life, where the tide must be taken at the flood, or the voyager end in shallows and in miseries, is a familiar image, and the obstacles to adventure are familiar and universal: the great burden of the family, voiced by the father, commanding and reproaching, the child who threatens supersession, and the wife who drains her husband's potency and represses even his memories of desire. Talk, storytelling, and bluff are equally familiar anaesthetics, which cannot prevail against the incoming tide. The play ends as the fire burns down to embers, the candle-flame gutters, and the human voice is worn down into silence.

The first sound of the play is the distant surge of the sea, coming louder and closer, while a booted Henry urges himself onward, slithering across the shingle beach, trying in vain to summon up a word from his dead father. Henry names for the audience the sound of the sea, and summons up for them the thudding hooves of passing horses. He must speak, he says, to drown the voice of the sea. But everything he says, in the attempt to voice his control, renews the misery of a life spent in submission, repression, and refusal.

At one time, he could talk to himself, inventing stories, none of them ever finished. His favourite story tells in vivid and realistic selective detail of an old man called Bolton, visited by Holloway, his doctor, with his little black bag. The two old men, in the great house, out of the snowstorm, warm themselves before the fire, looking out of the window on the cold silent world outside. The story runs towards an end where the flames die down to embers, and they are left still standing and gazing out, in an Impressionist soundscape of words, reverberating to create their perception of the whiteness that for them signifies the terrible silence of their imminent deaths, the void they can only apprehend, for as long as the fire still glows: 'looking out, white world, great trouble, not a sound, only the embers, sound of dying, dying glow'.[42]

The warm dream is cut through by Henry's present, with the sound of a drip, amplified, cut off, restored, amplified, and then silenced. The slow drip resolves itself into metaphor. The voices of Henry's family, internalised, ventriloquised, mimicked, and reinvented by him, spell out all the burdens these relationships, he says, have imposed on him. He imitates the contempt in his father's voice, whenever he refused his commands. He hands on his own misery to his daughter, Addie. He mimics Addie's refusal of his commands, and her long wails. His wife Ada contributed nothing worth remembering, just a stream of endless chatter.[43]

Henry asks himself why he lives on the brink of the sea, and gives his own answers, ranging from his professional commitments to, more honestly, 'Some old grave I cannot tear myself away from?'[44] He stays because this is the space marked out for him by his father. Ada's dead voice says they cannot leave because of their daughter. Addie is learning music and riding, at Ada's behest, living out Ada's unfulfilled desires as Henry lives out his father's. Henry acknowledges his own complicity in this handing down of torment through generations.

Henry trudges to the edge of the sea, but his attempt to stage a fresh challenge is accompanied by a series of 'Don't's' from Ada. These bring back to him, from twenty years earlier, her protests at his first sexual advances, his cry of triumph and her own cry, all amplified in the crashing sound of the sea. This, the highpoint of desire fulfilled, was undermined by Ada then, and now. Repressed, respectable, and dead, Ada appears to feel no terror at the sound of the sea and ridicules Henry's need to talk to drown it. Henry's response is violence, banging together two big stones from the beach, and rejoicing in the sound of their clashing and the thud of their fall. As it was for Mr Rooney, or the voice of *From an Abandoned Work*, both speaking out of a decaying body, violence is the best anaesthetic, though Henry, unlike Mr Rooney, stops short of murder – in Henry's narrative of life on the sea-edge there is, after all, no one left to kill.

The search in *Rockaby* for a familiar soul, where famished eyes seek out their other, is in radio terms a search for familiar, famished voices. Here there are none. In this version of the heterosexual couple, the woman speaks as tormentor, and the man as victim. Ada gloats over Henry's isolation and his approaching end, when he will be alone with no voice but his own.

Unexpectedly, she voices a story of her own. She came to visit Henry before they were married, to go swimming, but he was nowhere to be found. The family was thrown into uproar, and his father slammed out of the room and went to sit on a rock looking out to sea, as if turned to stone. Henry recognises this as a posture he too has often adopted. At his urging, she spins out her story as long as she can, and then abruptly gives up, abandoning him to his own resources, to be absorbed by the damning image of his father sitting on his rock, destroyed by his son, his whole body breathless and still.

Henry panics, his play with dead voices having thrown up images which cut too close to the fears and guilts that have shaped his life – not least the irrational guilt that the son always feels towards the father whose place he has taken. Words are slipping from him. He can no longer conjure up Ada or the sound of the hooves with a simple word, and he struggles to finish Ada's story about his father. His story of Bolton and Holloway struggles back slowly into shape. Bolton, formerly the strong old man peering out into the snow, now confronts the doctor, Holloway, eye to eye, begging for some resolution or cure. The poet searching for a familiar gaze is at the end of his powers, sight going from his glassy blue eyes, speech almost gone, all clarity dissolving, and the once fierce spotlight of consciousness reduced to the guttering candle shaking over his head. The narrative ends with the declaration that life was never more than that: dark, cold, and a flickering plea for rescue by another, to which there is no response.

The final image of that final look is reformulated into the conclusion of Henry's present performance, of the experience of life at the sea's edge. Still urging himself on, he pauses to read his diary, and the note that the plumber will come the next day: 'Ah yes, the waste. [*Pause.*] Words.'[45] The slow dripping of living erodes everything, leaving only the waste of words, and after that, Henry's diary shows nothing. The transmission fades out in the surge of the sea; but the underlying truth of Henry's condition is more desolate than the moving surge suggests. He told Barbara Bray that the title must be *Embers*, to provide his precise meaning: the ebb of the sea returns in flow, but after embers die down, there is nothing.[46]

It was during the production of *Embers* that Barbara Bray and Beckett became more closely involved. Her estranged husband had died in an accident, leaving her with two young daughters, and when she and Beckett first drew close, she was in a relationship with Donald McWhinnie. They saw a lot of each other in July 1959, when Beckett came over to England after receiving his honorary doctorate at Trinity College, and in October, by which time McWhinnie had a new girlfriend, she came over to Paris for a week to see him.[47] She produced his translation of Robert Pinget's *La Manivelle, The Old Tune*, broadcast on the Third Programme on 23 August 1960, with Jack MacGowran and Patrick Magee in the roles of the old men reminiscing and forgetting, the ends of their sentences trailing away unfinished. The old tune, played three times, is ironic: 'There's no Place like Home.'

In January 1961, at the age of 36, Bray gave up her job with the BBC, and told Beckett that she was planning to move to Paris with her daughters, to pursue a freelance career as a translator and reviewer.[48] Beckett immediately decided to marry Suzanne, then aged 61 (he was 54), to secure her financial position in relation to ownership of his literary rights, and perhaps also to reassure her; and the wedding took place in the Registry Office in Folkestone on 25 March.[49] Barbara Bray stuck to her plans. Their relationship was to last until he died in 1989, undisrupted by his commitments to Suzanne and his affairs with other women. They met frequently, sometimes in the company of Beckett's friends. He used to call in at her flat to talk or play classical music on the piano, and they also met in Beckett's country house in Ussy-sur-Marne, where Suzanne no longer went; they advised each other on their work, and exchanged hundreds of letters.[50] She typed his final work, 'Comment dire' (1989), which he composed when confined to the Tiers Temps nursing home in Paris.[51]

At the end of 1961, Beckett was writing radio plays that were far more focused than *Embers* on issues relating to the writing of poetic drama. The short sketch 'Rough for Radio I', written in French, in November 1961, and never performed, presents the unbridgeable gap between the artist and his public.[52] He allows She to turn the knobs on his radio, listen to the alternating and unceasing streams of words, music, and words-and-music. The process which for him has become a need is one that She cannot understand, and She leaves, commenting on his coldness. He returns to the radio, to urge on the words and music, which are beginning to fuse into some recognisable form, giving birth to a new work. A sequence of phone calls about meetings, appointments, deaths, departures, and in one case, a breech birth, interrupts the long slow process of the artist's listening, and is brushed aside; the trivia of life must yield priority to the making of art.

Two other plays written about the same time probe further the nature of listening, and also look more closely at what it is that the artist hears in the interplay of words and music, meaning and rhythm, and what he is aiming to create. *Words and Music*, broadcast on 13 November 1962, was a collaboration between Beckett and his musician nephew, John, set up by Barbara Bray at the request of the producer, Michael Bakewell.[53] The Creator, Croak, calls on his waiting servants, Words (Joe) and Music (Bob), with a shred of inspiration (the face on the stairs, in the tower) and hesitantly decides that the theme for tonight will be love. In the theatrical tradition, the thump of his club on the ground opens the performance. Words comes up with a ready-made text for all seasons, which the audience heard before Croak arrived, on the theme of sloth, rhetorical and repetitive, and Music provides an equally clichéd starting movement. In progressive response to Croak's thumps, curses, and cries of pain, the two play against each other, Words finding simpler language, following the better rhythms suggested by Music, until a softly sung verse emerges, in whose musicality Croak recognises the face of his original inspiration, in the form of a dream of lost love. The process is repeated, again passing through clumsy, clunky prose and bursts of noisy music, celebrating flamboyantly the hair, lips, eyes and breasts of a woman whom the anguished Croak names as Lily. A second verse makes its way through, softly sung by Words, of the dark of sexual congress, expressed discreetly, with no traces of the body parts that preceded it, all in negatives, building downwards to a glimpse of the source of all inspiration.[54] Croak, deeming the process done, abruptly drops the club and shuffles away, abandoning his instruments to their limbo.

Cascando, written originally in French in December 1961 to provide a text for a piece of music by Marcel Mihalovici, is an extended, far more detailed meditation on the same theme.[55] Mihalovici had been invited by the French broadcasting station ORTF to produce a composition. Beckett completed his text first, and Mihalovici responded to it with his music a year later. The work was first broadcast in French on 13 October 1963, with Roger Blin in the role of the Opener, and Roger Martin as the Voice. The English version was broadcast on the BBC's Third Programme a year later (6 October 1964). The piece states its inspiration from the start, in the title. As with *Words and Music*, in place of the crescendo to which music and drama conventionally build, Beckett scripted a cascando, a dying fall.

In this performance, the Opener is the counterpart of Croak, the will to create, and his definition of the starting point of the work, the month of May, strikes the keynote of renewal and growth.[56] He dictates the alternation of his instruments, Voice and Music, requires each of them to open and close, evaluates their interaction, and decides when the production has finally developed into a form that satisfies him. This time, the theme only appears half way through. The creative process is modelled as a never-ending story, a simple turning on and off of the flow of the words and the rhythms, to produce a text which names its own theme and writes itself. There is nothing in the Opener's head, though once he used to begin by setting the terms of the image and the shape of the story. Now all the images and shapes are already gathered together, and there is nothing to living and making but the flowing words, the musical evocation of movement, a perpetual springtime reawakening and reshaping. This is the state of being that the text declares its author inhabits. Audiences who bring only their eyes to his work have not truly seen it, or him; this radio audience is enjoined to try a different approach, and to listen:

> Opener: They don't see me, they don't see what my life is, they don't see what I live on, and they say, That is not his life, he does not live on that.
> [Pause.]
> I have lived on it … till I'm old.
> Old enough.
> Listen.[57]

There is a simple, regular structure, in which Voice and Music alternate, then sound out together. Their joint utterances throw into relief the key phrases of the writer's incessant, never-satisfied, always-resumed search for the 'right' speech, and as they advance, drawing their two worlds together, they draw the artist and his audience into a new place. Their final joint movement, into which the Opener chimes with his fervently approving 'Good!', trembles on the brink of catching 'the right one', which will be the end of all the stories, but never tips over, closing on a doubled 'come on', which reverberates into silence.[58]

The journey of being which in other texts is written as anguish and frenzy – *From an Abandoned Work*, for instance, where the decaying body and the disintegrating mind work through the terrors of ageing and dying – is in *Cascando* recuperated under the aegis of artistic form. The artist signals the opening of the work, and at its end, embeds himself into its resonating conclusion. He stands at its centre, explaining his relation to the double modes of his expression, words and music, and asserting his formal control. 'Story', the first word spoken by Voice, holds the journey in the distancing frame of fiction, and the tale of Woburn, pieced together from familiar fragments, is one of the reassuring old stories with which Beckett has long rocked himself to sleep. Woburn, ready to go, emerges from the limbo where all Beckett's images are now stored together – the darkness of night, but also the shed where the tools are kept. There is no evocation on this journey of the abjection of origins, with a shapeless subject tunnelling and crawling through the darkness and the mud. In the same old coat, with the same old stick, and same old broad-brimmed hat, Woburn goes on, falling and getting up, and both he and his journey are 'An image, like any other.'[59] This time though there is a difference. There was a choice between the sea and the hills, and Woburn chose to risk the sea, descending from the hills, onto the sand, over the stones, and into the boat that carries him towards the island. He goes on, falling, all the way; in the boat he is face down in the bilge, clinging on, heading, muses Voice, nowhere, anywhere, or elsewhere. Elsewhere is the best place to be. Woburn has nearly changed – but only, as the text repeats, nearly.

While writing new plays for radio, Beckett was still prepared to allow his stage dramas to be transferred to the very different medium. *Play*, which had opened at the National Theatre on 7 April 1964, offered substantial technical challenges. The visual impact of the identification of the three characters with their urns was one, but more important still was the representation of the spotlight which ranges across the three heads, with rigorous timing, to open each one's speaking. The file in the BBC archives contains a packet of the scripts used on stage, marked up for blackout, carefully timed, light switched on and off, or half on.[60] For the radio performance on 11 October 1966, Martin Esslin told listeners, Beckett had shared in the search for an appropriate substitute for the spotlight.[61] In an article he wrote later, he said it was the idea of the producer, Bennett Maxwell, to replace the beam of light with a continuous sound tape, made up of the voices of the three players, all saying 'I'. The tape was to cut out each time the spotlight was scripted to prompt a player into speech.[62]

How the play was understood by its radio audience is not clear. Esslin's broadcast 'Introduction' led the audience to expect an 'awesome metaphysical situation': 'Beckett has always been concerned with the problem of human consciousness and its relation to existence itself. To be, to him, is identical with being aware of oneself. And one of his nightmares is the impossibility of imagining the attainment of non-being, which to Beckett in many ways is a most desirable state.'[63] He added that the irony and the humour of *Play* was that in this situation were three characters in what could, differently constructed, be a conventional play about adultery. That Beckett extracted considerable humour from the clichés of adultery is certainly the case, but the convoluted account of the metaphysics of *Play* is less than helpful. In his article, Esslin ruefully describes Beckett, having heard the recording of the performance, telling him he had it all wrong.

By the mid-1960s, Beckett's rocketing stage reputation was earning him a considerable increase in BBC airtime, and the BBC's presentations of his work continued to help audiences to a better understanding of what they were listening to. A telegram from the BBC's Paris office to Norman MacDonald (2 March 1964), before the staging of *Endgame* in London, scheduled for June, suggested a discussion with the British cast (Magee, MacGowran, Nancy Cole, and Elvi Hale) and Barbara Bray about their attitudes to the new production, and to Beckett's work in general.[64] An Audience Research Report on the *New Comment* programme that was subsequently transmitted, on Tuesday 2 June 1964, reported for the sample of 65 listeners (6 per cent of the Listeners Panel) an Approval Index of 62 – two points better than the current average for *New Comment* programmes. Barbara Bray's conversation was described as lively, if over-intellectualising, and praised for provoking controversy, while comments from the two actors who took part apparently once again 'cleared some of the fog in which Beckett's plays are usually wrapped' and encouraged listeners to think they might go and see the play. The respondents liked the glimpses they were given of the personality of the 'enigmatic' Beckett.[65] The context of the responses is indicated by another report in the same file from Isa Benzie to the Chief Producer of Arts Talks, Philip French, which in the course of presenting arguments for a new kind of film programme transmits the observations of a young married professional, aged 25, who is on the lookout for more challenging intellectual fare. The young man, who prefers film, volunteers that he would also like to be offered the alternative of a more serious and different theatre. In London at the moment, he says, 'There is nothing between Beckett and "The Amorous Prawn".'[66]

The broadcasts of Beckett's work were not highly paid. The BBC at that time was well known for its low fees – a standard rate of £3 a minute, increased slightly for writers of high prestige, among whom Beckett seems to have figured from the start. For a poetry reading in 1966, for which the BBC had offered a little above the rate, John Calder wrote to Jack Beale, of the BBC Copyright Department, that one-third above the rate would be more acceptable, given that their client's poetry was of considerable importance, and the language highly concentrated. The Head of Copyright, Jack Leak, explained regretfully that the BBC could not change policy, 'even for Samuel Beckett'.[67] The policy held firm. *All That Fall*, which runs for seventy minutes, earned Beckett 200 guineas for a repeat in 1965; a broadcast in January 1970, marking Beckett's award of the Nobel Prize, was paid £250. Short extracts for the Schools department were paid slightly less than the normal £3 a minute; but the religious programme, 'Seeing is Believing', and the World Service, both paid standard rate for extracts from *Waiting for Godot*.[68]

The showcasing provided by *New Comment* attempted to ensure that Beckett's work established itself a place as challengingly avant-garde, but not totally out of reach. The programme broadcast on 9 March 1966, at 7.30 p.m., included Beckett's *Imagination Dead Imagine*, along with Donald Barthelme's experimental short story collection, *Come Back Dr Caligari* and Roy Bongartz's popular comic tales, *Twelve Chases on West 99th Street*.[69]

The difficulty of *Lessness*, first broadcast on 25 February 1971, was addressed by an 'Introduction' by the producer, Martin Esslin, which described the work as 'an intricately structured prose poem which describes a landscape of desolation after the collapse of a last refuge'.[70] The lines, a single block in the original, had here, he explained, been distributed over six voices, as indicated by Beckett himself. The voices (in this production, Donal Donnelly, Leonard Fenton, Denys Hawthorne, Patrick Magee, Harold Pinter, and Nicol Williamson) are not characters, but bearers of 'strands of connected images in a complex structure of thought and sound'. Importantly, the listeners were invited into the radio workshop where the final poem had been shaped. Each group, said Esslin, had been recorded separately 'so that the actual tapestry of the interweaving images only emerged in the tape cutting room. Thus the rhythmic pattern and the finely calculated structure of paragraphs and pauses demanded by the author could be far more accurately realised than if the whole piece had been recorded by the speakers in the conventional way.'

In a later essay, Esslin provided an illuminating insight into the thematic of the text, in a more detailed account of how Beckett originally constructed it: taking sentences from the original block of six, combining them at random, and then repeating the process. This was to generate a figure of eternity, in which time could be seen as endless variations on the same restricted building-blocks.[71] In Paris, it appears Esslin, Calder, and Beckett had discussed the play together, with Beckett stipulating the timing of intervals between sentences and paragraphs, and the need to create an effect of the piece emanating from the same voice: the different speakers must be distinguishable from each other, but the whole should be unified in tone.[72] Beckett was disappointed with the finished product, which did not in his view achieve the musical form he had aimed at, but listeners wrote in to indicate their appreciation.

In *Lessness,* language changes its nature, and words and sentences are transformed into musical notes. But the emphasis on rhythms, and Beckett's interest in creating a narrative form from randomness, does not completely eradicate semantic significance. The ruins of language are the 'true refuge' – not by any means a safe stronghold, but the best to be had, and all depends on what the artist does with the words that are his building blocks. Within these ruins, according to Esslin's broadcast 'Introduction', the six themes addressed are 'ruin, exposure, wilderness, mindlessness, past and future denied and affirmed', and the overall mood is of 'some loss: endlessness, hopelessness, helplessness'.[73] The key to the text that Beckett gave to his publisher, John Calder, is not much different.[74] But there is enough diverse material in the ruins to allow readers, and listeners, to hear the notes of affirmation inside the passing of language into music. With the creation of that music comes the abolition of external world, time and space, and the memory that makes and unmakes past and future. All is ash grey, sand, and ruins, sheets of sheer white alternating with blackout, and then an end to light, sound, and reason. They are, the text repeats, 'all gone from mind'; but this is not mindlessness, only the litany of refusal of the false distinctions mind created in its constructs of false reality, with its invented categories of time and space. In place of mind is the body, repeatedly evoked, in variations on 'Grey face two pale blue little body heart beating only upright'.[75] The body has legs, genitals, an arse, and a face, and its beating heart drives it on through the sand and ruins, stepping, falling, and still dreaming and imagining time, space, and the blue sky and rain of the outside world. The beat of the heart, oscillating between affirmation and denial, is the rhythm of life spoken into existence by the many unified voices of the text, celebrating the little body.

Only when the random combinations nominated by the author come to their end does it all draw to a close, with a new descriptor emerging, 'overrun'.[76] The penultimate line of the text is a minimalist celebration of the final condition of the body, 'genitals overrun arse', composing and composting, the origins of beginning and ending, both at the end running together and collapsing. The last line is a minimalist celebration of the final condition of the world outside the body, dawn and dusk, the human words defining the beginning and ending of nature's day. At the end, with everything reduced to its minimal form, time run out, beginning and ending are identified, and all that remains is the little body, and the 'figments' left by the mind it housed. But a word in a text is both 'figment' and 'dispeller of figments';[77] it is both fixed and fiction, and it can turn back on itself to disclose its double status, and in the process, liberate speaker and listener from the deceits of language. The chorus of voices falls silent on a note of neither hope nor hopelessness, only a statement of how it is. Esslin's formulation is a precise account of what Beckett is doing here and in each of his later works: using selected variations from the infinite possibilities surrounding the subject-in-time, to create a dynamic image of the situation of that subject enclosed in eternity, or as other texts term it, the void.

Beckett by this time was becoming very difficult to follow, even for the Third Programme audience, and even with all the help the broadcasters could offer. John Calder sent Martin Esslin the manuscript of *First Love*, which Beckett had just translated and which Calder was about to publish. He commented that, written at the same time as *Watt* and *Mercier et Camier*, it would be a nice piece for listeners who had difficulty with Beckett's later work. He was confident that it was appropriate for a Third Programme audience, although he was doubtful whether Mary Whitehouse would like it.[78] A record of what Mary Whitehouse thought about the brutal black comedy would be entertaining: the graphic account of 'anxiety constipation', the engraving of the loved one's name on a cowpat, the axiom that 'women smell the rigid phallus ten miles away', or the refusal to supply listeners with 'other reasons best not wasted on cunts like you'.[79] In early 1970, Beckett had fished the tale, in its original French, out of his collection of unpublished pieces, wanting to follow up on the award of the Nobel Prize, but not yet ready to produce anything new.[80] However, serendipitously the broadcast by Patrick Magee, in early May 1973, provided a gender counterpart – and stylistic contrast – to the first English production of *Not I* in January. The flood of words pouring from Mouth, telling her tale of unformed being, contrasts with the controlled syntax of the 'I' who inscribes his life in the frame of his father's house and his father's graveyard. While Mouth falls among the cowslips, he broods anally among cowpats, chamber pots, and the sweet smell of decaying corpses. She is never offered love; he has love thrust upon him, by Lulu, whom he despises, dispossesses of her room and her name, exploits, and finally abandons while she is giving birth. He has all the words for love (love-passion, platonic love, intellectual love), no doubt taught him by his father, who certainly taught him the only words he can remember for the stars, and gave him his hat, the only one he has ever owned: 'I may add it has followed me to the grave.'[81] He plays with his child's cries as he played once with its mother's song, walking backwards and forwards to change the volume, but unable, at the last, to make the cries stop. Unlike Mouth, he knows what he has done, and the knowledge runs painfully below the brutal words he has been taught. That's how it is: 'either you love or you don't.'[82]

Rough for Radio II, written in French in the early 1960s, was another reminder of how funny Beckett could be across the whole spectrum of comedy: from the blackest of black humour, sadistic and erotic, to the vulgar farce beloved by British audiences, double entendre, and self-indulgent jokes about translation questions. The twenty-minute piece was first broadcast for Beckett's seventieth birthday on Tuesday 13 April 1976, so the self-indulgence was forgivable.[83] It was one of a cluster of pieces gathered together on Martin Esslin's initiative, as a contribution to the birthday celebrations, with Harold Pinter as the Animator, Billie Whitelaw as the Stenographer, Patrick Magee as Fox, and Michael Deacon as Dick (who wields the bull's pizzle that beats the words out of Fox).[84] Esslin produced and directed.

Beckett was unhappy, as always, with the finished broadcast, and Billie Whitelaw thought her and Pinter's performances had not been very good.[85] Beckett gave his usual precise instructions about the sound effects, specifying that the bull's pizzle with which Fox is beaten into speech must operate with three different kinds of swish, depending on whether it had no impact, struck a hard surface, or struck flesh.[86] The aim, as the Stenographer says, is to torture a fresh story out of the familiar raw material. The Stenographer has a fresh pad and new pencils and is told to transcribe carefully the smallest syllable. But the Animator disobeys his own instructions and listens with prejudice: he looks back to yesterday's transcript before they begin; he looks for echoes of Dante and Sterne in today's 'new' utterance; and he looks, or rather leers at the Stenographer for inspiration, as she removes her overall. He is deaf to the comic double entendre of Fox's scream ('Let me out! Peter out in the stones!'),[87] and equally deaf to the implications of Fox's speaking for the first time of a brother inside him, an old twin. Instead of recognising this as an insight into the multiple aspects of the self, he homes in on Fox's mention of a woman, fantasises for her a pair of imagined breasts, and forces the Stenographer to add two invented kisses into her transcript. Like the Director of *Catastrophe*, the Animator is not interested in letting the story speak for itself and is instead preoccupied with shaping the image in his own image. And here too the joke turns against the audience, who will follow sexual and sadistic fantasies more cheerfully than a narrative of split subjectivity.

Beckett on Screen: Projecting Meaning onto the Void

Beckett's engagement with BBC television's drama department ran less smoothly. A number of his works for the stage were transferred to television, more or less effectively. A television version of *Waiting for Godot*, shot in a Birmingham TV studio on one camera, and transmitted in June 1961, disappointed him; he thought the play was not really suited to the medium, which in his view would work best for a play created for close-ups.[88] Audiences later agreed with his preference.[89] The production of *Krapp's Last Tape* transmitted in November 1963, poorly lit and edited, was the last straw; it convinced Beckett, for the time being at least, that his work could not be transferred from one medium to another.[90] He was happier with the version of *Not I* produced by Tristram Powell – a single-take, close-up on Billie Whitelaw's mouth – which was filmed on 13 February 1975 and broadcast in the autumn of 1976.[91] He was happier still with the work he wrote specially for television, which he could pre-record and edit.

In the summer of 1964, he went to New York to work with the director Alan Schneider on *Film*, an experiment in the visual representation of the two aspects of the self, perceived and perceiving, dramatised as the flight of the self from perception by others, forced finally to confront 'the inescapability of self-perception'.[92] Buster Keaton, the silent film star with the deadpan face, runs at comic speed through city streets, swerving away from others' gaze, tearing up and throwing away all images of himself, until finally, in solitude, he is forced to confront the eye of the camera, which is his own. Beckett was delighted by the beauty and power of the draft, noting that the result was visual, and plastic, and a long way from the abstract idea with which they had begun, but that the shift had given it 'a dimension and a validity of its own'.[93] Armed with this experience, which included helping with the edit of the first draft, Beckett wrote his first work conceived specially for television.

Eh Joe was offered to the BBC with the stipulation that Donald McWhinnie must direct, and Jack MacGowran play Joe, and this time his agent, Margaret McLaren (Curtis Brown), beat up the fee to £250, double the BBC's first offer. It was, as she pointed out, the first time Beckett had felt able to respond to the many requests he had received for an original television play.[94] The play was broadcast on BBC2 on 4 July 1966, and audience reaction was more positive than for earlier transmissions of *Waiting for Godot* and *Krapp's Last Tape*. A quarter of the sample audience liked the play for its representation of 'the pathetic condition of the isolated human being', and the expressive face of MacGowran, silently receiving the monologue from the Voice (Siân Phillips); it was said to be depressing, but compelling.[95] Here again is the subject confronted with his own perceptions of himself, but this time he is not seeking to flee them. Rather, he is shown in control of their construction. The structure implies the interpellation of the subject by the voice of his memories, but there is no indication whether these are memories or fantasies, and by the end, all that is clear is that Joe has a self-image that pleases him.

Joe, in his late fifties, is discovered sitting on the edge of his bed. He performs an anxious circuit of his room: checks the window, door, and cupboard, looks under the bed, and finally returns to his original position. Here is the chosen space – the solitary bed – in which Joe's desire for self-definition will take shape. The camera begins to close in on him, stopping each time that a woman's voice speaks. Camera and Voice between them, the perceivers, who are the visual equivalents of radio's *Words and Music*, construct the image, and Joe, the perceived, is Opener and Auditor. The sequence is repeated nine times, ending with a full close-up of his face. The Voice, Beckett explained to Alan Schneider, which is a dead voice in Joe's head, should be whispered, and have a minimum of colour.[96] Joe's face is unblinking and impassive, except, the stage directions say, 'in so far as it reflects mounting tension of *listening*'.[97] The Voice flows on, in a sequence of phrases broken by pauses, recalling for Joe the voices of those who once loved him – father, mother, and former lovers – all now strangled by Joe, in his head; and the many suicide attempts of one lover, who finally died on the shore with her face in the stones. Salacious and sadistic, the Voice calls Joe to imagine the eyes, lips, breasts, and hands of the dead girl, now wasted on the stones. Joe's facial language, despite the stage directions, is often staged as grimaces representing guilt, remorse, or torment for the loss of love, all attempts at 'strangling the voice in his head'.[98] But when Voice finally falls silent, Joe widens his eyes, and smiles, apparently satisfied with its representation of what love has meant for him: his cold heart, his cult of stony solitude, his ability to attract the love that is pity. In Voice's final line, the definition of love, for Joe, is in the rhythms that beat out a place for his own name: '*There's love for you* ... Isn't it, Joe? ... Wasn't it, Joe? ... *Eh Joe?* ... Wouldn't you say? ... Compared to us ... Compared to Him ... *Eh Joe?*'[99]

Jonathan Kalb has interesting things to say about the interplay of Voice and the camera, as it focuses on Joe's face, and the unanswered questions they raise for the audience about Joe's relationship to Voice (in particular, whether the throttling of his loved ones is real or imagined), and the nature of Joe's responses, which are strained and pitiful and skirt sentimentality. He refers to the German television production, where Beckett was closely involved in the direction, picking out the faintness of the light in the Stuttgart version. The lighting engineer said he could not get the light of the initial stages of the play faint enough for Beckett, who needed it because for the most part this was an evocation of things past, memory, and fantasy.[100] The darkness, Kalb points out, enables Beckett to communicate his concept of meaning as a subjective projection onto the void; and in the Stuttgart version, together with the movements of the camera and a more vicious tone to Voice, it creates a more dramatic, conflicted, inscrutable and malevolent version of Joe.[101]

For Gilles Deleuze, *Eh Joe*, with its emphasis on character, storytelling, and the flow of language, is a transitional piece between the novels and stage drama of earlier and later Beckett – the Beckett who had begun to find ways of dealing with the untrustworthiness of language. Deleuze's challenging study, *L'Épuisé*, explores Beckett's perception, expressed in his letter of 1937 to Axel Kaun, that what he wanted to do with language was to drill in holes and let the void – the absence of meaning that underpins and defines human existence, circumscribed by death – seep through.[102] This kind of language, which Deleuze calls Langue III, the third of the types of language he identifies in Beckett's work, is, he argues, present in all Beckett's projects, but its best realisation is in television, which makes visible the processes by which language operates: the image is seen taking shape inside the frame of a pre-recorded voice.[103]

The imperative is to strip referentiality out of words and use them in a different way, to create a 'true' image, one that carries no content or message, and is simply an organisation of forms, not an object but a process, trembling with the energy of its creation.[104] Truth emerges when the writing is made to foreground the framework that holds the image in place (that is, its origins in the artist's own imagination, and in the field of its production, and the parameters and limits of that field); to reduce to a minimum the signifying elements from which the image is synthesised (visual, verbal, and auditory); and to disconnect them from their conventional contexts and referents. All these factors are run through by Beckett in the performance that is the artwork, in all the combinations that are possible in this particular strictly-defined and limited configuration, until the combinations are exhausted, and what remains finally flickers into perception: the 'true' image of the Nothing that is all that is really doing. The themes, techniques and motifs of all Beckett's previous work reappear in these later experiments, condensed and simplified, and put to work in this new kind of production. Deleuze points to the recurrent figure in the later drama and prose, of the seated man, exhausted, head in hands, who is Author and Originator of the work,[105] and the ritualised indication of the (increasingly simplified) parameters of the field of production in which the work takes shape, exhausting its potential. He recalls their avatars in the set-pieces in the earlier comic novels, presented as mere games with pure form, played to fill and pass the time. Murphy probes the different combinations in which he can lay out his biscuits on the park bench, and Molloy moves his sucking stones from pocket to pocket, until there are no more moves left to make.

The producer Martin Esslin's account of Beckett's later drama describes it as creating a new genre in which language is reduced to the minimum, and the stage occupied instead by the sight and sound of a living image, an intense metaphorical production of human experience.[106] Illuminating in its descriptions of how the televised productions work, Esslin's study can usefully be read alongside that of Deleuze. At issue in both, couched in very different terms, is the underlying dynamic that Deleuze identifies: the desire of the artist to figure the energies of creative form, through which the longed-for realisation of 'nothing doing', the truth of all human experience, might finally tremble into perception.

The pieces Beckett wrote specially for television between 1975 and 1982 (*Ghost Trio, … but the clouds …, Quad,* and *Nacht und Träume*), are all representations of the process Deleuze describes, in their re-enactment of the patterns of ritual and repetition through which Beckett's 'true' images take trembling form.[107] In different spaces, and with different combinations of the basic televisual elements of sound and vision, each produces its distinctive, fleeting and intense image of some aspect of the human condition, which is desiring and losing.

Ghost Trio, written in English in 1975, uses movement and music and simple narrative motifs to evoke the anxiety and disappointment of desire that has fixed itself in waiting for the unattainable. The play, televised on BBC2 on 17 April 1977, is in three stages (Pre-Action, Action, Re-Action), with each stage scripted in short sequences of moves. The structure stretches time unendurably, building tension and mystery with its slow focusing on each detail of movement and setting. In Stage I, a faint female voice conducts the viewer on a tour of a grey, faintly luminous room, fixing on its floor, wall, window, pallet, repeating the tour, and ending on a seated male figure, listening to a cassette, the only living thing in this space.[108] The music playing is the Largo of Beethoven's Fifth Piano Trio, known as 'The Ghost'. The camera pans in, and then out again, and then moves into close-up on head, hands, and cassette; with the music growing louder and fainter to match its moves into, and away from, the trio of head, hands, and cassette, that together are creating the fantasy image. In Stage II, the voice instructs the figure that he will 'think he hears her', and he is shown looking and listening at all the points already toured, which define his space – which remains empty. But on his own initiative, and to the voice's surprise, he looks at himself in a mirror previously out of shot. Again, he is instructed that he thinks he hears her, he opens the door, and then he plays his cassette. In Stage III, with all parameters and elements of creation established, the voice is gone. The male figure switches the music on and off, and opens and closes the door and the window, to the sound of rain. The mirror is shown reflecting nothing. There is a knock on the door, which he opens to a small boy in black oilskins glistening with rain, who shakes his head, and disappears down a long receding corridor into the dark. The door closes. The figure goes back to bend his head over the cassette, and finally lifts his face; the camera pans away into its initial position, covering the whole room, whose contents have now been explored and exhausted. This is the trembling image of the ghost of desire, the frustrated longing that inhabits the empty space of human experience. Shaped to the rhythms of a recorded piece of music, its limits a gratuitous beginning and an unknown dark end, the first enfolded in someone else's voice, and the second enfolded in the brighter darkness of someone else's beginnings, man looks out for the reciprocal gaze of an Other who never appears. The eye never sees anything in the mirror, only its own face looking out: the face of a man who has come to terms with his given music, which is as much as can be done.

Written in 1976 and televised by the BBC in April 1977, *... but the clouds ...* works on multiple levels. Daniel Katz suggests that the play allegorises the operations of memory and also of losing and forgetting;[109] but as always, in Beckett, remembering, dreaming and creating are closely entwined.

The play begins with a shot from behind of a man on a stool, bent over an invisible table, like Krapp, a well-lit centre surrounded by shadows and darkness. In his own voice, he fantasises or, if Katz is correct, remembers, a variety of scenarios, each of which is performed in a separate shot, which are possible variants on the dream of a woman whom he tried to imagine in the long day's journey of his life. Each scenario operates with familiar elements from Beckett's storehouse. By day, he roams the roads, in everyday hat and greatcoat; by night, he labours to exhaustion, begging her image to appear. In the first scenario, her face flickers briefly into sight; then it flickers into sight twice more, and then appears murmuring inaudibly the phrase of the play's title. The sequence is repeated, and then the voice reports how, most often, the face never appears until he gives up hope, occupies himself with other tasks, and sets out again, this time on the back roads. Then only, in a final image, the woman's face appears, and the man's voice speaks the complete line, which closes Yeats's poem 'The Tower', celebrating the moment when, at the end of a life recounted, all that mattered in the living of it fades away, to become no more than clouds on the vanishing horizon, darkening shadows, a faint bird-note. At the end, all the forms of mind, memory, dream, and desire, must blur into the indifferentiation of their beginning. The shot dissolves to the man, their maker, and the final fade-out.

In this visual metaphor of the human condition, all experience is loss and longing, the unrequited desire for an Other, who can only be a flickering projection. The images formed in this projection, memories or fantasies, are shaped to the rhythms not this time of borrowed music, but of a borrowed poem. In the process of production, 'personal' emotion works its way into the form of the collective cultural inheritance. As in *Ghost Trio*, the borrowed form is made the author's own: the plangent nostalgia that drew him to Yeats's poem is transposed into the rhythms and rituals of his own voice, clothed in the coat and hat of his own life experience.

Quad, scripted in English in 1981, for four dancers, and written and directed by Beckett for Süddeutscher Rundfunk, works inside a stage space of six paces square, overlooked by a fixed camera.[110] The process here consists of no words, only rhythmic movement, light, and percussive sound. The figures, of indeterminate gender, small and thin, probably adolescent, are identical, except that each has its own colour for its costume and the light that tracks its movement, its own muted percussion accompaniment (in shadow at the back of the stage), and its distinctive footstep, heard intermittently when the percussion pauses.[111] A precisely-scripted combination of sequences directs the four pacing out their own courses, one pace a second, individually and then together. The series is repeated, after which all combinations are exhausted, and the light fades on one figure completing a last solitary course. There is no contact, and no crossing of paths. When they approach the centre, they swerve to circle round it, always in a clockwise direction. With the human figures stripped of individual identifiers, the strongest elements are the abstracts: rhythm, colour and movement. The effect is of a comic frenzy, an encapsulation of human being, going through the motions, with no pretence of significance or referent but the motion itself – a minimalist evocation of being, as nothing doing, everything passing. The piece became, in production in Stuttgart, *Quadrat I and II*, the first in colour, and the second in black and white, decided on after the German producer showed Beckett the monochrome monitor in the production box.[112] Without percussion, only the sound of shuffling feet, and taken at slower speed, this was a demonstration that form, even when exhausted, can still find a different form and be further diminished.

Nacht und Träume, written in 1982 for Süddeutscher Rundfunk, is a piece almost without words, but nevertheless loaded with cultural referents. It opens and closes with snatches of the melody of the last few bars of Schubert's song, hummed in a male voice, and a few sung words from his 'Holde Träume'. A grey-haired Dreamer, in an empty room with his hands on a table, sits in the foreground, faintly lit, and bows his head into his hands. On a higher podium, middle stage, is the mirror of his dream self, sitting in the same posture, but lit by a better light. A hand brings his dream self a cup, wipes his brow, joins hands with him, and gently touches his head. The dream fades out, the Dreamer is faded in, and the sequence is repeated. Here at last is an evocation of the human desire for love and tenderness, at last finding fulfilment – in a form that clearly signals mere dream, and tips into irony with the sentimental choice of music, and the clichés of a Christian consolation which Beckett himself never sought.

NOTES

1 Ronald Hayman, 'Radio meets theatre', *The Listener*, 2812 (9 June 1983), p.32. For an extended account of Beckett's broadcasting activity with the BBC, see Clas Zilliacus, *Beckett and Broadcasting: A Study of the Works of Samuel Beckett for and in Radio and Television* (Åbo: Åbo Akademi, 1976); see also Donald McWhinnie, *The Art of Radio* (London: Faber, 1959).

2 See Everett C. Frost, 'Fundamental Sounds: Recording Samuel Beckett's Radio Plays', *Theatre Journal*, 43, 3 (October 1991), p.366. (http://www.jstor.org/stable/3207590. Consulted 15 April 2011.)

3 Martin Esslin, 'Martin Esslin on Beckett the Man', Knowlson and Knowlson, *Beckett Remembering*, p.150.

4 See above, Chapter 6, p.142.

5 RCONT 1. Patrick MAGEE ARTIST. File 1: 1955–1962. (BBC Written Archive, Caversham Park.)

6 Andrew Todd 'Obituary' [for Barbara Bray], *The Guardian* (4 March 2010). (http://www.theguardian.com/tv-and-radio/2010/mar/04/barbara-bray-obituary. Consulted 2 October 2013.)

7 Marek Kędzierski, 'Barbara Bray: In her Own Words', *Modernism/ modernity*, 18, 4 (November 2011), p.891.

8 Talks. File 1: June 61–64. 'New Comment.' R51/893/1. (BBC Written Archive, Caversham Park.)

9 Letter from Beckett to Nancy Cunard, 4 July 1956, *Letters* II, p.631.

10 Letter from Beckett to Aidan Higgins, 6 July 1956, *Letters* II, p.633.

11 Sleeve notes to *Samuel Beckett: Works for Radio. The Original Broadcasts* (London: British Library Publishing Division, 2006).

12 RCONT 1. Patrick MAGEE ARTIST. File 1: 1955–1962 (BBC Written Archive, Caversham Park.)

13 Roy Walker, 'Critic on the Hearth. Sound Drama', *The Listener*, 1451 (17 January 1957), pp.131–2.

14 Letter from Beckett to Donald McWhinnie, 18 December 1956, *Letters* II, p.688, pp.688–9, n.1.

15 Everett C. Frost, Project Director of The Beckett Festival of Radio Plays, which was launched in April 1989, wrote that the aim of the recordings was to exploit to the full the radio potential of each play, and in the process to respect Beckett's original intentions for the sound (Frost, 'Fundamental Sounds' p.363). See the review of the collection by Katharine Worth, '*The Beckett Festival of Radio Plays.* Directed and produced by Everett C. Frost for Voices International, 2 Washington Square Village, 16-J, New York, NY 10012. *All That Fall, Words and Music, Cascando,* and *Rough for Radio II', Theatre Journal,* 42, 3 (October 1990), pp.385–8.

16 Frost, 'Fundamental Sounds', p.367.

17 See also the discussion by Jeff Porter, 'Samuel Beckett and the Radiophonic Body: Beckett and the BBC', *Modern Drama,* 53, 4 (Winter 2010), pp.431–46. Porter sees the representation of the body here as an exception in Beckett's work, which otherwise, he argues, writes towards its abolition. I have argued throughout the present book that the materiality of the human condition is a factor with which Beckett is always negotiating, even when his writing is at his most abstract. See also the analysis in Ulrike Maude, *Beckett, Technology and the Body* (Cambridge: Cambridge University Press, 2009), of the significance of the body in Beckett's work as the foundation of subject identity; Maude is especially interesting on Beckett's emphasis on the different forms of sensory perception, especially vision and hearing.

18 Samuel Beckett, *All That Fall* (1957); *CDW* 1986, p.174.

19 Beckett, *All That Fall* (1957); *CDW* 1986, p.175.

20 Letter from Beckett to Barney Rosset, 1 December 1956, *Letters* II, p.681.

21 Knowlson, *Damned to Fame,* p.430.

22 Kalb, *Beckett in Performance,* p.231. In the original broadcast, the actors were Irish: J.G. Devlin and Mary O'Farrell played Mr and Mrs Rooney.

23 Beckett, *All That Fall* (1957); *CDW* 1986, p.185.

24 Christopher Ricks, *Beckett's Dying Words* (Oxford: Clarendon Press, 1993), p.102.

25 Beckett, *All That Fall* (1957); *CDW* 1986, p.182.

26 Ibid.

27 Beckett, *All That Fall* (1957); *CDW* 1986, p.183.

28 Beckett, *All That Fall* (1957); *CDW* 1986, p.195.

29 Beckett, *All That Fall* (1957); *CDW* 1986, p.196.

30 Whitelaw, cit. Frost, 'Fundamental Sounds', p.368.

31 Policy R34/1, 639/1 (BBC Written Archive, Caversham Park).

32 RCONT 1. Patrick MAGEE ARTIST. File 1: 1955–1962 (BBC Written Archive, Caversham Park).

33 Beckett, *From an Abandoned Work*; *CSP* 1995, p.156.

34 Beckett, *From an Abandoned Work*; *CSP* 1995, p.158.

35 Beckett, *From an Abandoned Work*; *CSP* 1995, p.161.

36 Beckett, *From an Abandoned Work*; *CSP* 1995, p.163.
37 Beckett, *From an Abandoned Work*; *CSP* 1995, p.164.
38 RCONT 1. 910. Samuel Beckett. Source File. E1/2, 119/1. Italy. Italia Prize: *Embers* (BBC Written Archive, Caversham Park).
39 Knowlson, *Damned to Fame*, p.446.
40 Samuel Beckett, *Embers* (1959); *CDW* 1986, p.258.
41 E1/2, 119/1 Italy. Italia Prize: *Embers*. Italia Prize 1959 BBC Entry: *Embers* (BBC Written Archive, Caversham Park).
42 Beckett, *Embers* (1959); *CDW* 1986, p.255
43 Beckett, *Embers* (1959); *CDW* 1986, p.256.
44 Beckett, *Embers* (1959); *CDW* 1986, p.258.
45 Beckett, *Embers* (1959); *CDW* 1986, p.264.
46 Letter from Beckett to Barbara Bray, 11 March 1959, cit. Lois More Overbeck, 'Letters', in *Samuel Beckett in Context*, Anthony Ullman (ed.), Cambridge and New York: Cambridge University Press, 2013.
47 Knowlson, *Damned to Fame*, p.470.
48 Knowlson, *Damned to Fame*, p.480.
49 Knowlson, *Damned to Fame*, pp.481–4.
50 Marek Kędzierski, 'Rue Samuel Beckett', *Evergreen Review*, 122 (March 2010), (http://www.evergreenreview.com/122/rue-sam-beckett.html. Consulted 26/04/2013.) Kędzierski refers to a memoir written by Barbara Bray about her life with Beckett, which he helped her put together from her correspondence with him. For extracts from the memoir, see Kędzierski, 'Barbara Bray: In Her Own Words', n.7 above. The unattributed obituary in *The Telegraph* (18 April 2010), said the memoir was commissioned by Harvill Press (http://www.telegraph.co.uk/news/obituaries/culture-obituaries/tv-radio-obituaries/7604308/Barbara-Bray.html. Last consulted 13 November 2014.)
51 Andrew Todd 'Obituary' [for Barbara Bray].
52 The English translation, 'Sketch for Radio Play', was published in *Stereo Headphones*, 7 (Spring 1976).
53 RCONT 1. Barbara Bray Scriptwriter. File 1: 1955–62 (BBC Written Archive, Caversham).
54 Samuel Beckett, *Words and Music* (1962); *CDW* 1986, p.294.
55 Marcel Mihalovici, a French composer born in Romania, was married to the pianist Monique Haas. He had already written an operatic version of *Krapp's Last Tape*, working with Beckett to fit together the musical and textual phrases.
56 Samuel Beckett, *Cascando* (1963); *CDW* 1986, p.297.
57 Beckett, *Cascando* (1963); *CDW* 1986, p.300.
58 Beckett, *Cascando* (1963); *CDW* 1986, p.304.
59 Beckett, *Cascando* (1963); *CDW* 1986, p.303.

60 R19/1492. Entertainment. *Play* by Beckett. 1st b/c 11 October 1966 (BBC Written Archive, Caversham Park).

61 Introduction script, by Martin Esslin, in R19/1492. Entertainment. *Play* by Beckett. 1st b/c 11 October 1966 (BBC Written Archive, Caversham Park).

62 Martin Esslin, 'Samuel Beckett and the art of broadcasting', *Encounter* (September 1975), p.44. (http://www.unz.org/Pub/Encounter-1975sep-00038. Consulted 1 November 2013.)

63 Introduction script, by Martin Esslin, in R19/1492. Entertainment. *Play* by Beckett. 1st b/c 11 October 1966 (BBC Written Archive, Caversham Park).

64 R51/893/1. Talks. File 1: June 61–64. New Comment (BBC Written Archive, Caversham Park).

65 Ibid.

66 Ibid.

67 Letter from John Calder to Jack Beale, 21 October 1966; Letter from Jack Leak to Margaret McLaren, 25 October 1966 (Rcont18. Samuel Beckett Copyright File. File I: 1965–69 [BBC Written Archive, Caversham Park]).

68 See correspondence in Rcont18. Samuel Beckett Copyright File. File I: 1965–69 (BBC Written Archive, Caversham Park).

69 R51/194/1. Talks. File 2: 1965 - . New Comment (BBC Written Archive, Caversham Park).

70 Introduction script by Martin Esslin, in SF (Subject File) Entertainment. R19/1491 Entertainment. *Lessness* by Samuel Beckett (BBC Written Archive, Caversham Park).

71 Martin Esslin, 'Samuel Beckett and the Art of Radio', in S.E. Gontarski (ed.), *On Beckett. Essays and Criticism*, rev. edn. (London and New York: Anthem Press, 2012), p.283.

72 Ibid., p.284.

73 Introduction script by Martin Esslin, in SF (Subject File) Entertainment. R19/1491 Entertainment. *Lessness* by Samuel Beckett (BBC Written Archive, Caversham Park).

74 See Mark Nixon (ed.), Introduction to *Texts for Nothing*, pp.xxiii–iv, n.18.

75 Samuel Beckett, *Lessness* (1971); *TN* 2010, p.129.

76 Beckett, *Lessness* (1971); *TN* 2010, p.132.

77 Ibid.

78 Letter from John Calder to Martin Esslin, 23 March 1973, in RCONT 15. Samuel Beckett Scriptwriter. File 4: 1973–82 (BBC Written Archive, Caversham).

79 Samuel Beckett, *First Love* (1973); rpt. in Samuel Beckett, *'The Expelled' and Other Novellas* (Harmondsworth: Penguin Books, 1980), p.12; p.15; p.17.

80 Knowlson, p.574.

81 Beckett, *First Love*, p.19.

82 Beckett, *First Love*, p.30.

83 Production details are in R19/1492 Entertainment. *Rough for Radio* (BBC Written Archive, Caversham Park).

84 Letter from Martin Esslin to Beckett, 9 February 1976, in RCONT 15. Samuel Beckett Scriptwriter, File 4: 1973–82 (BBC Written Archive, Caversham Park).

85 Whitelaw, *Billie Whitelaw*, p.162.

86 Letter from Beckett to Martin Esslin, 13 February 1976, in RCONT 15 Samuel Beckett Scriptwriter File 4 1973–82 (BBC Written Archive, Caversham Park).

87 Samuel Beckett, *Rough for Radio II* (1976); *CDW* 1986, p.281.

88 Knowlson, *Damned to Fame*, p.533. See for production details of this project the extensive file in the BBC archives, which also indicates preliminary reluctance from BBC senior administrators to approve of Beckett's work – despite their pleasure in noting that *Waiting for Godot* would make a very cheap production (TELI/C 985/8958 Television Subject File T5/2, 420/1 DRAMA WAITING FOR GODOT TX 61.06.26, B/C 26.6.61 (BBC Written Archive, Caversham Park).

89 See Audience Research Report on 'Beginning to End', ed. Jonathan Miller, in RCONT1 910. Samuel Beckett Source File TELI/C/1415/12473 Television Registry Talks Subject File T32/1, 089/1 MONITOR TX 65.02.21 B/C 23.2.65 (BBC Written Archive, Caversham Park). Miller's programme consisted of a monologue made up of extracts from Beckett's plays and novels, all read by a single voice, which many respondents declared baffling and boring. The expenses on file for Miller's preparatory visit to Paris for this programme were high; two dinners with Beckett, and one lunch with Beckett and four others, including drinks, left little change out of £400. Beckett flew over and back from Berlin, first class, to attend rehearsals.

90 See TELI/C/838/6344 Television Subject File T5/2, 144/1 DRAMA *Krapp's Last Tape* TX 63.11.13 B/C 63.11.13 (BBC Written Archive, Caversham Park).

91 Knowlson, *Damned to Fame*, p.620.

92 Letter from Beckett to Alan Schneider, 29 September 1964, in Harmon (ed.), *No Author Better Served*, p.167. Letter © the Estate of Samuel Beckett, reproduced by kind permission of the Estate of Samuel Beckett c/o Rosica Colin Limited, London. Beckett attached to his letter extensive notes on the draft of the film (*Film*; *CDW* 1986, p.323).

93 Ibid. *Film* was awarded the Prie Filmcritice at the Venice Film Festival in October 1965 (Harmon [ed.], *No Author Better Served*, p.16, n.2).

94 Letter from Margaret McLaren to Edward Caffery, 1 July 1965, in Rcont18. Samuel Beckett Copyright File I: 1965–69 (BBC Written Archive, Caversham Park).

95 Audience Research Report, Eh Joe? (T5/1, 296/1. Subject File Drama B/C 4.7.66 (BBC Written Archive, Caversham Park). A German version, directed by Beckett, was broadcast by Süddeutscher Rundfunk three months earlier, because of the slowness of the BBC in finding a place on its schedules (Knowlson, p.535).

96 Letter from Beckett to Alan Schneider, 7 April 1966, in Harmon (ed.), *No Author Better Served*, p.201.

97 Samuel Beckett, *Eh Joe* (1967); *CDW* 1986, p.362.

98 Richard Toscan, 'MacGowran on Beckett' [interview], *Theatre Quarterly*, 3, 2 (July–Sept. 1973), p.20.

99 Beckett, *Eh Joe* (1967); *CDW* 1986, p.367.

100 Kalb, *Beckett in Performance*, p.109.

101 Ibid.

102 Letter from Beckett to Axel Kaun, 9 July 1937, *Letters* II, p.518.

103 Deleuze, *L'Epuisé*, p.74. See also Mary Bryden, 'Deleuze Reading Beckett', in Lane, Richard J. (ed.), *Beckett and Philosophy* (London: Palgrave, 2002), pp.80–92.

104 Deleuze, *L'Epuisé*, p.72.

105 Deleuze, *L'Epuisé*, p.64.

106 Martin Esslin, 'Towards the Zero of Language', in Acheson, J. and Arthur, K. (eds), *Beckett's Later Fiction and Drama*, (New York: St Martin's Press, 1987), p.46.

107 The first two were produced by Beckett for the BBC and Süddeutscher Rundfunk. *Quad*, and *Nacht und Träume* were both written for Süddeutscher Rundfunk and directed by Beckett.

108 Samuel Beckett, *Ghost Trio* (1976); *CDW* 1986, p.409.

109 Daniel Katz, 'Mirror Resembling Screen: Yeats, Beckett and "... *but the clouds* ..."', in Catharina Wulf (ed.), *The Savage Eye/ L'Oeil fauve. New Essays on Samuel Beckett's Television Plays, Samuel Beckett Today/ Aujourd'hui*, 4 (Amsterdam and Atlanta, GA: Editions Rodopi, 1995), p.83.

110 Esslin, 'Towards the Zero', p.42. The play was first transmitted by Süddeutscher Rundfunk, and then on BBC2, 16 December 1982.

111 Mary Bryden's discussion of *Quad*, which uses Beckett's handwritten drafts of the play in Reading University Library, includes a discussion of the gender implications of the performance. She points out that in a later annotation Beckett indicates the indifference here of gender, and argues that this gender fluidity is intrinsic to his primary engagement with movement, sound and light (Mary Bryden, '*QUAD*: Dancing Genders', in Catharina Wulf [ed.], *The Savage Eye/ L'Oeil fauve*, pp.109–122).

112 Knowlson, *Damned to Fame*, p.674.

Coda

Life and writing, always following the same paths, between the mystery of the necessary start and the mystery of the inevitable end, reached the final threshold in the 1980s. Beckett's cohort of friends and collaborators, already much diminished, was tragically reduced in 1984 by the deaths of Roger Blin, his first producer, and the stage director Alan Schneider, killed in a car accident, who was one of his last. Beckett himself began to suffer from emphysema, and from 1986 needed an oxygen cylinder to help him breathe; he suffered frequent falls.[1] He wrote on, with increasing difficulty; already in 1980, he had written to Alan Schneider that 'I feel drained as dry as an old herring bone'.[2] *Stirrings Still*, the collection of fragments published in 1988, is a compendium of familiar themes: loss, longing for consolation, falling, getting up again, and waiting for death.

After a fall in July 1988 that left him unconscious, he was taken to hospital, and then settled in a nursing home. He translated *Stirrings Still* into French, and 'Comment dire' into English ('what is the word'). There were regular visitors, including numerous newer friends, and always Barbara Bray. Suzanne, who had become increasingly frail, irritable, and hostile, never came to visit. She died on 17 July 1989, and Beckett was able to attend her funeral. He collapsed in his bathroom on 6 December, and on 22 December died peacefully in hospital. There were many obituaries in the national and international press. Most mentioned *Waiting for Godot* as the play that transformed the London stage. Some spoke feelingly of the friend. Leslie Hill, writing in *Radical Philosophy*, noted of his writing that:

> what emerges most clearly is the power of Beckett's commitment to an ethics of writing, his respect for the trace of otherness, the alterity and

> difference at the heart of assumed identity that, for Beckett, was what was at stake in literature.[3]

Here is Samuel Beckett's distinctive attribute: an engagement with language and form which enables him to establish a true understanding of how it is to be human, writing out an end to self-possession. His 'own' voice is inseparable from that of the 'other' voices with which it conducts its endless dialogue. The subject, never fixed, endlessly moving, finally grasps itself as a plethora of changing positions, in the form of notes resonating together in a chord, or better still, the form of the bees' dance, bodies all in motion. That time spent doing nothing, doing time, slips through the rhythms of Beckett's writing into the time of undoing, the real form of human time.

NOTES

1 Knowlson, pp.700–4, traces Beckett's last two years of life.

2 Letter from Beckett to Alan Schneider, 5 September 1980, in Harmon (ed.), *No Author Better Served*, p.391. This letter, © the Estate of Samuel Beckett, reproduced by kind permission of the Estate of Samuel Beckett c/o Rosica Colin Limited, London.

3 Leslie Hill, 'Samuel Beckett (1906–1989)', p.62.

References

I) Samuel Beckett: Texts Cited

Texts in each section are in chronological order of publication. Date of first publication in English (UK or US) is given in brackets after the title, followed by publication details of the edition used for references. Mark Nixon, in his Preface to his edition of *Texts for Nothing and Other Shorter Prose, 1950–1976* (London: Faber and Faber, 2010), and S.E. Gontarski, in his Introduction to his edition of *The Theatrical Notebooks of Samuel Beckett, Vol. IV, The Shorter Plays* (London: Faber and Faber Ltd, and New York: Grove Press, 1999), have useful discussions alerting readers to the variants between texts due to the number of Beckett's publishers and the changes the writer himself constantly made to manuscripts and new printed editions. Date of first publication in French is given in main text or endnotes.

Collections of works by Samuel Beckett

The Beckett Trilogy. Molloy, Malone Dies, The Unnamable (London: Pan Books, Picador Edition, 1979). Abbreviated as *Trilogy* 1979.

Disjecta. Miscellaneous Writings and a Dramatic Fragment, ed. and intro. Ruby Cohn (London: John Calder, 1983). Abbreviated as *Disjecta* 1983.

The Complete Dramatic Works (London: Faber and Faber, 1986). Abbreviated as *CDW* 1986.

Samuel Beckett. The Complete Short Prose 1929–1989, ed. and intro. S.E. Gontarski (New York: Grove Press, 1995). Abbreviated as *CSP* 1995.

Samuel Beckett: The Grove Centenary Edition, Vol. I, Novels, ed. Paul Auster and intro. Colm Tóibín (New York: Grove Press, 2006). Abbreviated as *Grove* 2006.

Company, Ill Seen Ill Said, Worstward Ho, Stirrings Still, ed. Dirk Van Hulle (London: Faber and Faber, 2009). Abbreviated as *Van Hulle* 2009.

Texts for Nothing and Other Shorter Prose, 1950–1976, ed. Mark Nixon (London: Faber and Faber, 2010). Abbreviated as *TN* 2010.

The Collected Poems of Samuel Beckett, eds Seán Lawlor and John Pilling (London: Faber and Faber, 2012). Abbreviated as *CP* 2012.

Poetry

Whoroscope (1930); *CP* 2012.

Echo's Bones and Other Precipitates (1935); *CP* 2012.

Poèmes '38-39 (1946); *CP* 2012.

Fizzles (1976); *TN* 2010.

Drunken Boat (1976); *CP* 2012.

Poèmes suivis de Mirlitonnades (1978); *CP* 2012.

'what is the word' (1989); *CP* 2012.

Prose

'Assumption' (1929); *CSP* 1995.

'Dante ... Bruno. Vico ... Joyce' (1929); *Disjecta* 1983.

Proust (1931); rpt. in *Proust and 'Three Dialogues: Samuel Beckett & Georges Duthuit'* (London: John Calder, 1965).

'Ding-Dong', in *More Pricks than Kicks* (1934); *More Pricks than Kicks*; rpt. London: Calder & Boyars, 1973, pp. 39–40.

'Recent Irish Poetry' (pseud. Andrew Belis, 1934); *Disjecta* 1983.

Murphy (1938); *Grove* 2006.

Three Dialogues: Samuel Beckett & Georges Duthuit (1949); rpt. in *Proust and 'Three Dialogues Samuel Beckett & Georges Duthuit'* (London: John Calder, 1965).

Watt (1953); *Grove* 2006.

Molloy (1955); *Trilogy* 1979.

From an Abandoned Work (1956); *CSP* 1995.

Malone Dies (1956); *Trilogy* 1979.

The Unnamable (1959); *Trilogy* 1979.

How It Is (1964); rpt. Edouard Magessa O'Reilly (ed.), *How It Is* (London: Faber and Faber, 2009).

Imagination Dead Imagine (1965); *TN* 2010.

Enough (1967); *TN* 2010.

Ping (1967); *TN* 2010.

Texts for Nothing, in Samuel Beckett, *No's Knife: Collected Shorter Prose,* 1945–66 (London: Calder and Boyars, 1967) and Samuel Beckett, *Stories and Texts for Nothing* (New York: Grove Press, 1967); TN 2010.

Lessness (1970); *TN* 2010.

The Lost Ones (1972); *TN* 2010.

The North [extract from *The Lost Ones*], illustrated by Avigdor Arikha (London: Enitharmon Press, 1972).

First Love (1973); rpt. in Samuel Beckett, *The Expelled and Other Novellas* (Harmondsworth: Penguin Books, 1980).

Mercier and Camier (1974); *Grove* 2006.

All Strange Away (1976); *TN* 2010.

Fizzles (1976); *TN* 2010.

Company (London: John Calder, 1980).

Ill Seen Ill Said (1981); *Van Hulle* 2009.

Worstward Ho (1983); *Van Hulle* 2009.

Disjecta. Miscellaneous Writings and a Dramatic Fragment, ed. and intro. Ruby Cohn (London: John Calder, 1983).

Stirrings Still (1989); *Van Hulle* 2009.

Nohow On (London: John Calder, 1989).

Dream of Fair to Middling Women, Eoin O'Brien and Edith Fournier (eds) (Dublin: The Black Cat Press, 1992).

Echo's Bones, ed. Mark Nixon (New York: Grove Press/ Atlantic Monthly Press, 2014).

Drama

Waiting for Godot (1954); *CDW* 1986.

Ó Briain, Liam, and Ó Carra, Seàn (trans.), *Ag Fanacht Le Godot* (*Waiting for Godot*), staged 28 November 1971 (Playography Ireland, Irish Theatre Institute, www.irishplayography.com/play.aspx?playid=3376. Consulted 18 September 2013.)

All That Fall (1957); *CDW* 1986.

Endgame (1958); *CDW* 1986.

Krapp's Last Tape (1958); *CDW* 1986.

Act Without Words I (1958); *CDW* 1986.

Act Without Words II (1959); *CDW* 1986.

Embers (1959); *CDW* 1986.

Happy Days (1961); rpt. James Knowlson (ed.), *Happy Days/ Oh Les Beaux Jours* by Samuel Beckett (London and Boston: Faber and Faber, 1978).

Words and Music (1962); *CDW* 1986.

Cascando (1963); *CDW* 1986.

Play (1964); *CDW* 1986.

Eh Joe (1967); *CDW* 1986.

Film (1967); *CDW* 1986.

Breath (1970); *CDW* 1986.

Not I (1973); *CDW* 1986.
Rough for Radio I (1976); *CDW* 1986.
Rough for Radio II (1976); *CDW* 1986.
Rough for Theatre I (1976); *CDW* 1986.
Rough for Theatre II (1976); *CDW* 1986.
That Time (1976); *CDW* 1986.
Footfalls (1976); *CDW* 1986.
Ghost Trio (1976); *CDW* 1986.
... but the clouds ... (1977); *CDW* 1986.
Rockaby (1981); *CDW* 1986.
Ohio Impromptu (1981); *CDW* 1986.
Catastrophe (1984); *CDW* 1986.
Quad (1984); *CDW* 1986.
What Where (1984); *CDW* 1986.
Nacht und Träume (1984); *CDW* 1986.
Eleutheria, trans. Barbara Wright (London: Faber and Faber, 1996).
The Theatrical Notebooks of Samuel Beckett, Vol. IV, The Shorter Plays, ed. and intro. S.E. Gontarski (London: Faber and Faber Ltd, and New York: Grove Press, 1999).

Letters

Martha Dow Fehsenfeld, Lois More Overbeck, George Craig and Dan Gunn (eds), *The Letters of Samuel Beckett, Volume I: 1929–1940* (Cambridge and New York: Cambridge University Press, 2009). Abbreviated as *Letters* I.

George Craig, Martha Dow Fehsenfeld, Dan Gunn, Lois More Overbeck (eds), *The Letters of Samuel Beckett, Volume II: 1941-1956* (Cambridge and New York: Cambridge University Press, 2011). Abbreviated as *Letters* II.

Maurice Harmon (ed.), *No Author Better Served. The Correspondence of Samuel Beckett and Alan Schneider* (Cambridge, Massachusetts and London, England: Harvard University Press, 1998).

Electronic media

The Beckett Festival of Radio Plays, Directed and produced by Everett C. Frost for Voices International, 2 Washington Square Village, 16-J, New York, NY 10012. Launched in 1989.

Beckett on Film (4 DVDs), produced by RTE, Channel 4, and the Irish Film Board (London: Clarence Pictures, 2001).

Samuel Beckett: Works for Radio. The Original Broadcasts (London: British Library Publishing Division, 2006). NSACD. 4 disks.

II) Secondary Sources

Ackerley, C.J. and Gontarski, S.E. (eds), *The Grove Companion to Samuel Beckett. A Reader's Guide to his Works, Life and Thought* (New York: Grove Press, 2004).

Adorno, Theodor W., *Negative Dialectics* (London: Routledge, 1990).

Aldington, Richard, *Life for Life's Sake* (1940); rpt. London: Cassell, 1968.

Andrew, Nigel, 'Meremost Minimum', *The Listener*, 2821 (11 August 1983), p.26.

Anon., 'Barbara Bray' [Obituary], *The Telegraph* (18 April 2010) (http://www.telegraph.co.uk/news/obituaries/culture-obituaries/tv-radio-obituaries/7604308/Barbara-Bray.html. Last consulted 13 November 2014.)

Anon., 'Billie up to her neck in Beckett,' *Arts Guardian* (30 May 1979), p.12.

Anon., [Review of *Murphy*], *Dublin Magazine*, 14.2 (April–June 1939), p.98.

Anon., 'Samuel Beckett Class Offshore Patrol Vessels, Ireland', *naval-technology.com* (http://www.naval-technology.com/projects/samuel-beckett-class-offshore-patrol-vessels-opvs/. Consulted 28 August 2014.)

Artaud, Antonin, *Le théâtre et son double* ([1938] Paris: Gallimard, 1964).

Atik, Anne, *How It Was. A Memoir of Samuel Beckett* (London: Faber and Faber, 2001).

Bair, Deirdre, *Samuel Beckett. A Biography* (London: Jonathan Cape, 1978).

Barth, John, 'The Literature of Exhaustion', *Atlantic Monthly*, 220, 33 (August 1967), pp.29–34.

Baudelaire, Charles, 'Une Charogne', *Les Fleurs du mal* (Paris: Poulet-Malassis et de Broise, 1857).

'Beckett Shorts', Brochure for the French Theatre Season, 30 September–20 December 1997.

Bennett, Susan, *Theatre Audiences. A Theory of Production and Reception,* 2nd edn (London and New York: Routledge, 1997).

Ben-Zvi, Linda, '*Not I*: Through a Tube Starkly', in Linda Ben-Zvi (ed.), *Women in Beckett: Performance and Critical Perspectives* (Urbana and Chicago: University of Illinois, Illini Books Edition, 1992), pp.243–8.

Benveniste, Émile, *Problèmes de linguistique générale*, 1966; trans. Mary Elizabeth Meek, *Problems in General Linguistics* (Coral Gables: University of Miami Press, 1981).

Billington, Michael, 'Plays for Today. Beckett wrote four masterpieces. The rest will soon be forgotten', *The Guardian* (1 September 1999) (http://archive.is/TxK4. Consulted 24 October 2013.)

'Bing Beckett Blin Bordeaux 2012.' Essai filmique. Texte de Samuel Beckett (1966, Editions de Minuit), voix de Roger Blin sur France-Culture 1965, images des trois cimetières juifs de Bordeaux (1724 à nos jours). Published on 29 October 2012. (http://www.youtube.com/watch?v=x3Zyt4XLHs0. Consulted 9 July 2013.)

Birkett, Jennifer and Ince, Kate (eds), *Samuel Beckett* (London and New York: Longman, Longman Critical Readers, 2000).

Bradby, David, *Beckett, 'Waiting for Godot'* (Cambridge: Cambridge University Press, 2001).
Bradby, David and Delgado, Maria M. (eds), *The Paris Jigsaw. Internationalism and the City's Stages* (Manchester: Manchester University Press, 2002).
Brook, Peter, *The Empty Space* (1968); rpt. Harmondsworth: Penguin Books, 1990.
Brooker, Peter and Thacker, Andrew (eds), *The Oxford Critical and Cultural History of Modernist Magazines. Volume I: Britain and Ireland 1880–1955* (Oxford: Oxford University Press, 2009).
Bryden, Mary, *Women in Samuel Beckett's Prose and Drama. Her Own Other* (Houndmills, Basingstoke: The Macmillan Press, and Lanham: Barnes & Noble, 1993).
Bryden, Mary, 'Beckett/ Deleuze/ Guattari: Gender in Process', in *Women in Samuel Beckett's Prose and Drama*, pp.58–69.
Bryden, Mary, '*QUAD*: Dancing Genders', in Catharina Wulf (ed.), *The Savage Eye/ L'Oeil fauve. New Essays on Samuel Beckett's Television Plays, Samuel Beckett Today/ Aujourd'hui*, 4 (Amsterdam and Atlanta, GA: Editions Rodopi, 1995), pp. 109–122.
Bryden, Mary, 'Deleuze Reading Beckett', in Richard J. Lane (ed.), *Beckett and Philosophy* (London: Palgrave, 2002), pp.80–92.
Bryden, Mary and Topping, Margaret (eds), *Beckett's Proust/ Deleuze's Proust*, (Houndmills, Basingstoke and New York: Palgrave Macmillan, 2009).
Cixous, Hélène, 'Une Passion: l'un peu moins que rien', in Tom Bishop and Raymond Federman (eds), *Samuel Beckett, Cahiers de l'Herne*, Special Issue, 31, 1976, pp.326–35.
Cixous, Hélène, 'La Missexualité: où jouis-je?' *Poétique* 26 (1976); rpt. in *Entre l'écriture* (Paris: éditions des femmes, 1986), pp.75–95.
Connor, Steven, *Samuel Beckett: Repetition, Theory and Text* (Oxford: Basil Blackwell, 1988).
Coughlan, Patricia, '"The Poetry is Another Pair of Sleeves": Beckett, Ireland and Modernist Lyric Poetry', in Patricia Coughlan and Alex Davis (eds), *Modernism and Ireland: The Poetry of the 1930s* (Cork: Cork University Press, 1995), pp.173–208.
Cronin, Anthony, 'A Vote for the Little World. *Watt* by Samuel Beckett', *TLS*, 3231 (30 January 1964), p.81.
Cunard, Nancy (ed.), *Negro. An Anthology* (1934); ed. and abridged with an Introduction by Hugh Ford (New York and London: Continuum, 2002).
Deleuze, Gilles, 'L'Épuisé', in Samuel Beckett, *'Quad' et autres pièces pour la télévision, suivi de 'L'Épuisé' par Gilles Deleuze* (Paris, Editions de Minuit, 1992).
Driver, Tom, 'Beckett by the Madeleine', *Columbia University Forum* 4.3 (1961), pp.21–5.
Dwan, Lisa, 'Beckett's *Not I*: how I became the ultimate motormouth', *The Guardian* (8 May 2013) (http://www.theguardian.com/culture/2013/may/08/beckett-not-i-lisa-dwan. Consulted 28 October 2014.)
Esslin, Martin, 'Samuel Beckett and the art of broadcasting', *Encounter* (September 1975), p.44 (http://www.unz.org/Pub/Encounter-1975sep-00038. Consulted 1 November 2013.)

Esslin, Martin, 'Towards the Zero of Language', in J. Acheson and K. Arthur (eds), *Beckett's Later Fiction and Drama* (New York: St Martin's Press, 1987), pp.35–49.

Esslin, Martin, 'Martin Esslin on Beckett the Man', in James and Elizabeth Knowlson (eds), *Beckett Remembering/ Remembering Beckett* (London: Bloomsbury Publishing Plc, 2006).

Esslin, Martin, 'Samuel Beckett and the Art of Radio', in S.E. Gontarski (ed.) *On Beckett. Essays and Criticism*, rev. edn (London and New York: Anthem Press, 2012), pp. 273–91.

Eyre, Richard and Wright, Nicholas, *Changing Stages. A View of British Theatre in the Twentieth Century* (London: Bloomsbury Publishing Plc, 2000).

'Fathoms from Anywhere.' A Samuel Beckett Centenary Exhibition, The Harry Ransom Humanities Research Center, The University of Texas at Austin. (http://www.hrc.utexas.edu/exhibitions/web/beckett/share/. Consulted 9 September 2013.)

Friedman, Alan Warren (ed.), *Beckett in Black and Red: The Translations for Nancy Cunard's* Negro *(1934)* (Lexington: University Press of Kentucky, 2000).

Frost, Everett C., 'Fundamental Sounds: Recording Samuel Beckett's Radio Plays', *Theatre Journal*, 43, 3 (October 1991), pp.361–76 (http://www.jstor.org/stable/3207590. Consulted 15 April 2011.)

Gardner, Lyn, '*Waiting for Godot*, Haymarket, London', *The Guardian* (26 January 2010).

Gibbons, Luke, *Transformations in Irish Culture* (Notre Dame, Ind.: University of Notre Dame Press, in association with Field Day, 1996).

Gierow, Karl Ragnar, 'The Nobel Prize in Literature 1969. Samuel Beckett. Award Ceremony Speech.' The Nobel Foundation. (http://www.nobelprize.org/nobel_prizes/literature/laureates/1969/press.html# Consulted 3 December 2012.)

Girodias, Maurice, *Une Journée sur la terre. II Les Jardins d'Éros* (Paris: Editions de la Différence, 1990).

Glendinning, Alex, '*More Pricks than Kicks*', *TLS*, 1695 (26 July 1934), p.526.

Glendinning, Alex, 'The New Novels', *TLS*, Spring Books Number, 1884 (12 March 1938), p.172.

Gontarski, S.E. (ed. and intro.), *The Theatrical Notebooks of Samuel Beckett, Vol. IV, The Shorter Plays* (London: Faber and Faber Ltd, and New York: Grove Press, 1999).

Gordon, Lois, *The World of Samuel Beckett (1906–1946)* (New Haven and London: Yale University Press, 1996).

Gormley, Anthony, 'Observations: I made a tree because Beckett means a lot to me', *The Independent* (25 August 2012) (http://www.independent.co.uk/arts-entertainment/art/news/observations-i-made-a-tree-because-beckett-means-a-lot-to-me-8076584.html. Consulted 11 November 2011.)

Hall, Peter, 'Godotmania', *The Guardian* (Saturday 4 January 2003) (http://www.theguardian.com/stage/2003/jan/04/theatre.beckettat100. Consulted 9 September 2013.)

Harmon, Maurice (ed.), *No Author Better Served. The Correspondence of Samuel Beckett and Alan Schneider* (Cambridge, Mass.: Harvard University Press, 1998).

Harvey, Lawrence E., *Samuel Beckett: Poet and Critic* (Princeton, New Jersey: Princeton University Press, 1970).

Hawksley, Rupert, 'Samuel Beckett's *Not I* to be performed on television', *The Telegraph* (27 June 2013) (http://www.telegraph.co.uk/culture/tvandradio/10146406/Samuel-Becketts-Not-I-to-be-performed-on-television.html. Consulted 29 October 2014.)

Hayman, Ronald, 'Radio meets theatre', *The Listener*, 2812 (9 June 1983), p. 32.

Higgins, Jennifer, *English Responses to French Poetry 1880–1940. Translation and Mediation* (Oxford: Legenda, 2011).

Hill, Leslie, *Beckett's Fiction: In Different Words* (Cambridge: Cambridge University Press, 1990).

Hill, Leslie, 'Samuel Beckett (1906–1989)', *Radical Philosophy*, 55 (Summer 1990), pp.61–2.

Iser, Wolfgang, *Prospecting: From Reader Response to Literary Anthropology* (Baltimore, MD and London: Johns Hopkins University Press, 1989).

Jeffers, Jennifer M., 'Deviant Masculinity and Deleuzian Difference in Proust and Beckett', in Mary Bryden and Margaret Topping (eds), *Beckett's Proust/ Deleuze's Proust*, pp. 171–82.

Jones, David Houston, *Samuel Beckett and Testimony* (Houndmills, Basingtoke: Palgrave Macmillan, 2011).

Joyce, James, *Ulysses* (Paris: Shakespeare & Company, 1922).

Joyce, James, *Finnegans Wake* (London: Faber and Faber; New York: Viking, 1939).

Kalb, Jonathan, *Beckett in Performance* (Cambridge: Cambridge University Press, 1989).

Karpf, Anne, 'Radio', *The Listener*, 2785 (4 November 1982), p. 29.

Katz, Daniel, 'Mirror Resembling Screen: Yeats, Beckett and "... *but the clouds* ..."', in Catharina Wulf (ed.), *The Savage Eye/ L'Oeil fauve. New Essays on Samuel Beckett's Television Plays, Samuel Beckett Today/ Aujourd'hui*, 4 (Amsterdam and Atlanta, GA: Editions Rodopi, 1995), pp.83–92.

Kędzierski, Marek, 'Rue Samuel Beckett', *Evergreen Review*, 122 (March 2010) (http://www.evergreenreview.com/122/rue-sam-beckett.html. Consulted 26/04/2013.)

Kędzierski, Marek, 'Barbara Bray: In Her Own Words', *Modernism/modernity*, 18, 4 (November 2011), pp. 887–97.

Kelley, Paul, *Stories for Nothing: Samuel Beckett's Narrative Poetics* (New York, Bern, and Frankfurt am Main: Peter Lang, 2002).

Kennedy, Seán (ed.), *Beckett and Ireland* (Cambridge: Cambridge University Press, 2010).

Kenner, Hugh, 'The Terminator', in *A Colder Eye. The Modern Irish Writers* (Harmondsworth: Penguin Books, 1984), pp.329–42.

Kiberd, Declan, *Inventing Ireland: The Literature of the Modern Nation* (London: Vintage, 1996).

Knowlson, James, *Damned to Fame. The Life of Samuel Beckett* (London: Bloomsbury Publishing Plc, 1996).

Knowlson, James and Knowlson, Elizabeth (eds), *Beckett Remembering/ Remembering Beckett* (London: Bloomsbury Publishing Plc, 2006).

Knowlson, James and Leakey, Felix (eds), *Samuel Beckett 'Drunken Boat': A Translation of Arthur Rimbaud's poem 'Le Bateau ivre'* (Reading: Whiteknights Press, 1976).

Kristeva, Julia, 'Le Père, l'amour, l'exil', in Bishop, Tom, and Raymond Federman (eds), *Samuel Beckett, Cahiers de l'Herne,* Special Issue, 31, 1976, pp.246–52; 'The Father, Love and Banishment', in Leon S. Roudiez (ed.), *Desire in Language: A Semiotic Approach to Literature and Arts,* trans. Thomas Gora, Alice Jardine, Leon S. Roudiez (New York: Columbia UP; Oxford: Basil Blackwell, 1980), pp.148–58.

Lane, Richard J. (ed.), *Beckett and Philosophy* (London: Palgrave, 2002),

Lawlor, Seán, '"That's how it was and them were the days": Beckett's early publications with Samuel Putnam and Nancy Cunard', in Mark Nixon (ed.), *Publishing Samuel Beckett,* pp.23–34.

Lennon, Peter, 'Evenings with Sam', *Review Guardian* (25 January 1990), pp.23–4.

Lezard, Nicholas, 'People will shudder …', Review Supplement, *The Saturday Guardian* (10 May 2014), p.20.

Lichtenfels, Peter, 'Afterword. British Intersections with Paris', in Bradby and Delgado, *The Paris Jigsaw,* pp.277–86.

Lloyd, David, *Anomalous States: Irish Writing and the Post-Colonial Moment* (Durham, NC: Duke University Press, 1993).

Macklin, Gerald M., '"Drunken Boat": Samuel Beckett's Translation of Arthur Rimbaud's "Le Bateau ivre"', *Studies in 20th-Century Literature,* 27, 1 (January 2003) (http://dx.doi.org/10.4148/2334-4415.1549).

Mahon, Derek, 'An Image from Beckett', *Poems 1962–68* (Oxford and New York: Oxford University Press, 1979).

Mahon, Derek, 'Burbles', *The Hudson Letter* (Oldcastle: The Gallery Press, 1995), pp.21–2.

Mahon, Derek, 'Watt is the word. The "brief scattered lights" of Beckett's poems', *TLS,* 5405 (3 November 2006), pp.12–13.

Manifesto for 'The Revolution of the Word', *transition* 16–17 (June 1929).

McDonald, Rónán, 'Beckett and Irish Studies', in Seán Kennedy (ed.), *Beckett and Ireland,* pp.16–30.

Mars-Jones, Adam, '"Not I"', *London Review of Books,* 36, 5 (6 March 2014), p.22.

Maude, Ulrike, *Beckett, Technology and the Body* (Cambridge: Cambridge University Press, 2009).

Mays, J.C.C., 'Brian Coffey's Review of Beckett's *Murphy*: "Take Warning while you praise"', in Benjamin Keatinge and Aengus Woods (eds), *Other Edens. The Life and Work of Brian Coffey* (Dublin and Portland, Oregon: Irish Academic Press, 2010), pp. 82–100.

McDonald, Rónán, 'Beckett and Irish Studies', in Seán Kennedy (ed.), *Beckett and Ireland*, pp.16–30.

McWhinnie, Donald, *The Art of Radio* (London: Faber, 1959).

Monk, Craig, 'Eugene Jolas and the translation policies of *transition*', *Mosaic: a Journal for the Interdisciplinary Study of Literature*, 32, 4 (December 1999), pp.17–34.

Mood, John J., 'The Personal System – Samuel Beckett's *Watt*, *PMLA*, 86, 2 (March 1971), pp.255–65.

Mooney, Sinéad, *A Tongue Not Mine: Beckett and Translation* (Oxford: Oxford University Press, 2011).

Morin, Emilie, *Samuel Beckett and The Problem of Irishness* (London and New York, NY: Palgrave Macmillan, 2009).

Murphy, P.J., 'Beckett and the Philosophers', in John Pilling (ed.), *The Cambridge Companion to Beckett* (Cambridge: Cambridge University Press, 1994), pp.222–39.

Nixon, Mark, '"A brief glow in the dark": Samuel Beckett's Presence in Modern Irish Poetry', *Yearbook of English Studies* 35 (2005), pp.43–57.

Nixon, Mark (ed.), *Publishing Samuel Beckett* (London: The British Library Publishing Division, 2011).

Nixon, Mark, 'George Reavey – Beckett's first literary agent', in Mark Nixon (ed.), *Publishing Samuel Beckett*, pp. 41–56.

Nixon, Mark and Feldman, Matthew (eds), *The International Reception of Samuel Beckett* (London: Continuum, 2009).

O'Brien, Kate, 'Fiction. *Murphy*. By Samuel Beckett', *The Spectator* (25 March 1938), p. 50 (http://archive.spectator.co.uk/article/25th-march-1938/50/fiction. Consulted 27 August 2013).

O'Neill, Eoin, *The Beckett Country: Samuel Beckett's Ireland* (New York: Arcade Publishing, 1993).

Oppenheim, Lois (ed.), *Directing Beckett* (Ann Arbor: University of Michigan Press, 1997).

Overbeck, Lois More, 'Audience of Self/ Audience of Reader', *Modernism/modernity*, 18, 4 (November 2011), pp.721–37.

Overbeck, Lois More, 'Letters', in Anthony Ullman (ed.), *Samuel Beckett in Context* (Cambridge and New York: Cambridge University Press, 2013).

Peake, Charles H. 'In pursuit of failure', *TLS*, 3589 (11 December 1970), p.1442.

Philips, Deborah, 'Interview: Billie Whitelaw', *Women's Review*, 4 (February 1986), pp.6–8.

Pilling, John (ed.), *The Cambridge Companion to Beckett* (Cambridge: Cambridge University Press, 1994).

Pilling John, 'Guesses and Recesses: Notes on, in and towards *Dream of Fair to Middling Women*', in Marius Buning, Danielle de Ruyter, Matthijs Engelberts and Sjef Houppermans (eds), *Beckett versus Beckett, Samuel Beckett Today/ Aujourd'hui* (Amsterdam-Atlanta, GA: Rodopi, 1998), pp.13–23.

Pilling. John and Lawlor, Seán, 'Beckett in Transition', in Mark Nixon, *Beckett and Publishing,* pp.83–96.

Porter, Jeff, 'Samuel Beckett and the Radiophonic Body: Beckett and the BBC', *Modern Drama,* 53, 4 (Winter 2010), pp.431–46.

Proust, Marcel, *A la recherche du temps perdu* (1913–27); rpt. Jean-Yves Tadié and Florence Callu (eds), (Paris: Gallimard, Editions de La Pléiade, 4 vols, 1987–89).

Putnam, Samuel, Darnton, Maida Castelhuhn, Reavey, George and Bronowski, Jacob (eds), *The European Caravan, A Critical Anthology of the New Spirit in European Literature,* Vol. I (New York: Brewer, Warren & Putnam, 1931).

Putnam, Samuel, *Paris Was Our Mistress. Memoirs of a Lost and Found Generation* (1947; rpt. Carbondale IL: Southern Illinois University Press, Arcturus Books Edition, 1970).

Reavey, George (ed.), *Thorns of Thunder* (London: Europa Press & Stanley Nott, 1936).

Ricks, Christopher, *Beckett's Dying Words* (Oxford: Clarendon Press, 1993).

Rimbaud, Arthur, 'Le Bateau ivre', in Paterne Berrichon (ed.), *Oeuvres de Arthur Rimbaud: Vers et proses* (Paris: Mercure de France, 1912).

Robbe-Grillet, Alain, 'Samuel Beckett, Auteur Dramatique', *Critique* 9 (February 1953), pp.108–114.

Robinson, Michael, *The Long Sonata of the Dead: A Study of Samuel Beckett* (New York: Grove Press, 1969).

Rushdie, Salman, *Imaginary Homelands* (London: Granta Books, 1991).

Schoene, Berthold, 'The Union and Jack: British Masculinities, Pomophobia, and the Post-nation', in Glenda Norquay and Gerry Smith (eds), *Across the Margins: Cultural Identity and Change in the Atlantic Archipelago* (New York: Palgrave Macmillan, 2002).

Sesame Street – Monsterpiece Theater, 'Waiting for Elmo', *Beckett Shorts,* YouTube. (http://www.youtube.com/playlist?list=PLFA3C073738DAC946. Consulted 9 September 2013.)

Shloss, Carol Loeb, *Lucia Joyce. To Dance in the Wake* (London: Bloomsbury Publishing Plc, 2005).

Smith, David, Carter, Imogen, and Carnwath, Ally, 'In Godot we trust', *The Observer* (Sunday 8 March 2009). (http://www.theguardian.com/culture/2009/mar/08/samuel-beckett-waiting-for-godot. Last consulted 11 November 2014.)

Spencer, Charles, '*Waiting for Godot,* Haymarket Theatre Royal', *The Telegraph* (8 May 2009).

Taylor-Batty, Juliette, 'Imperfect Mastery: The Failure of Grammar in Beckett's *L'Innommable*', *Journal of Modern Literature* 30, 2 (2007), Indiana University Press, pp.163–79.

Thomas, Dylan, 'Recent Novels', *New English Weekly*, 12 (17 March 1938), pp. 454–5.

Todd, Andrew, 'Obituary' [for Barbara Bray], *The Guardian* (4 March 2010) (http://www.theguardian.com/tv-and-radio/2010/mar/04/barbara-bray-obituary. Consulted 2 October 2013.)

Toscan, Richard, 'MacGowran on Beckett' [interview], *Theatre Quarterly*, 3, 2 (July–Sept. 1973), pp.15–22.

transition (eds Eugene Jolas, Elliot Paul).

Transition (ed. Georges Duthuit).

Tucker, David, *Samuel Beckett and Arnold Geulincx. Tracing 'a Literary Fantasia'* (Continuum: London and New York, 2012).

Ullman, Anthony (ed.), *Samuel Beckett in Context* (Cambridge and New York: Cambridge University Press, 2013).

Vine, Barbara, *The Chimney Sweeper's Boy* (Viking 1998, Penguin Books, 1998, reissued 2007).

Walker, Roy, 'Critic on the Hearth. Sound Drama', *The Listener*, 1451 (17 January 1957), pp.131–2.

Watson, David, *Paradox and Desire in Samuel Beckett's Fiction* (Houndmills, Basingstoke: Macmillan, 1991).

Whitelaw, Billie, *Billie Whitelaw … Who He? An Autobiography* (London: Hodder and Stoughton, 1995; Sceptre Paperback, 1996).

Williams, David, '"Towards an art of memory": Peter Brook, a foreigner in Paris', in Bradby, David and Delgado, Maria M. (eds), *The Paris Jigsaw*, pp.37–52.

Worth, Katharine, '*The Beckett Festival of Radio Plays.* Directed and produced by Everett C. Frost for Voices International, 2 Washington Square Village, 16-J, New York, NY 10012. *All That Fall, Words and Music, Cascando*, and *Rough for Radio II*', *Theatre Journal*, 42, 3 (October 1990), pp.385–8.

Wulf, Catharina (ed.), *The Savage Eye/ L'Oeil fauve. New Essays on Samuel Beckett's Television Plays, Samuel Beckett Today/ Aujourd'hui*, 4 (Amsterdam and Atlanta, GA: Editions Rodopi, 1995.

Zilliacus, Clas, *Beckett and Broadcasting: A Study of the Works of Samuel Beckett for and in Radio and Television* (Åbo: Åbo Akademi, 1976).

III) Archives and Collections Consulted

BBC Written Archive Centre, Caversham Park

University of Reading Library Special Collections: Beckett Collection

Times Literary Supplement (*TLS* Historical Archive 1902–2009: online)

IV) Web Resources

The Samuel Beckett On-Line Resources and Links Page: http://www.samuel-beckett.net/

The Beckett Circle. Official Newsletter of the Samuel Beckett Society: http://www.beckettcircle.org/

The Samuel Beckett Endpage at the University of Antwerp: https://www.uantwerpen.be/en/rg/the-samuel-beckett-endpage/

The Beckett International Foundation at the University of Reading: http://www.beckettfoundation.org.uk/

University of Reading Library Special Collections: Beckett Collection: http://www.reading.ac.uk/special-collections/collections/sc-beckett.aspx

'Beckett Shorts', YouTube: http://www.youtube.com/playlist?list=PLFA3C073738DAC946.

Also consulted: *Samuel Beckett. Apmonia*, The Modern Word website: http://www.themodernword.com/beckett/beckett_links.html (site not available at last consultation 14 November 2014).

Index